THE ROYAL SOCIETY
OF MINIATURE PAINTERS SCULPTORS
AND GRAVERS

ONE HUNDRED YEARS

All the miniatures in this book are actual size

This book has been a difficult project for all concerned. Collecting material from contributors took time and persuasion and editing the biographies to readable pieces of reasonable length was a long and painstaking task. Desiring perfection, it was hard for me to learn and accept short-comings inherent in film and colour reproduction when controlled by budget restrictions.

I would like to thank all those whose dedicated help has made the book the best attainable: Rado Klose, the photographer, for much extra unprofitable care; David Gatehouse for excellent colour judgement; Brian Nicholson of Surdaw Press with Alan Peapell, Marion Nicholson, Maria Hughes who deciphered endless corrections; Julian Nettley, David Hurlow, Richard Sercombe and Pauline White whose happy voice on the telephone cheered my darkest days. Finally my thanks to Margaret Hayward, without whose two years of constant help at every stage, patience and remarkable memory, this volume would still be struggling towards the light of day.

We are grateful for sponsorship from
Joan Ayling, former Vice President; Laura Staniland Roberts, former Associate Member;
Llewellyn Alexander (Fine Paintings) Ltd, London

Frontispiece – Portrait of The Queen on her Accession by Lily A. Ogilvie RMS

Portrait of the Founder President by Dora Webb RMS

Portait of the President by Pauline Gyles RMS

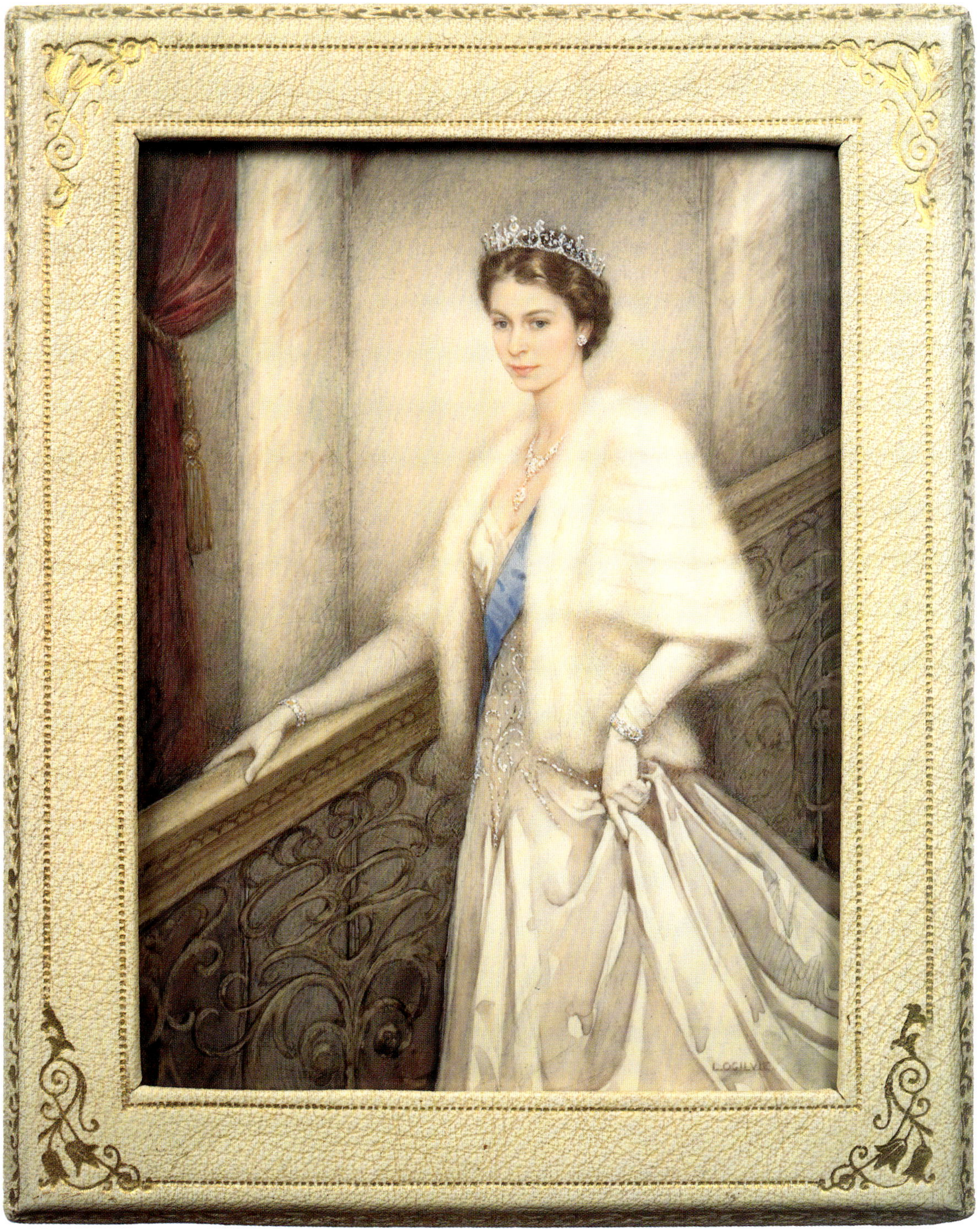

Her Most Excellent Majesty
The Queen
Patron of the Society

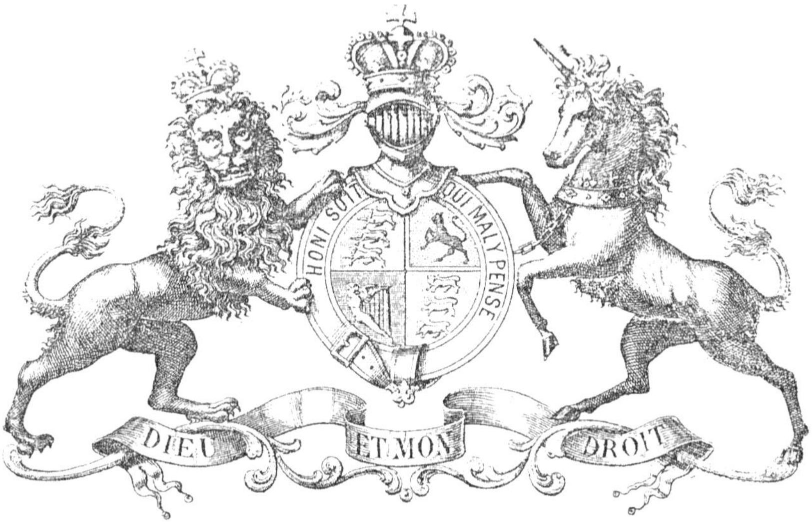

THE ROYAL SOCIETY
OF MINIATURE PAINTERS SCULPTORS
AND GRAVERS

ONE HUNDRED YEARS

Commemorating The One Hundredth Anniversary
of the Royal Society of Miniature Painters Sculptors and Gravers

Lucas Art

THE ROYAL SOCIETY
OF MINIATURE PAINTERS SCULPTORS AND GRAVERS

ONE HUNDRED YEARS

Written and Edited by Suzanne Lucas
FLS PRMS FPSBA SWA HSF Médaille de la France Libre

Published by Lucas Art, Manor Road,
Mere, Warminster, Wiltshire BA12 6HQ
for the Royal Society of Miniature Painters, Sculptors and Gravers

First published in Great Britain July 1995 by Lucas Art

Designed by Lucas Art and Printed by Surdaw Press
Station Road, Gillingham, Dorset SP8 4PR

Printed Offset Litho onto Sovereign Gloss from
Howard Smith Papers Limited

Colour Separations by Radstock Reproductions Yeovil Limited

Bound by Cedric Chivers Limited, Bristol

British Library Cataloguing in Publication Data
A catalogue record for this book is available from the British Library

ISBN 0-9520456-9-9

Lucas Art

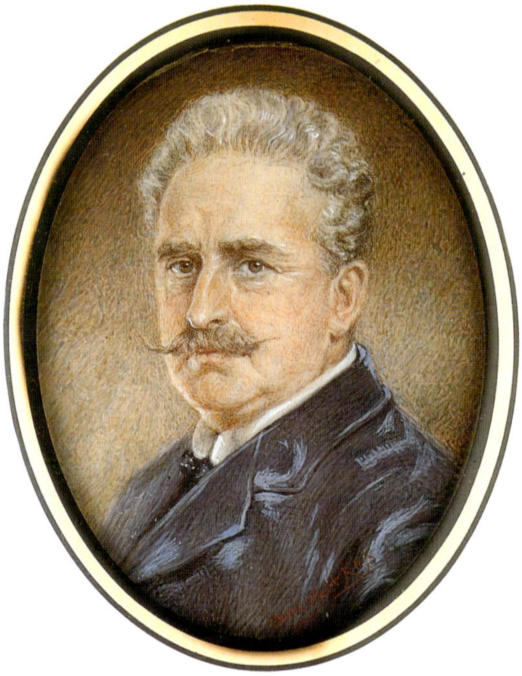

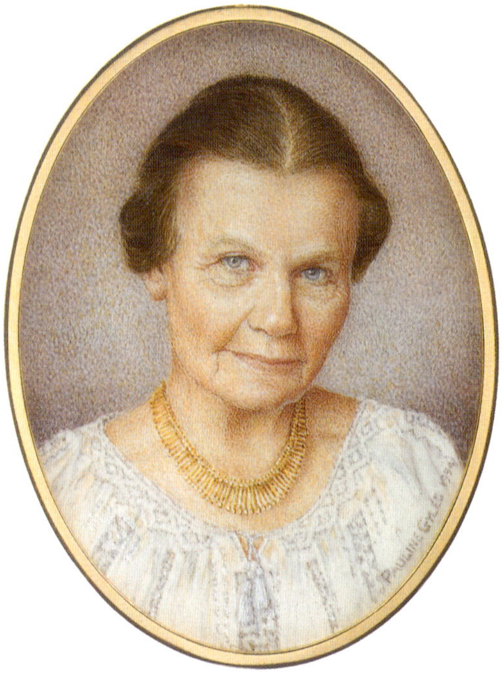

Introduction

by Suzanne Lucas FLS PRMS FPSBA SWA HSF
Médaille de la France Libre

Miniature art is a particular skill of exquisite precision in colour, composition and technique. To fulfil its demands the artist must follow the traditional disciplines, of which this is one of the last purist strongholds in a world where anything goes and we are instructed to consider those wild experiments as art. The miniaturist regards them with mild surprise and returns to his home ground. Mild because self-control is an essential part of his character, surrounded and supported by stillness in search of perfection which must be approached in quietude, with infinite patience and courage.

The origins of this lovely discipline are lost in time, at least so in the East, but miniatures as they are known to-day date from the Middle Ages. However, the modern idea of a Society bringing together those practising the art began with our foundation, and that of the Society of Miniaturists, at the end of the nineteenth century. We worked steadily and with much honour, visited by members of the Royal Family, including the Prince and Princess of Wales, and counting the Presidents of the Royal Societies among our Honorary Members. But success in those days was dignified and not expected to set the world on fire with publicity as now. The destruction of war did that for us most disastrously and it was a slow recovery afterwards, with no noticeable growth until the Sixties, but a membership of superb quality.

Now there is a renaissance, a flowering of the art of the miniature, with an ever growing interest and number of enthusiastic collectors. Societies have sprung up in England, the United States, Australia, South Africa and France, all of which will be represented in the World Exhibition of Miniature Art which is a celebration, as is this book, of our Hundred Years of creative life.

As to the practicalities of the book's production, which has taken almost two years' work, the aim was perfection. The realization must, of necessity, fall short of that ideal goal, but at least to reach for the heights means a greater measure of achievement than initial acceptance of inevitable imperfections. In the Orient it is considered unwise to make a perfect thing lest it attract the vengeance of the gods who alone may be perfect. Let this be my apology for any faults, which are not for want of months of care, arranging, research and revision. As to the reproduction one point is important to remember. A framed miniature cannot be put on a drum for direct laser action. There are, therefore, three steps down from the original - photography, colour separation, printing and the short-comings of each with which to contend. All those concerned have done their utmost to fulfil my hopes for a book which is, in essence, a gallery in your hand.

Miniature Artists are a steadying influence on the rest of human character in a turbulent and insecure world. Endowments of perseverance, observation and deep love of all that is excellent, make them valuable when so many standards are falling in an age where the best is no longer the only acceptable criterion.

Any further communication on the subject of this letter should be addressed to—
THE UNDER SECRETARY OF STATE,
HOME OFFICE,
LONDON, S.W.,
and the following number quoted :—

B24,307/2

WHITEHALL

30th May, 1904.

Sir,

I am directed by the Secretary of State to acquaint you that the application of the Society of Miniature Painters to be allowed to use the prefix "Royal" has been graciously acceded to by His Majesty who has signified His Pleasure that the Society be known as the Royal Society of Miniature Painters.

I am,

Sir,

Your obedient Servant,

Henry Cunynghame

The Secretary,
Royal Society of Miniature Painters,
The Modern Gallery,
175 Bond Street,
W.

P.S.B.

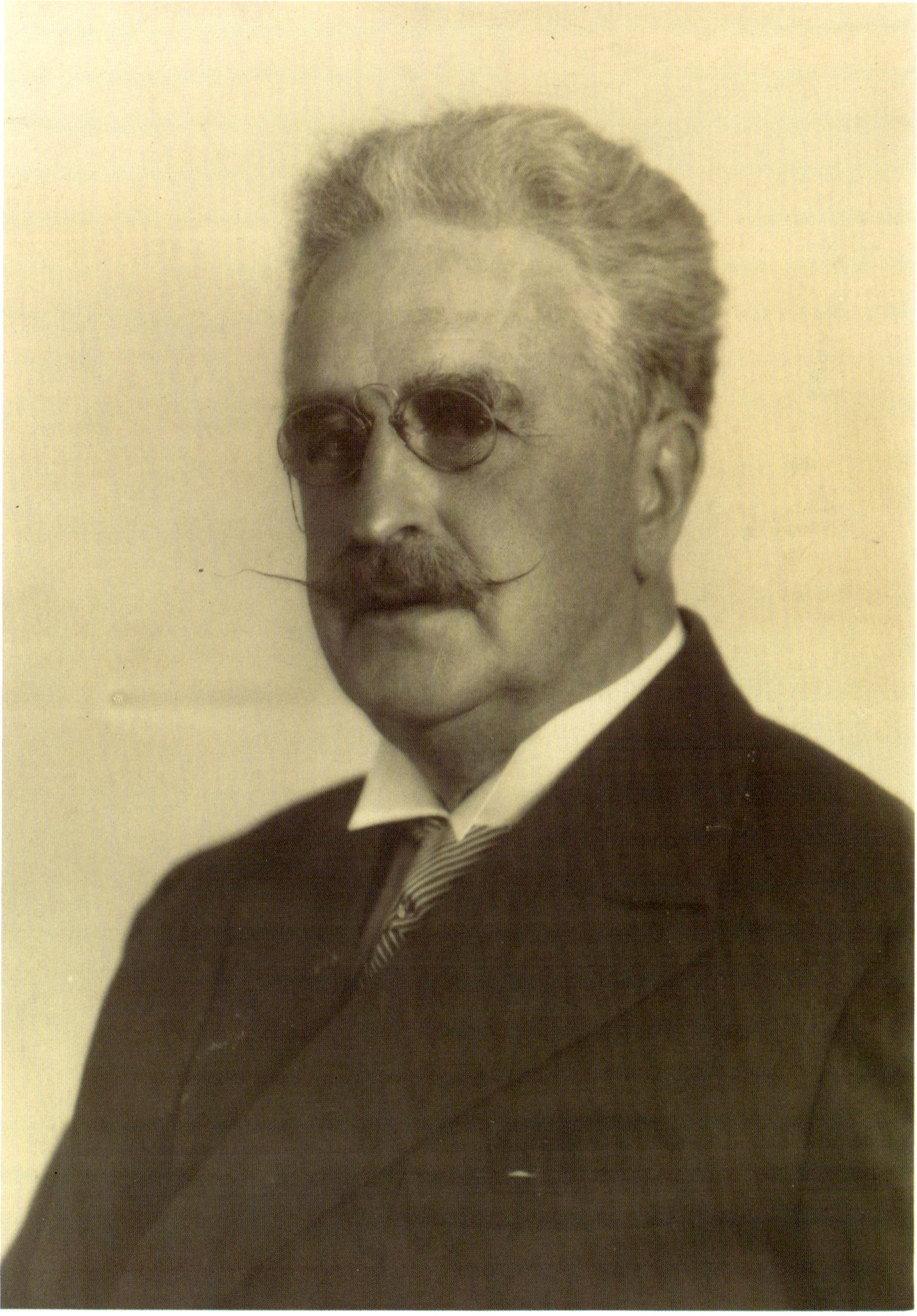

Alyn Williams

The Founder President of the Society

The Royal Society of Miniature Painters, Sculptors and Gravers

One Hundred Years

For one hundred years of Minutes, Catalogues and a dozen files bursting with relevant papers, four pages is clearly inadequate. A comprehensive history is planned later on when the fascinating detail of the characters which live in the old pages, tensions and arguments, enthusiasm, plans, above all devotion, as ever of the few, will emerge. They were dedicated to the Society and the work entailed in making it live for as long as the world of art encompasses the exquisite detail and steady self-discipline needed by the artist working in miniature.

This book celebrates the Hundredth Anniversary of a Society which is not only alive after two world wars and a series of depressions and recessions - the present being one in a long line - but has grown out of all recognition. It counts turnover in tens of thousands where there were hundreds and, despite money being devalued every year, it has more than kept pace, proud not only of its artistic traditions, but also the many years of success and fame.

Striving to bring together deliberations and events over so long a time span makes one think that in truth history is but a repetition. There is a strange impression of an echo before one has spoken - a mirror echo of the present. All has been said and met before, a recurrent chorus interjected at intervals into the song, making the past relevant and familiar.

At the beginning Minutes were short, an Honorary Secretary's dream, but this brevity did not last despite the frequency of Council Meetings, often each fortnight. Within days of the foundation on May 7th. 1896 the founder, Alyn Williams, and his Council were challenged by another Society of Miniature Painters, claiming prior right to the title. In diplomatic exchanges on May 20th. our Society suggested a meeting at which the representatives of the other failed to attend. Other offers of amalgamation with equal rights brought no response and again delegates failed to appear. So the Council decided to give up the useless effort and concentrate on its own Society which, at the Inaugural Exhibition, had welcomed the Princess of Wales and other members of the Royal Family, of whom Her Royal Highness Princess Louise, Marchioness of Lorne (later Duchess of Argyll) gave her accolade to the Society by becoming an Honorary Member. A selection of works were submitted to Her Majesty Queen Victoria. By 1897 the Presidents of all the Royal Art Societies had accepted Honorary Membership and the Society was well born to wide recognition and acclaim. The first Exhibition was at The Gallery, 175 New Bond Street, which moved to 6 Pall Mall, then back again becoming the Modern Gallery, and in 1913 one was at the Maddox Street Galleries where the Society hoped to have a permanent home but decided otherwise. It sub-let to the Lyceum Club at that time.

It is clear from the Minutes that the date of foundation has been misquoted ever since, between 1922 and '25 (the catalogues of 1922-1924 are missing) Dr. George C. Williamson, appointed Hon. Librarian, wrote his foreword and, miscounting the number of exhibitions, pronounced 1895 to be the date. A variety of imaginative combinations including 1894 and 1895 have been asserted even by experts such as Daphne Foskett and Raymond Lister, nobody having consulted the Minutes. The facts are as now stated and corroborated by the 21st. Anniversary celebrated in 1916 and the 80th. in 1975, though even that catalogue gives the foundation as in 1894. Later this was eliminated by the President who had mistakenly trusted bygone experts and left the date in place. The history itself is hampered by the disappearance of some catalogues and minutes, gaps of about ten years. In 1940 the Arlington Gallery, the Society's home, disappeared in the Blitz and with it our archives. An appeal later asked Members to replace catalogues, many of which came to hand, and an inspired person, probably the Secretary, seems to have had most of the Minutes elsewhere on that fateful night. Despite that one book from 1922-1931 is still lost. In 1975 the President, then a Member of Council, pleaded for a request for some Royal recognition, but was told there was no charter and it might draw attention to an unauthorised title. Permission to consult the archives was refused her, so the incorrect date persisted.

The first Minutes were written by Alyn Williams himself and he was meticulous in giving a full President's Address to the Members each year. If he were away it was sent and read. He was the elected President and with him the first Vice Presidents were Hal Hurst RBA and Rob Sauber RBA, the Hon. Secretary Mary, Mrs. Theo Smith-Dorrien, the Hon. Treasurer Thomas McKeggie and Members of Council Miss M. Josephine Gibson, Miss Mabel Hobson, Richard Jack, A. Dampier May, Hugh Nicholson, Cecil W. Quinnell and Edward Tayler. The Secretary was Edward Freeman of the Modern Gallery who, with the President, worked indefatigably for the Society's welfare and success, and the subscription was fixed at ten shillings and sixpence for the first twelve Members.

Alyn Williams VPRBA, RCA, ARCA, VPIAL, at whose studio the preliminary ideas for the Society were discussed, was a young man of much talent, great enthusiasm and tenacity of purpose, the perfect character for the task of, to quote the Artist in 1899, "giving miniature painters everything they desire to promote their art and by this means the art of miniature painting is certainly being resuscitated." He tended his Society with love and determination and had many of the right friends and acquaintance. His Majesty King Edward VII honoured him with his friendship and in 1916, at the Twenty-first Anniversary Exhibition, Queen Alexandra attended on May 8th, bringing with her the Princess Royal and Princess Victoria, and bought five miniatures. Alyn painted several portraits of both Their Majesties and fulfilled a commission placed by the King for miniatures of the Queen's eyes on his cuff-links so that "she could watch over him wherever he might be." Alyn travelled widely and was received by the Pope, whose portrait he painted, among other famous names such as President Coolidge, Cardinal Gibbons and Sir Gardner Engleheart, a descendant of George. All his best work is in the United States with two at the Smithsonian Institute.

In 1916 his only son was killed and after that he spent many years in the United States with a second marriage to an artist who was also a spiritualist, which may have helped him in his loss. It was then, in 1921 (history's repetition) that he proposed an International Society of Miniature Painters, founded by his Society with the American and Philadelphia Societies of Miniature Painters, for which he drew up a Constitution and plans for the first exhibition in the United States. This was unfulfilled but there, recently, a suggestion for an International Federation of Miniature Societies was proposed. A single Society now would hardly be possible for so many flourishing bodies with separate existences.

In 1899, supposedly to increase the Society's prestige, Alyn Williams stood down in favour of Sir William Blake Richmond KCB, RA who, extraordinarily, was elected both Member and President at the same AGM. Apart from being an artist of note (his father George, a Royal Academician, and grandfather Thomas who studied with George Engleheart, were both miniaturists), he was one of fifteen children resulting from his father's romantic Gretna Green elopement and marriage to Miss Julia Tatham, who was accompanied to the tryst by George's elder brother Thomas.

George was also a friend of Calvert, Palmer and Blake (hence Sir William Blake Richmond) with work at the Victoria and Albert Museum and National Portrait Gallery. It was a renowned family of artists and though Sir William did not attend meetings, his name and influence were of value.

In 1898 a petition for the bestowal of the prefix Royal was submitted to the Queen but was unsuccessful until on May 30th. 1904, supported by well-known signatures, it was granted by His Majesty King Edward VII. Sir William was still President, though suggesting already in 1900 that Val Princeps should succeed him. Fortunately this injustice was not done, and after the title of Acting President from 1907 to 1911 Alyn was again President and remained so until his death in 1941, an example of dedication followed by S. Arthur Lindsey and Scott Shepherd with Lt. Colonel Goddard feeling he could perhaps retire at ninety to become Hon. President.

In those days the Society was very active. Apart from its Annual Exhibition in the Capital, there were provincial ventures such as Liverpool (a regular venue) Plymouth and overseas exhibitions in Toronto, the United States, South Africa under discussion and in 1916, Dublin. In 1916 much happened: the Twenty First Anniversary Exhibition at the Grafton Gallery; the tragic death of Alyn's son; the danger to, but safe return of the Dublin Exhibition during the Rebellion, with a note of regret that there were no sales; and the death of Sir James Linton PRI who had always been good and of great assistance to the Society. During 1914 and '15 there was some Society activity despite the call-up of Members and the President's illness. The trouble with unpaid subscriptions, recurring since 1898, was dealt with severely, an Hon. Librarian was appointed and the bye-law on size amended to 7 x 5 ins. Members in the armed forces were accorded Honorary Membership, subscriptions reduced to £2.2.0 and special writing paper was printed to request Princess Louise's acceptance of the Honorary Presidency.

The understanding of the size of a miniature is a problem since it is the technique which defines its nature. Size is therefore dependent on exhibition space. The Society started with much room, therefore a size of 12 x 10 ins. This was quickly reduced to 10 x 7 ins, then remained at 7 x 5 ins, to which one could add mount and frame, until the Sixties. As miniatures began to proliferate with space no more accommodating, further steps were taken to 7 x 5 ins. overall and then, perforce, in the face of seven hundred or more miniatures to place, to 6 x 4½ ins. overall where it is to-day. Full Members may exceed this a little but are requested to keep to the rules as far as possible. The only rule on subjects is that heads or single objects shall not measure more than two inches.

The affairs of the Society continued with some exhibitions in conjunction with the Royal Society of Portrait Painters, later in the Royal Institute Galleries, an arrangement drawing more clients but the miniature work, overpowered by large paintings, escaped the notice of critics, another recurrent situation for the last hundred years. Critics are able to assess the large and obvious but, except for the first years of the Society when much was written in art magazines and newspapers, they have ignored miniatures, finding their technique and value, in so small a space, too much trouble to understand. It is not otherwise to-day. Critics who find much to say about a single line, or even a blank canvas, cannot be persuaded to consider something which will require thought and understanding, nor even to visit our Exhibitions.
In 1953 the Hon. Secretary wonders "if that is because they hesitate to show their lack of knowledge of our work" and in 1954 there is an appeal to Members to make the Society known and "overcome the lethargy of Art Critics."

Another constituent of the recurring chorus is the extraordinary, not to say unjust, treatment miniaturists suffer at the hands of the Royal Academy, despite this country's world position as the leading exponent of miniature art. Though the Academy was founded to foster all branches of art, aside from ten years under Sir Charles Wheeler's Presidency when quality above all was strongly upheld and eccentricities were unacceptable, the miniatures have been badly shown, not shown, grudgingly shown or mixed with small works painted without any resemblance to miniature techniques. All that miniatures ask is fair selection by knowledgeable judges for reasonable exhibition. These facts have their place here, threaded through one hundred years of enthusiasm from the people opposed to rejection by "experts". It is a thousand pities that Sir William Charles Ross RA flourished too soon to give us the sure support he would certainly have offered. He painted two thousand two hundred miniatures, among them most of Europe's crowned heads, including Queen Victoria and Louis Philippe of France with their families. He was knighted in 1842 and in 1843 won the prize at the Westminster Hall Competition with others from the Society of Artists.

His miniatures are in all the great collections including the Victoria and Albert Museum, the Wallace Collection and that of Her Majesty the Queen.

Already in 1905 Associate Members were instituted and they have come far since then, for they not only had no voice but were not allowed to attend meetings. This they do now and may give opinions and make suggestions, though not propose these or vote. Their ideas are often of use and their membership has now been increased up to seventy, with eighty full members, extra places imposed by the ever-growing numbers of talented miniaturists. Much has happened in the last fifteen years as before then the Society moved little, with no real incentive for change. It was comfortable as it was and static compared with its first animated years under its Founder's leadership. In 1920 the historic President's Jewel, an excellent example of Art Nouveau, was created by Lyndhurst Pocock who worked with Fabergé. The pendant was presented to the President at a celebratory musical evening and the names of all those contributing were beautifully inscribed by Miss Mary Kimber on a designed scroll which must have been destroyed by the 1940 bomb.

At this time there was much activity encouraging craft and sculpture work with appeals for more of high quality. By 1926 it had grown so much to the satisfaction of His Majesty King George V that he gave his Royal Command for the name to become the Royal Society of Miniature Painters, Sculptors and Gravers. Here it is appropriate to mention one shining star whose goldsmith's work was of supreme beauty, Omar Ramsden. Two of his works are now a part of history: the wonderful gold and jewelled badge and chain he created in 1929 for His Royal Highness the Prince of Wales, the First Master of the Honourable Company of Master Mariners, and a mazer bowl in 1936 to commemorate the year in which the country had three Kings, therefore our Society had three Royal Patrons, George V, Edward VIII and George VI. Edward VIII awarded us his Patronage on May 5th 1936. There are a few pictures of Omar's work in the catalogues, where the reproductions are a gallery of fame which could merit a book of their own. There is a rare foray into colour for a miniature by May B. Lee of the Hon. George Lascelles, son of Her Royal Highness Princess Mary, the Princess Royal. Members of this Society have been commissioned throughout the Society's life to paint the Royal Family, amongst them Stella Marks M.V.O. who painted fourteen portraits, especially one of the young Princess Elizabeth commissioned by the Duke of Edinburgh, and Patricia Nichols has also been in much demand. That we are not permitted to show the portraits in our Exhibitions, as does the Royal Society of Portrait Painters, is a matter for regret as our Members take most particular care with such work. One to be shown was a portrait of the Duke of Edinburgh by W.P. Mundy.

In 1933, the Society was sorely tried by the Stock Market collapse, the President advising the utmost economy in face of falling sales. A Press Preview Day was first mentioned and there was talk of Exhibitions in Toronto and Australia. Members heard of the necessity of making their voluntary contributions to the Diploma Collection more importantly representative. The Victoria and Albert Museum was among leading Galleries to invite the Collection and Members should do their best, not only to enhance the Society's reputation, but also to perpetuate their names through future ages. The Collection fell into abeyance many years ago but in 1994 the President suggested its revival for the Hundredth Anniversary. A number of works have been added. They make up for some which were missed, on checking, after years when Society Officers had not made a regular inventory.

In 1938 there were bad times when miniatures were not in vogue and coloured photographs were, with little heed paid to the difference. An article in The Times regrets the miniature's "photographic lines" and failure "to exploit the decorative possibilities of gleaming colours on a basis of line." This is certainly not true to-day where an exhibition has exactly what the Times required, "the light jewelled effect," and is a brilliant and entrancing display of colour, form and imaginative beauty. Added to this the war was to strike and the 1940 Minutes end with a proposed exhibition at the RWS Galleries, then blank pages until 1943. All our other papers were lost with our gallery and even some Members, of whom the founder Vice President Cecil W. Quinnell.

S. Arthur Lindsey was elected President in 1943, a much admired artist both for his character and work and also the creator of, as far as is known, the only modern anamorphosis, of King George V. Its whereabouts is unknown to us, but it was in the old tradition of a flat and incomprehensible painting which, when a reflective cylinder was placed in the middle, resolved itself into a portrait. It was valuable to the Jacobites who could carry the separate pieces safely, setting them together for a picture of their Prince at secret meetings.

In this year the Society moved to the RWS Galleries in Conduit Street and Harry Philp became Secretary in place of Lucy MacDonald, who retired after years of devoted and efficient service. He took his work most seriously and his reports are honest and to the point. Above all it concerned him that Members did not appreciate the high honour of membership of the Society and how little they considered their obligations to it in return. This attitude, in some cases, has not changed. Nor should one wonder at it for if the world does not learn how should the Society Members ?

By 1944, the Society was under way and a peaceful era began. It dealt with long overdue subscriptions by striking ten names from the Membership List and, in 1945, a simplification of the top-heavy and complicated Rules. Janet Haughton presented two much-needed sculpture cases and in 1951 Albert Cousins designed the Society's Diploma, first presented in 1953 and still used to-day.

In 1950 a new catalogue, very "economy" in looks and lacking the list of illustrious Honorary Members, was the third sort and happily changed to the fourth in 1958, with a cover designed by Daisy Borne. Illustrations did not re-appear until the Eightieth Anniversary in 1975. In 1982 the President, elected in 1980, introduced the Society's colours of blue and gold which were used for the catalogue until 1990 when she proposed cream and gold, the title designed by Vera Ibbett, which Members found so satisfactory that they voted to use it for the Hundredth Anniversary. The Royal Arms, which first appeared on the 1910 edition, were re-drawn by the President and used in gold.

In 1952 the much-loved President died after long illness and on December 3rd. Lieutenant Colonel F.A. Goddard OBE was elected to the Presidency, still fulfilling his work as Hon. Treasurer for a while longer. A year later Nellie M. Hepburn Edmunds, whose name runs through the Society's history from 1902, also died. She was a great artist, the only one living to have a miniature in the Victoria and Albert Museum Permanent Collection at that time, an invited contributor to the Queen's Dolls House, a Vice President till 1952 and before then a meticulous Hon. Treasurer and a tireless, completely devoted worker for the benefit of her Society. Her presence threads together its life for fifty years and she seems to step out of the pages, becoming a valued and much-admired friend. She died only a year before the present President was elected to membership, leaving a sense of regret that she did not meet her.

The choppy seas of gallery ups and downs, constant bye-law changes and small but important concerns of the formative years, but also two world wars, were followed by the peace of steady occupation at the RWS Gallery on Conduit Street under the intelligent guidance of Harry Philp. He took a deep interest in Society affairs until 1958 when the RWS dispensed with his services, which broke his heart, and gave us notice to leave. In 1957 an agreement with Maurice Bradshaw had sent our Archives to the Art Exhibitions Bureau at 23 Albermarle Street and Mr. Bradshaw was to manage our Exhibitions, with Mr. Philp, for a fee of £75. The Exhibition ran for one more year at the RWS. In 1959 it moved to the Alpine Gallery and, after discussions with Maurice Bradshaw, to the RBA Galleries at 6½ Suffolk Street where his plans were afoot for the creation of the Federation of British Artists, incorporated in 1961, of which our Society became a Member.

Quietude set in, the Society was managed by Maurice and we had little to worry about apart from the decision on new covering for the screens entrusted to the present President, then a Member of Council. There were some excellent miniature painters and the sculpture section stood out at that time with the highest quality of glass-engraving, sculpting and ceramics the Society has seen, to be looked back on now with nostalgia. Much of the work was of real beauty and outstanding artistic worth: Peter Dreiser's glass and Joyce Bidder's ivory carvings to mention but two whose work now appears in important auction sales.

But change was in the air for Maurice Bradshaw who dreamed of a new gallery in the Mall, towards which he worked untiringly, and in 1970 the whole Federation upped stakes and took possession of the Mall Galleries, its new home, which was opened by Her Majesty The Queen in February 1971. We lost our delightful oval room, but supported the new venue with donations from Members for furnishing and lighting. With deep regret we saw the Royal Institute of Painters in Water Colours leave its beautiful daylight galleries to join us, but continued to exhibit with gratitude a special case of miniatures at their Exhibitions, allowed by an agreement between Suzanne Lucas and their President Rowland Hilder.

The atmosphere settled and work was made easy by appointed staff. Colonel Scott Shepherd OBE, MC, elected President in 1957 and regarded with affection for his kindly interest in all Members, died in 1969 and in 1970 Raymond Lister was elected. During the ten years until her election to the Presidency in 1980, Suzanne Lucas served a hard-working apprenticeship as Hon. Secretary and Vice President, writing all the required articles and reports, also Minutes until the appointment of a new Hon. Secretary.

In 1985 the President gave the Gold Memorial Bowl in memory of her Mother, Winifred Beeby RMS. Crafted in 18ct. gold by Garrard the Crown Jewellers, it is the most prestigious honour in the world of miniature art, given each year to the creator of the best work in the Exhibition and the President makes a personal gift to the artist of a silver-gilt replica.

But financial trouble was brewing which finally came to a head, a meeting of the Governors was called and a board of five Executive Governors appointed which included the President. It was a stormy time with a great deal of hard work and difficult argument, factions forming and dissolving, with insistence that the Federation should declare itself bankrupt which the President's firm refusal to concur prevented, and her plan to save the FBA being passed at a full Governors' meeting, all had a profound effect on the Society. The original Executive Board resigned in protest at new turns of events and finally a meeting of other Societies voted this Society out of the Federation with a rider that we might be allowed, nevertheless, to use the gallery as an "outside let". The same had happened earlier to the Society of Women Artists, so the two in co-operation set about finding a home. This was to be the creation of a new Gallery at Westminster Central Hall. The President worked in agreement with the management to accomplish plans and, on a fine June day, cases and all the Society property were loaded quietly into a pantechnicon and spirited away. It was quite dramatic, particularly watching our two large and fragile vitrines being manoeuvred down a long steep flight of stone steps to the basement at the Hall. The Society inaugurated the Westminster Gallery in 1987.

So again a new venue, a new life and a great deal more work with the return of total independence. But the Society flourished. The larger room gave more space to patrons, new cases were ordered to accommodate the seven hundred or more miniatures on show and the turnover increased year by year. People of importance, including several Right Worshipful Lord Mayors of Westminster, honoured us by opening our Exhibitions and each year we are complimented on the ever higher standard of the work. The variety of subjects, the real excellence of the portraits, the wonderful use of colour and technique by a group of consummate and dedicated artists, bring the Society to its memorable Hundredth Anniversary Celebration, with a sense of worth and achievement, along the hard road towards the unattainable, but ever desirable lodestar of perfection.

It is in this striving that the characters of miniaturists mature, making them most useful to the world for their honesty, peaceful endeavours, delight in beauty and deep contemplation of loveliness in even the smallest and most delicate creation.

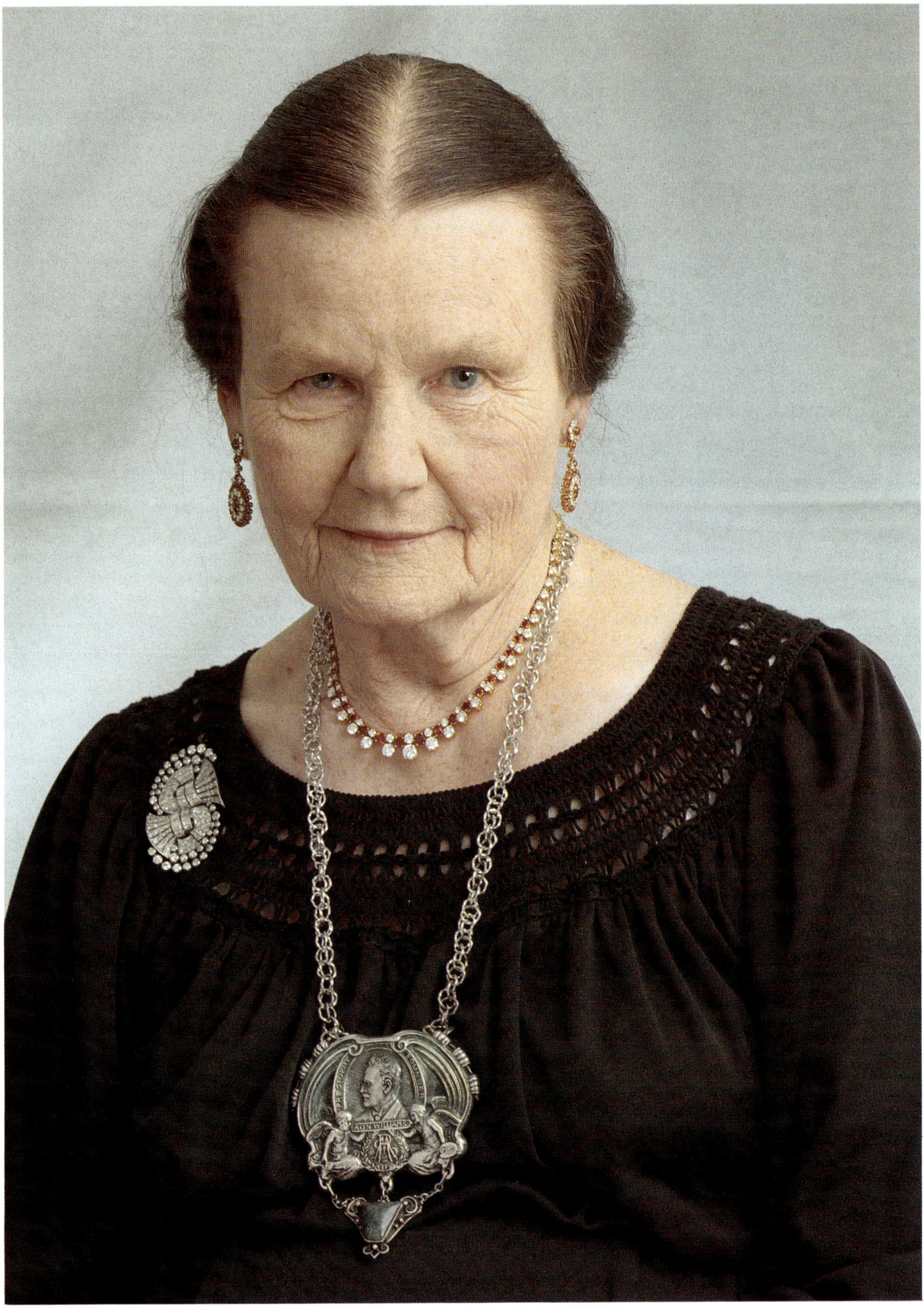

Suzanne Lucas

President of The Royal Society of Miniature Painters Sculptors & Gravers

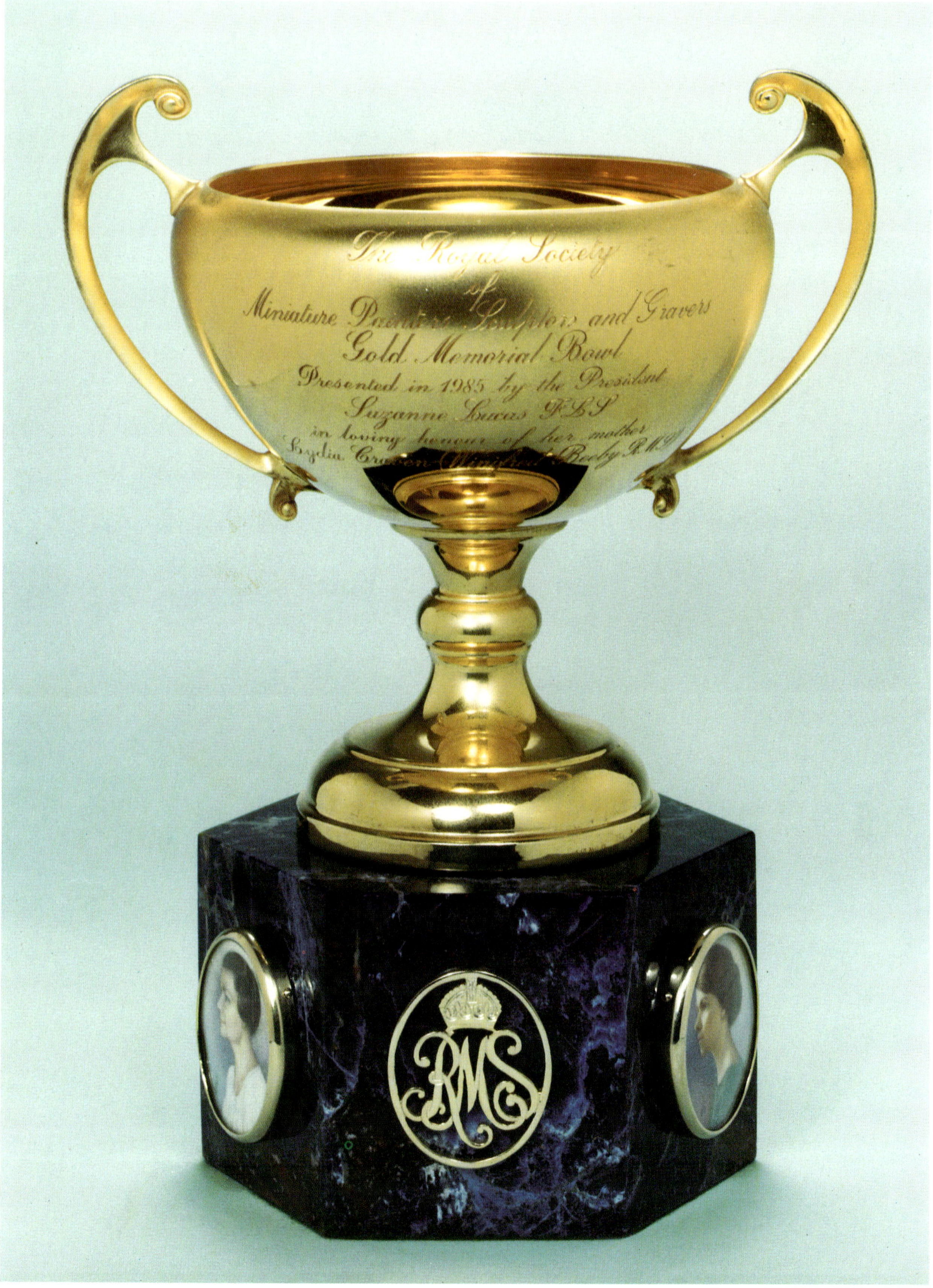

The Gold Memorial Bowl

A gift to the Society from the President Suzanne Lucas
in honour of her Mother Winifred Beeby R.M.S

Jennifer Buxton

Hon. RMS (retired) HSF Gold Memorial Bowl 1985

Musette
(water-colour on ivory)
kindly lent by the President

Katherine and Folly
(water-colour on ivory)
kindly lent by Rear-Admiral and Mrs. Pirnie

Rupert
(water-colour on ivory)

Winifred Beeby, RMS
(water-colour on ivory)
kindly lent by the President

Jennifer began drawing studies, when she was ten years old, with Marguerite Frobisher at the Bushey School of Animal Painting. A scholarship to the Byam Shaw School led to a prize for head portraiture in her final year.

After years of full-size work in oil and pastel, she was encouraged to paint miniatures and was caught by the enchantment of watching a sitter come to life on the fine ivory surface. Working from a pastel portrait painted from life, or photographs taken, developed and printed personally, she painted freely on the ivory or vellum. She delighted in the pleasure of sitters and their relatives when shown the miniatures, yet she always looked forward to the next one and the constant quest for improvement towards perfection. Only many years later, when she had to use glasses and a magnifier, did she feel that something came between her and her sitters and she returned to larger work.

She enjoyed her twenty years' active membership of the Royal Miniature Society where she found a feeling of good comradeship among the members. She was elected an Associate in 1969 and a Member in 1970. In 1985 she was awarded the Gold Memorial Bowl, in its inaugural year, for a miniature of Winifred Beeby, and the Mundy Sovereign Award followed in 1987. She won the Bell Award for Best Portrait the next year at the Hilliard Society Exhibition as well as the First in Portrait Prize in 1993 at the exhibition of the Miniature Art Society of Florida.

On becoming an Honorary RMS (retired) she devoted her time to larger painting and was commissioned to create six portraits of a submarine, to be presented to the ship by the sponsor, Lady Eberle. This work led to exciting car journeys around Scottish lochs to achieve sketches of the submarine as she steamed past. The finished pictures accompanied her to the Falklands. The painting of HMS Vanguard, first of the Trident Class, commissioned by VSEL, was hung in the main reception room ready for the day when Princess Diana named the vessel.

A visit to Canada created an interest in landscapes, followed by a journey to the geologically interesting Flinders Range in Australia, all of which made an unusual contrast to the many portraits of animals on the Cumbrian Fells.

Jennifer's paintings and miniatures are in many collections, at home and abroad, and are much treasured by their owners.

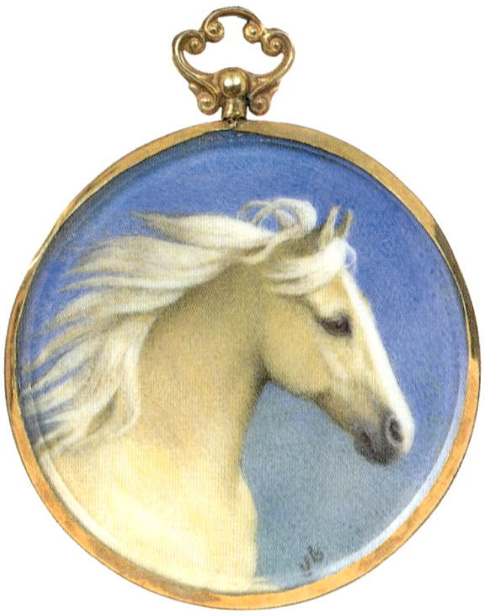

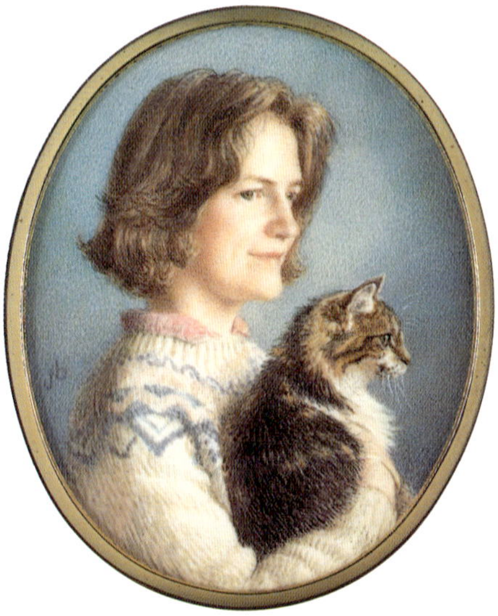

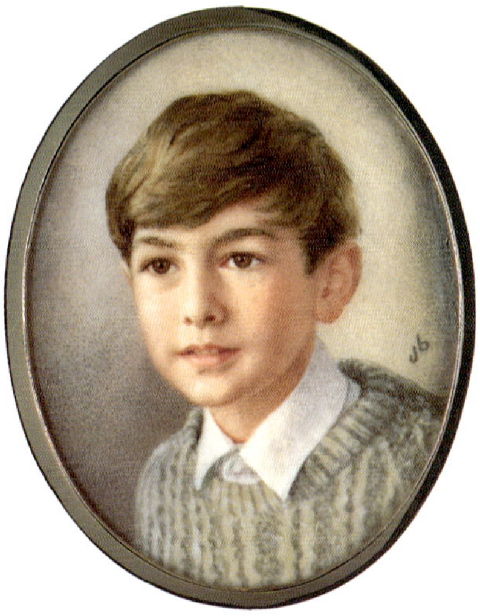

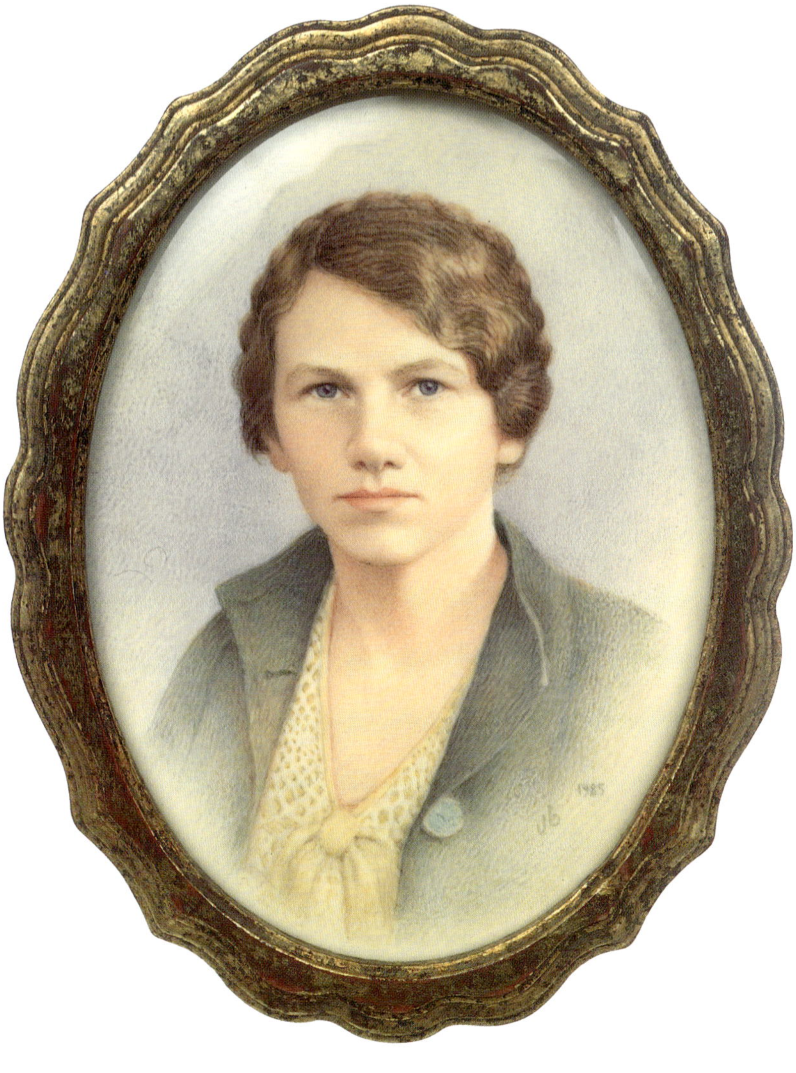
1985

William P. Mundy

RMS MASF HSF MAA Gold Memorial Bowl 1986

Spike Milligan
(water-colour on ivory)

Red Hesser
(water-colour on ivory)

Gilbert Adams
(water-colour on ivory)

His miniature portraits are in Royal, public and private collections throughout the world. He paints in a distinctive stippled style, reminiscent of pointillism in miniature.

Born in Berkshire in 1936, Bill Mundy started painting before his fifth birthday. After a five year apprenticeship as a lithographic artist he became a cartographer in the Far East during the Malayan Emergency in 1956.

His career in advertising spanned twenty years from 1960 on. An Art Director in Singapore, Creative Director in Hong Kong and Bangkok, he became the Area Director for Asia for an International United States Advertising Agency.

A miniature portrait of HRH The Sultan of Johor was exhibited at the Royal Academy in 1977. After being The Court Painter to the Johor Royal Palace in Malaysia he returned to England in 1978 to paint full-time.

His water-colour Early Apples was voted the Exhibit of the Year at the Royal Academy Summer Exhibition in 1980. In 1982 his painting The Picture Framer was voted Exhibit of the Year and he won a Silver Medal at the Paris Salon. Two years later the Game Conservancy commissioned a large sepia portrait of HRH The Duke of Edinburgh who granted a sitting at Buckingham Palace. The world's most prestigious prize for miniature painting is the Gold Memorial Bowl, awarded to Bill Mundy in 1986 for his portrait of Edwin Hunt, Bargemaster to Her Majesty the Queen. This was bought by Sotheby's for the Cincinnati Museum of Art. In 1987 he won the Bell Best Portrait Award at the Hilliard Society and a portrait miniature of David Money-Coutts was acquired by the Victoria and Albert Museum for their permanent collection. In 1992 he was elected a member of the Miniature Artists of America.,

At the Chitralada Palace in Bangkok in 1989 he presented a miniature portrait of HM King Bhumibol Adulyadej of Thailand and, in 1990 at a further Audience, two miniature portraits of HRH Princess Maha Chakri Sirindhorn.

Portrait in Time, an unusual larger portrait exhibited at the Royal Academy in 1991 and at the Royal Society of Portrait Painters in 1992, pictured a watch, on Royal Academician Anthony Green's hand, which moved and kept perfect time.

Bill Mundy is a prolific artist having painted nearly three hundred miniatures, many larger portraits and Trompe l'Oeil paintings. He lives and paints in his riverside studio at Henley-on-Thames in Oxfordshire.

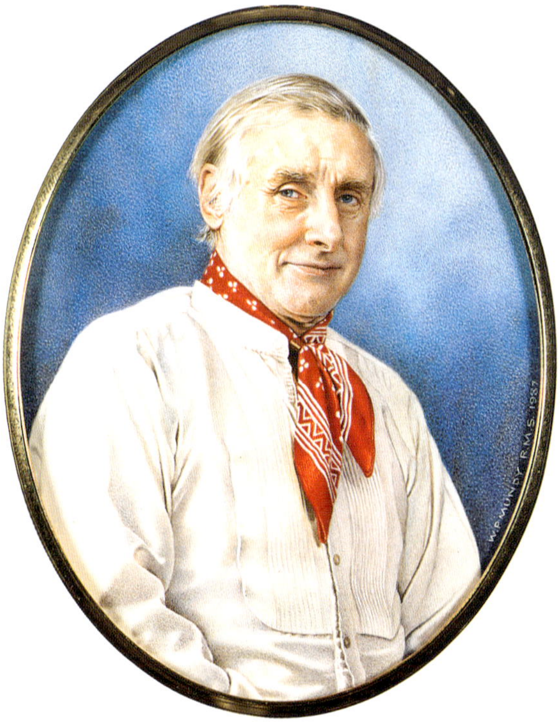
W.P.MUNDY R.M.S. 1987

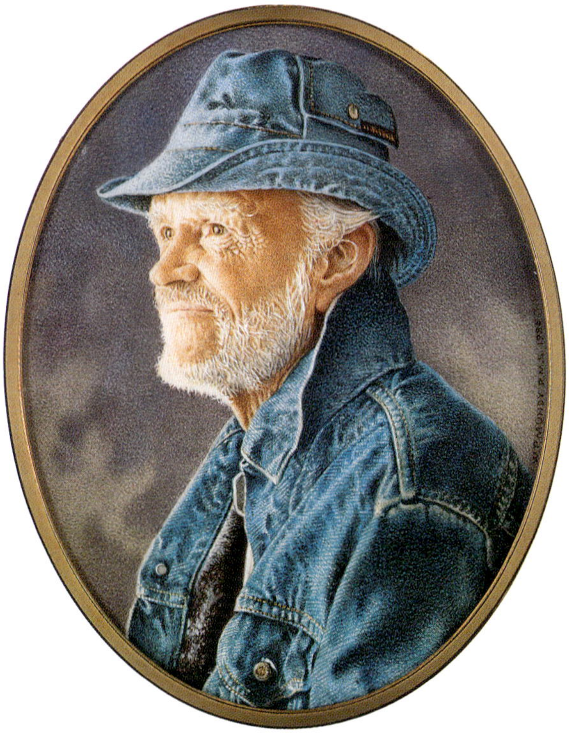

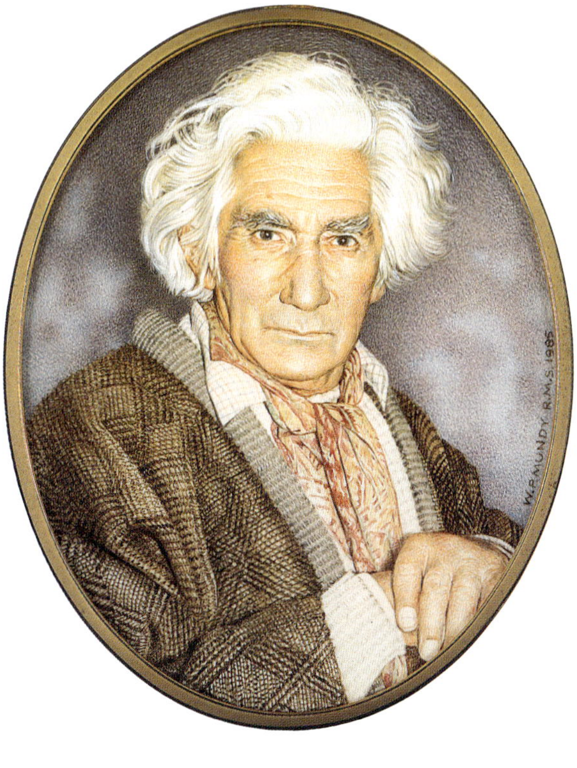
W.P.MUNDY R.M.S. 1985

Henry Saxon

RMS HSF MAA Gold Memorial Bowl 1987

A Hymn
(water-colour and gold leaf on Bristol board and Ivorine)

A Poem
by Jonathan Poley his eight year old grandson
(water-colour and gold leaf on Bristol board)

Henry Saxon was born in Ashton-under-Lyne in Lancashire in 1918. He was encouraged in his early years, by his grandfather, to take an interest in art and at the age of fourteen studied at the Manchester School of Art. It was there that he first developed his skills in calligraphy. Later, on the commercial side, he was introduced to the illuminator's art and studied this fine skill over a number of years. At that time he was also involved in hand drawn lithography on both stone and plate.

The interruption of war led him into the army medical corps in September 1939 for over six years. His artistic talents were always on call and early in 1940 he illustrated a text book on radiography.

In 1946 he returned to the reproduction side of the printing industry and it was in Chesterfield that he was first introduced to miniature painting, by the late John Spencer Hon. RMS, when he was the manager of the reproduction department of the famous firm of Waterlow's. Years later when he was involved in reproductions of miniatures to appear in the Country Life Magazine for Suzanne Lucas, President of the Royal Miniature Society, she re-introduced him to miniature art and he began exhibiting with the Society. In 1982 he was elected to Associate Membership and in 1985 became a Member of the Royal Society of Miniature Painters, Sculptors and Gravers. He was greatly honoured in 1987 when he was awarded the Gold Memorial Bowl, the most important prize in the world of miniatures. He has also won the Gordon Drummond and the Fairman Members Subject Miniature Awards and is a Founder Member of the Hilliard Society of Miniaturists.

In 1992 he was elected a Signature Member of the Miniature Artists of America winning awards both in Georgia and Florida. Together with miniature work he loves outdoor water-colour sketching and has exhibited work in France, Germany and Israel. He is a do-it-yourself enthusiast, making his own frames, and his other interests include woodwork, gardening, fly-fishing and photography. He spends time on demonstrations for local art clubs and has been the Chairman of Dunstable Art Club for over fifteen years.

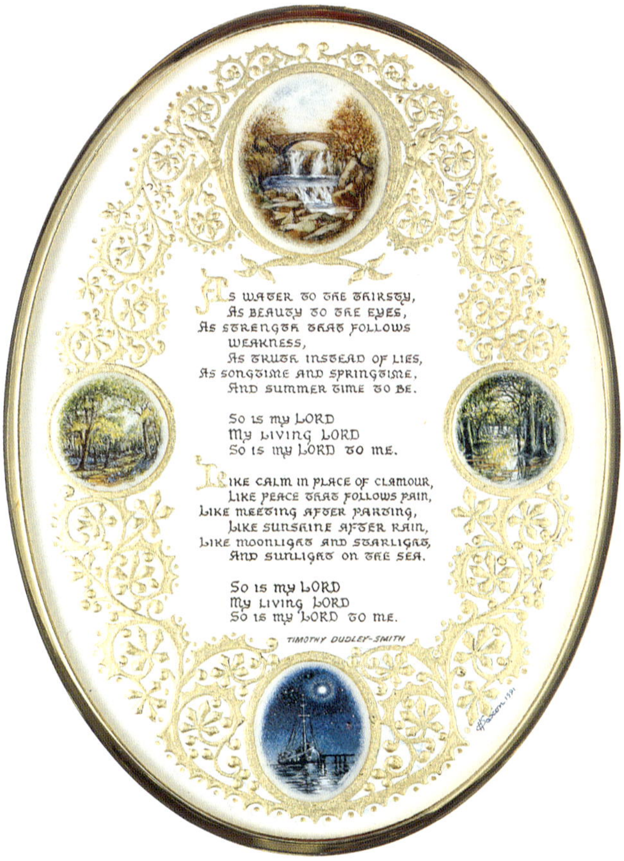
As water to the thirsty,
As beauty to the eyes,
As strength that follows weakness,
As truth instead of lies,
As songtime and springtime,
And summer time to be.
So is my LORD
My living LORD
So is my LORD to me.
Like calm in place of clamour,
Like peace that follows pain,
Like meeting after parting,
Like sunshine after rain,
Like moonlight and starlight,
And sunlight on the sea.
So is my LORD
My living LORD
So is my LORD to me.
TIMOTHY DUDLEY-SMITH

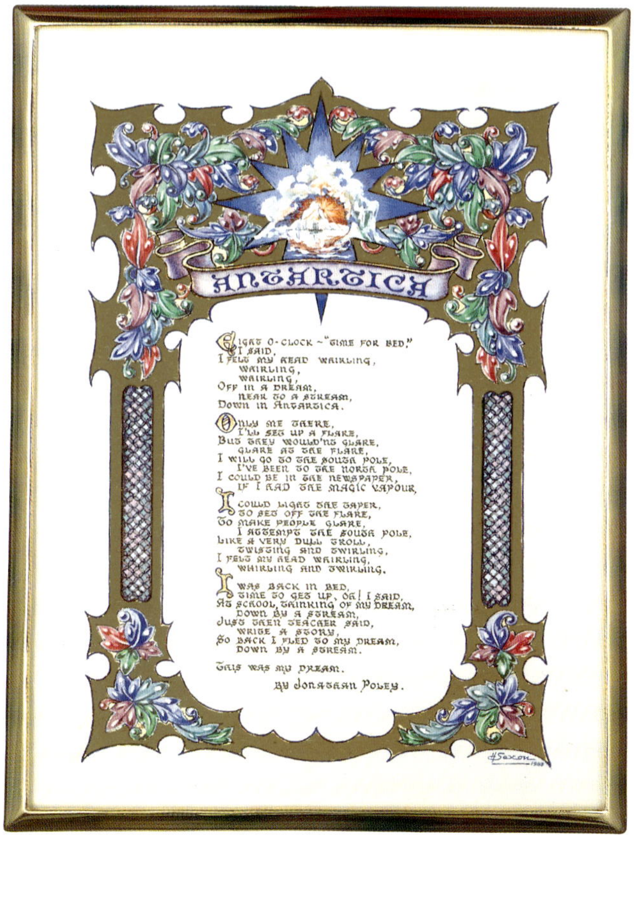
ANTARTICA
Eight o-clock ~ "Time for bed,"
I said,
I felt my head whirling,
whirling,
whirling,
Off in a dream,
near to a stream,
Down in Antartica.
Only me there,
I'll set up a flare,
But they would'nt glare,
glare at the flare,
I will go to the south pole,
I've been to the north pole,
I could be in the newspaper,
if I had the magic vapour,
I could light the taper,
to set off the flare,
To make people glare,
I attempt the south pole,
Like a very dull troll,
twisting and twirling,
I felt my head whirling,
whirling and twirling.
I was back in bed,
time to get up, oh! I said,
At school, thinking of my dream,
down by a stream,
Just then teacher said,
write a story,
So back I fled to my dream,
down by a stream.
This was my dream.
By Jonathan Poley.

Phyllis Arnold

RMS PPUSWA UWS HS Gold Memorial Bowl 1988

Portrait of Eithna
(water-colour on vellum)

Seánin and Gráinne Gilmore in Profile
(gouache on plaster)

Portrait of Carolyn Julia Berry
(water-colour on vellum)

Phyllis Arnold worked in a commercial art studio in Belfast for a short time in the late fifties, then left to marry a chartered aeronautical engineer. She has two sons and a wayward pekinese!

Now a leading portrait miniaturist, her first drawing in silhouette was made by mistake. Fate took a hand and, since 1968, she has been a self-employed artist, while working half of the week in her antique and fine art gallery in Greyabbey, County Down.

Phyllis is the only present-day artist to specialize in portrait silhouettes painted on plaster with gouache, combining a sharp profile outline with diaphanous hair, lace and transparency of costume as in the Georgian shades. These are traditionally presented in black and gold acorn frames.

Her jewellery portrait silhouettes are scaled down from four by three inches to half an inch for rings and are overpainted with shell gold and enhanced with gold and silver antique settings.

She has done profiles of many renowned figures in public life. In 1977 Coalport Porcelain commissioned her to paint a profile of Her Majesty the Queen to celebrate her Jubilee. Over a dozen different porcelain pieces carried the Queen's profile, mostly limited editions. She presented two original paintings to Her Majesty of her likeness.

Finding herself alone as the only miniature painter in Ireland, it was the annual visit to the Royal Miniature Society private view which never failed to inspire her for another year. She found it tempted her to try colour portraits. With no books or classes available, it was back to the trial and error method. Now her commissions are for silhouettes and colour portraits equally, both winning awards.

All through the lonely years her driving ambition was to hold a Royal Miniature Society Member's Diploma. To her surprise and delight in 1988 she reached her goal and was also awarded the prestigious Gold Memorial Bowl, her most coveted award.

She has won many prizes, including three Hunting Group Finalist certificates, the Gold Memorial Bowl Honourable Mention in its inaugural year of 1985 and a Llewellyn Alexander award for the Best Miniature in 1993. She is a Past President of the Ulster Society of Women Artists and Founder President of the Ulster Society of Miniaturists.

Lately, she has found enjoyment in painting rare breeds of poultry and discovered that, with their colours and textures, research into them between portrait work is a relaxation.

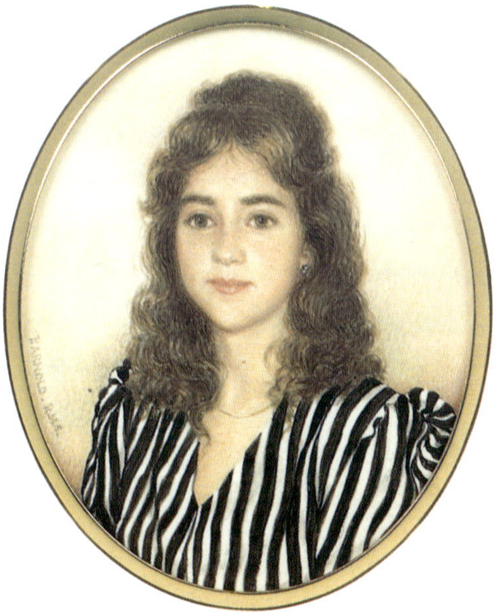

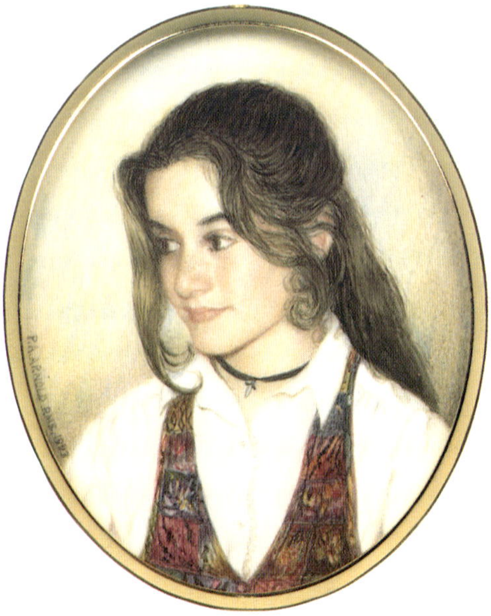

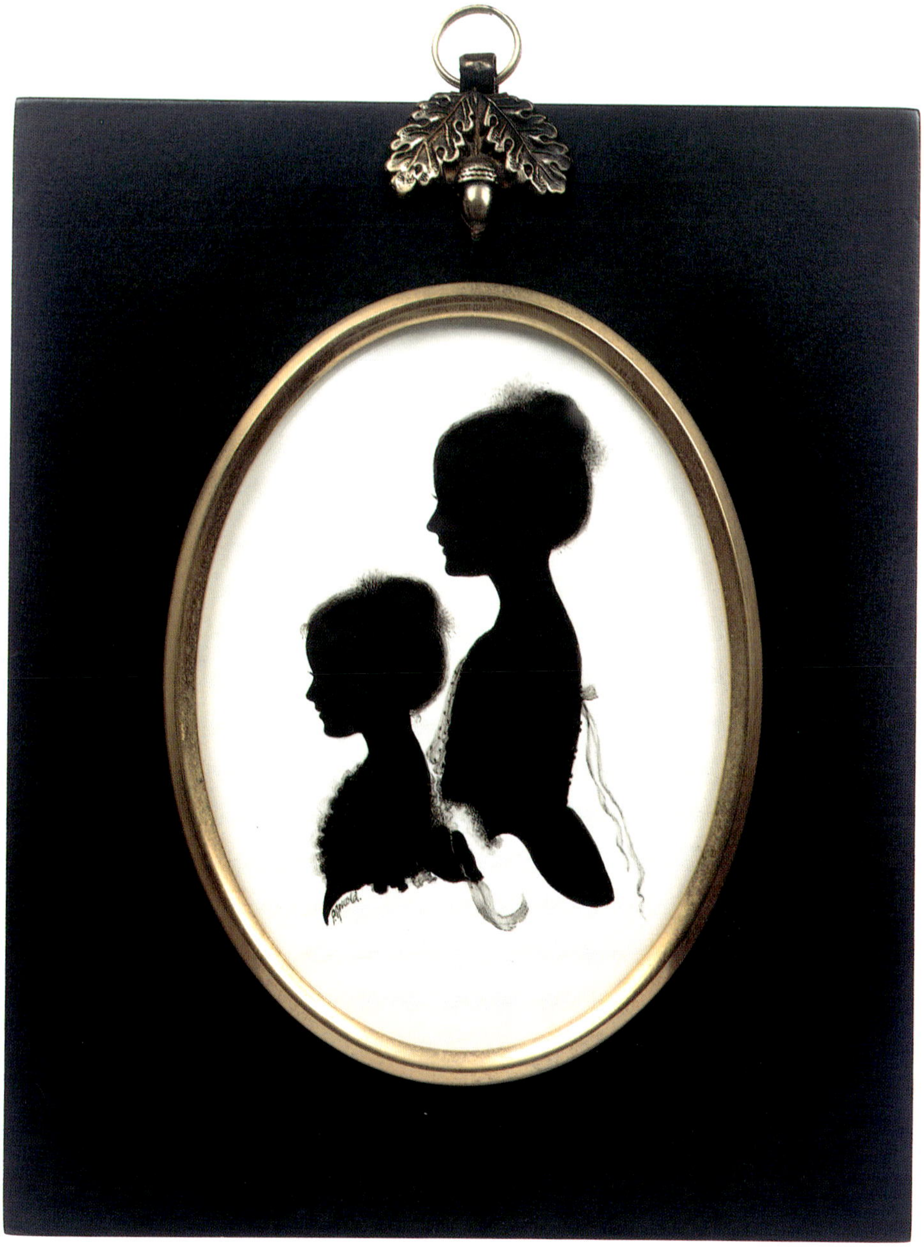

Sheila Fairman

RMS SWA FSBA HSF Gold Memorial Bowl 1989

Danish Iced Pastries
(oil on Ivorine)
from the Diploma Collection

Harvest Mouse
(oil on Ivorine)

Sweets and a Walnut Whirl
(oil on Ivorine)

Fruit with Willow Pattern China
(oil on Ivorine)

Born in August 1924, she lives in Leigh-on-Sea, Essex. She won a scholarship to the Southend-on-Sea College of Art in 1939. She took up painting seriously in 1969, pursuing her interest in both drawing and painting, mainly in the study of portraiture and life-drawing at college. She also designed and painted the scenery for local dramatic societies.

Her interest in still life dates back many years to a visit to the Fitzwilliam Museum in Cambridge, where she fell in love with Fantin-Latour's study of a white cup and saucer. This is a painting of the utmost simplicity which opened her eyes to the beauty of everyday objects. Her love for miniature painting stems from her eye for detail and a delight in everything that is small.

Her 'Shells and Feathers' series of paintings was exhibited for many years in the Royal Society of Marine Artists exhibitions and for three years at the Royal Academy Summer Exhibitions. She works in oil on Ivorine, which produces a glow similar to that given by ivory. Oil is a good medium for blending colours easily and for glazing, when the under paint is dry, to create extra transparency and glow. Darker areas of colour are best left in thin layers, but thicker paint can be used to good effect in the lighter parts and for highlights.

Sheila exhibits widely in London both with Societies and in galleries, including the Royal Institute of Painters in Water Colours and the Royal Institute of Oil Painters. She has been both a finalist and a prize winner with the Hunting Group Art Awards in 1981, 1982 and 1983, and received the Gordon Drummond Subject Miniature Award in 1985. She was awarded the Gold Memorial Bowl in 1989 and won the Llewellyn Alexander Subject Miniature Award in 1991 with a Commendation of Excellence in 1995.

Through the years her miniatures have covered a wide range of subjects, showing her talent to be various in its interest as well as excellent in quality, including her most unusual and appealing portraits of cakes, remarkable for their realism.

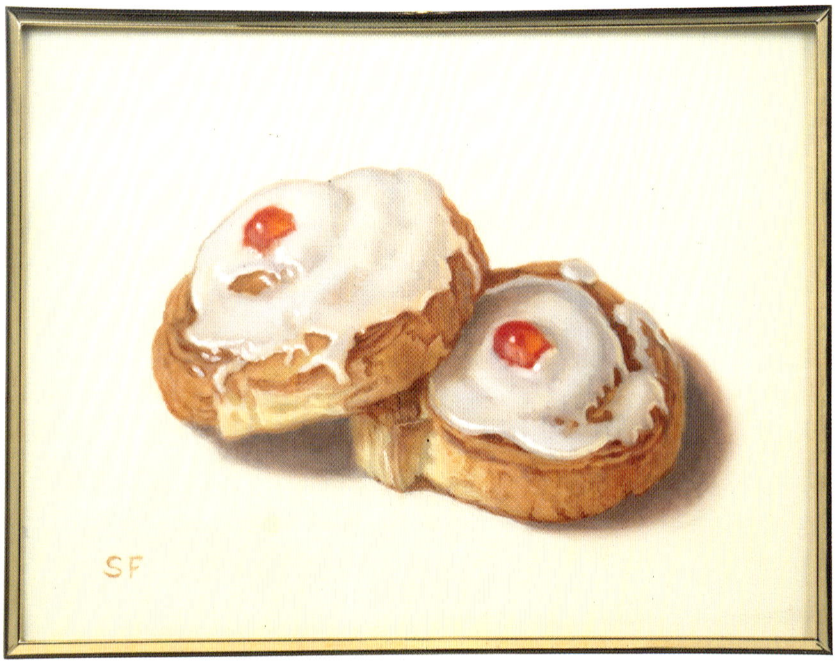
SF
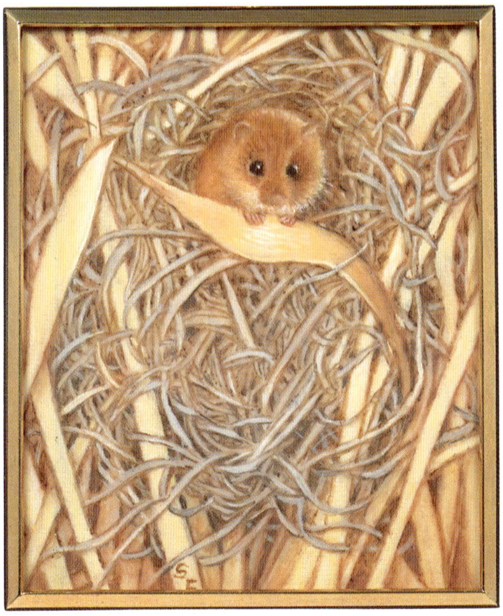
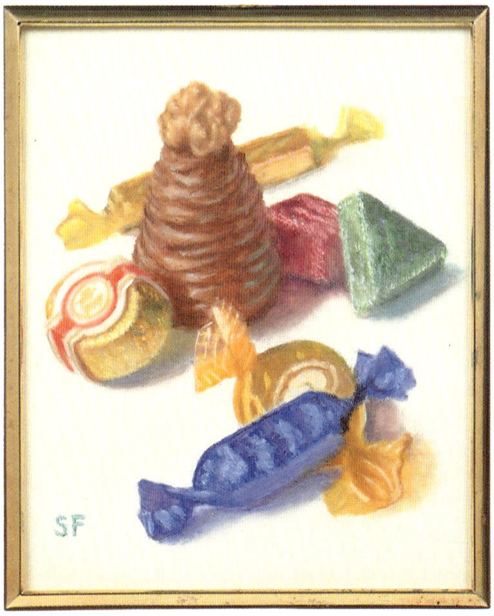
SF
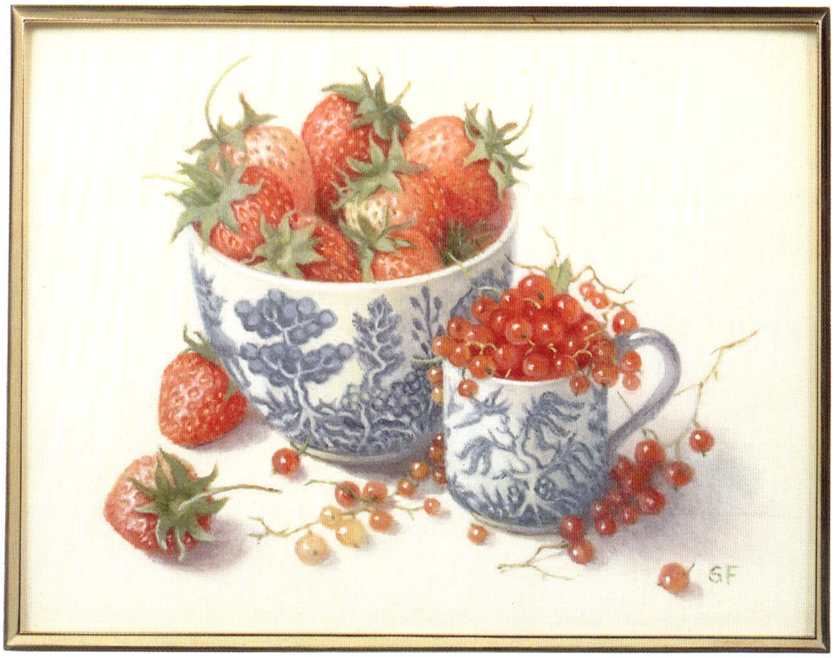
SF

Pamela Davis

VPRMS SWA FSBA HSF Gold Memorial Bowl 1991

Late Summer Roses
(acrylic on Ivorine)

Pansies
(acrylic on Ivorine)
from the Diploma Collection

After gaining a scholarship to Twickenham School of Art, Pamela studied commercial art for three years, subsequently working for a London studio.

Leaving there to get married she developed a freelance connection working on a variety of commercial subjects and designs.

In 1970 she found herself in a position to abandon commercial art and devote herself exclusively to painting the subjects of her choice, chiefly flowers and landscapes of the English countryside.

The entirety of her work is executed with great attention to detail which is the hallmark of her painting. She works in all media, favouring acrylic, oil and gouache. Her pictures are used extensively as reproductions for greetings cards and calendars.

She was a finalist in the Hunting Group art prizes in 1982, 1983 and 1984 and she received the distinction of a Gold Memorial Bowl Honourable Mention at the Royal Miniature Society Exhibitions of 1985, 1986, 1987, 1988, 1989 and 1990.

Pamela won the Royal Society of Miniature Painters Sculptors and Gravers Gold Memorial Bowl Award in 1991.

A miniature by her was judged the joint best in show at the Hilliard Annual Exhibition of 1987, receiving the Suzanne Lucas Award. Further honours included the Best in Show in the international section of the Ulster Society of Miniaturists in 1987, the second prize of the Fairman Members Subject Award in 1992 and the Llewellyn Alexander Award in 1994.

She is a Vice President of the Royal Society of Miniature Painters, Sculptors and Gravers, a Member of the Society of Women Artists, a Founder Member of the Society of Botanical Artists and the Hilliard Society of Miniaturists.

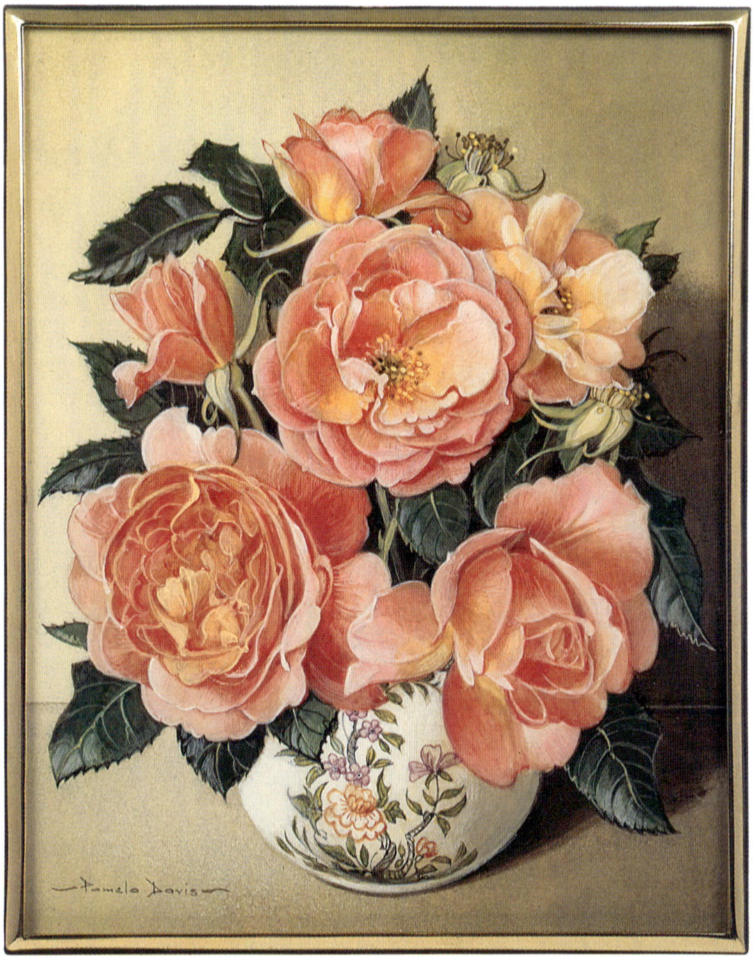
Pamela Davis

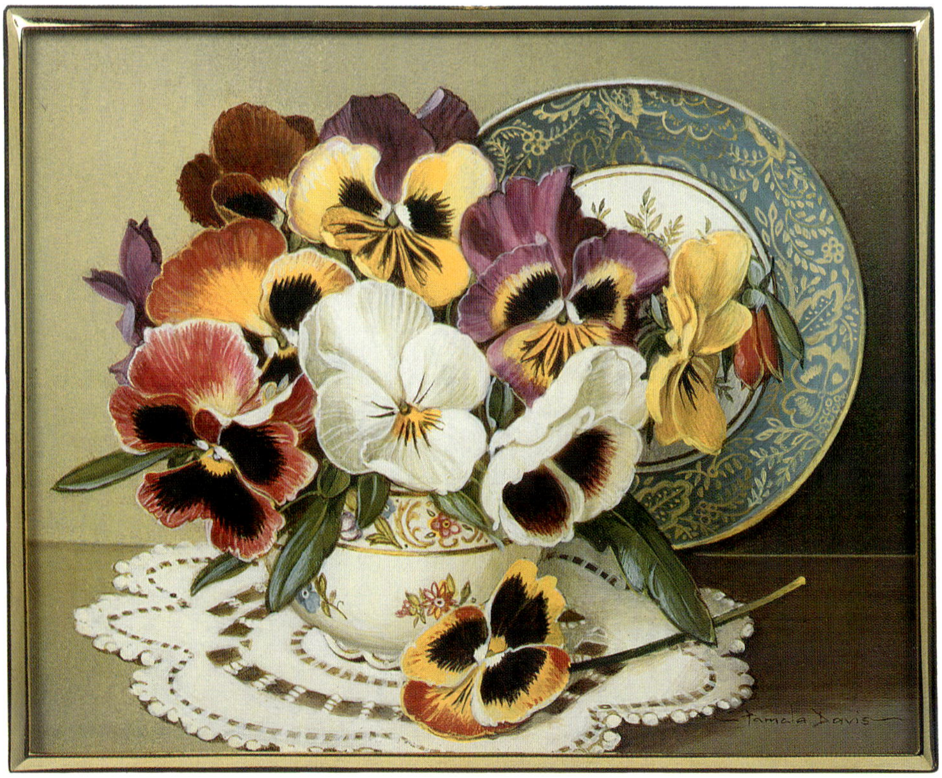
Pamela Davis

Michael R.P. Bartlett

RMS HS SLm. Gold Memorial Bowl 1992

Alisdair Gayne
(water-colour on Ivorine)

Colin del Paul
(water-colour on Ivorine)

Trained in commercial art he worked in various advertising studios before deciding to become a freelance artist. Clients included airlines, shipping companies, engineering and electrical concerns and textile manufacturers.

He became involved in exhibition stand design which led to working for architects, producing water-colour paintings of interiors and exteriors of hotels, bars, offices and domestic premises.

His interest in miniature painting began when he was asked to repair an antique miniature. Restoration work for Sotheby's, Christie's and collectors provided an excellent opportunity to study at close hand the techniques of English, American and Continental miniature painters of past centuries before painting portraits on his own account.

As well as winning a Gold Memorial Bowl Honourable Mention in 1991 with the Bowl itself in 1992, he had won the Mundy Sovereign Portrait Award in 1990 and a Llewellyn Alexander Award in 1993.

Whether working from life or photographs, he makes preliminary water-colour sketches to the size of the proposed final painting, for choice of pose and colouring, before transferring the composition onto vellum, Ivorine or paper.

Costume and background are often completed before the head and hands. Finished heads on pale grounds lose weight when dark or strong colours are added, for the background or costume, and additional flesh-tone working afterwards can lead to a muddy appearance. Painting from life needs several sittings.

Backgrounds can often be very time-consuming but powdered pastels, blended and rubbed onto the painting surface, give soft tonal or cloud effects and speed up the process. Careful masking of the figure is necessary to prevent colour spreading to it. The pastel is sprayed with a fixative, before the masking is removed, and can be overpainted with water-colour. A portrait is rarely shown to the sitter in an unfinished state: to encounter oneself, half bald and with only one eye, can be disturbing and certainly unflattering! It is best to present the pleasant surprise of the finished work to the client.

Michael Bartlett is now a very well-known portrait artist and is invited by such institutions as the Victoria and Albert Museum to give lectures on miniature painting to-day.

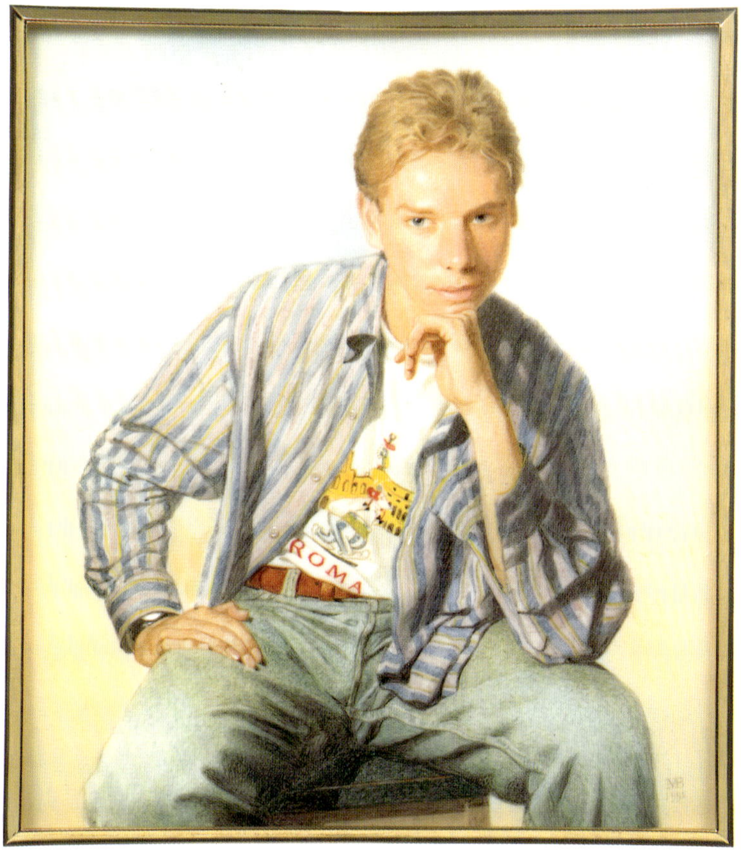
ROMA

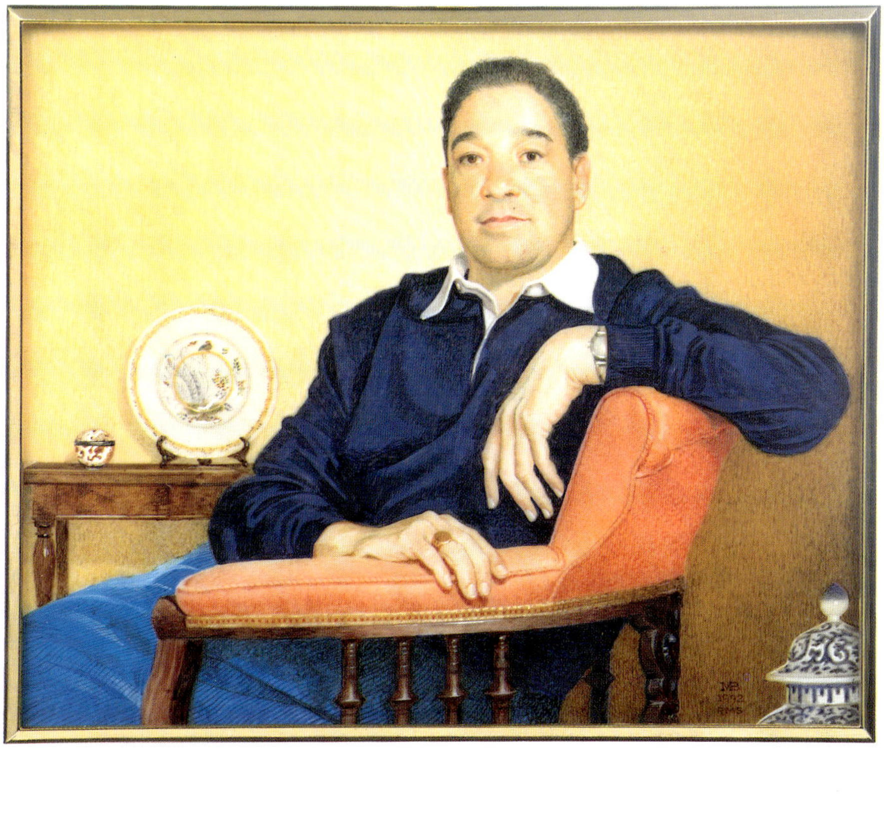

Pauline Gyles

RMS FSBA HS Gold Memorial Bowl 1994

Josephine
(water-colour on Ivorine)

Apples with Poole Pottery
(water-colour on Ivorine)

Pauline has lived all her life in the Bournemouth area. Her father was the senior partner in a firm of estate agents, founded by her great-grandfather, with offices all along the south coast.

She married her husband, a hotelier, in 1955. During the winter months when the hotel was closed they would take off in their sports car for Spain, driving thousands of miles with no set itinerary along unmade roads, visiting present-day holiday resorts long before airports or tourists came onto the scene.

Living so close to beautiful Poole Harbour it was only natural that they should own a boat, enjoying all the associated activities and social life.

Only after the sale of the hotel was there more time to devote to painting and the discovery of miniature work turned her into a compulsive artist.

She did not follow any formal art school training but has specialized in miniature painting for the past eighteen years. She exhibited with the Royal Miniature Society for the first time in 1976, was elected an Associate Member in 1981 and a Member in 1985. At present she is the Honorary Secretary of the Society. She was awarded two Gold Memorial Bowl Honourable Mentions in 1987 and 1992 and at the Hilliard Society exhibitions of 1989 and 1991 she won the Suzanne Lucas Best Painting and the Bell Best Portrait Awards. In 1990 the second prize Fairman Award was presented to her and in 1994 the Mundy Sovereign Portrait Award with a Commendation of Excellence from the Llewellyn Alexander Gallery in 1995. She is a Founder Member of the Society of Botanical Artists and paints flower and plant studies for exhibition with the Society as well as miniatures. She has always lived in Dorset and her work is shown widely in both local and London galleries. The Russell Cotes Art Gallery and Museum in Bournemouth and the Society of Apothecaries of London have examples of her paintings in their collections.

Her miniatures have been reproduced for fine art publications and she is well-known for the delicacy of her portraits. Her still life work is particular in the shapes and colours of the china or earthenware vessels which she collects for it, often with a future picture in mind. She enjoys her portrait and still life work very much, but also finds time to teach the art of miniature painting and lecture on it regularly, as well as creating her larger flower studies.

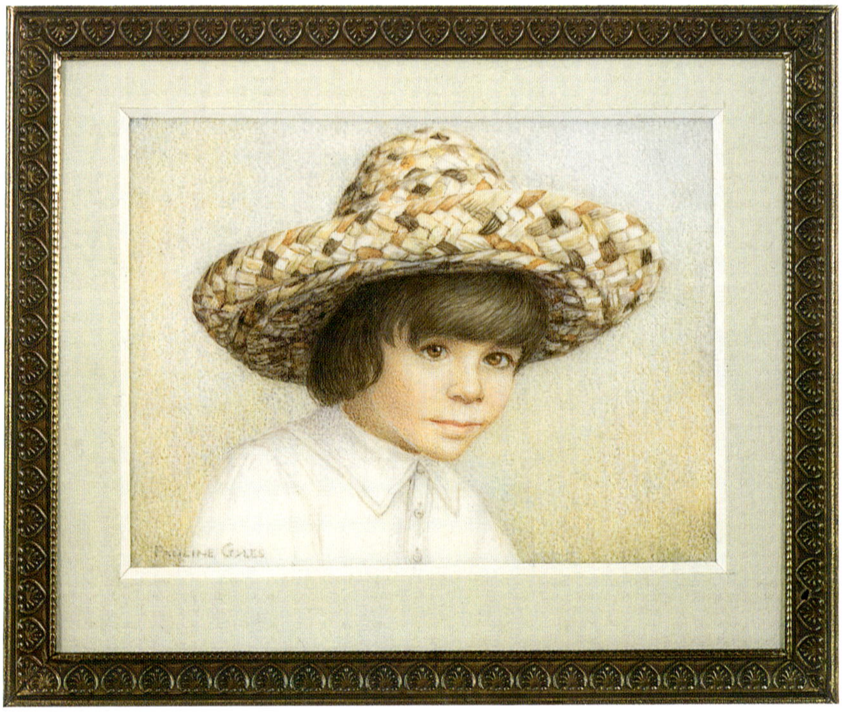
PAULINE GYLES

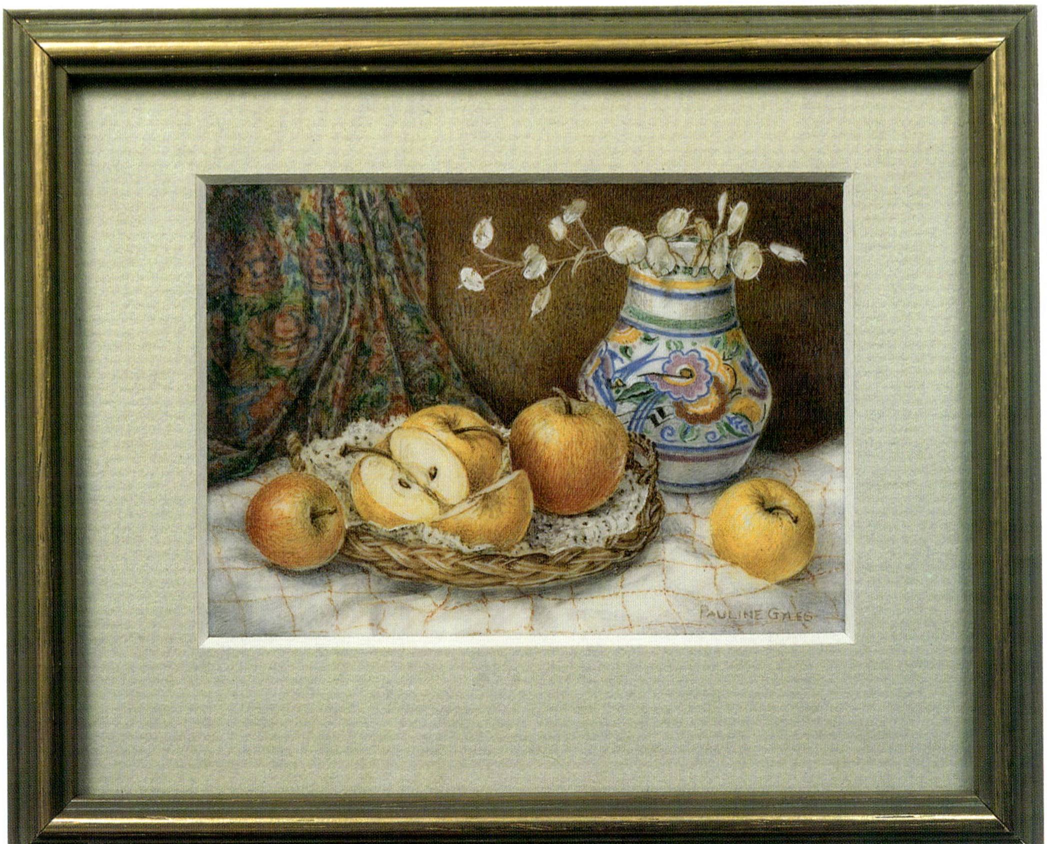
PAULINE GYLES

Suzanne Lucas

FLS PRMS FPSBA SWA HSF
Médaille de la France Libre

Alpine Flowers
(water-colour on ivory)

Toadstools and Autumn Leaves
(water-colour on ivory)

Born in India and surrounded by the vibrant colours of saris, butterflies, birds and flowers, her first love was an exquisite tropical bird. Childhood memories include a vast cloud of golden butterflies, sunset over the Himalayas and the revelation of the stars. She returned home to Devon and was sent to Roedean School and Edinburgh University. Her mother, who believed in travel as excellent education, then took her through Europe including language courses at Grenoble and Munich Universities. They met Hitler and were deluded by the magnificent presentation of Nazi dogma. In Berlin the illusion was dispelled by the murder of an anti-Nazi friend.

Back in Italy she sailed from Venice to join her father, posted to Egypt by the Royal Air Force. The romantic social life of the Suez Canal Headquarters town, Ismailia, ended at the outbreak of war just before she married the Director of Navigation. Under threat of imminent German invasion she was on half-hour notice to evacuate the family.

Her husband had founded the Free French Movement in Egypt leading to a dangerous flight to join Général de Gaulle in London. He took part in the invasion and, after promotion to Admiral, became Governor of Brest. There she saw the devastation of a city flattened by bombs, then in contrast a liberated Paris where art lived again in extra-ordinary beauty and enthusiasm.

On retirement she bought an enchanted cottage where she tamed the animals and birds and began a serious art career. She was elected by the Royal Miniature Society in 1954 and, after being a constant Council Member, served as Honorary Secretary and Vice President until becoming President in 1980.

Exhibiting at the Royal Academy, Paris Salon, Royal Institute, the Linnean Society of London and, most recently, the Presidents' Exhibition at the Royal Birmingham Society of Artists, her one-man shows were at the Stadmore Gallery, Liberty's, Atlanta U.S.A. and three at the Mall Galleries where she was a Director of the Federation of British Artists and four times a Hunting Group Prize finalist.

She was awarded thirteen Gold Medals during her eighteen years painting toadstools, promoting their beauty and interest. She wrote, illustrated and published a book 'In Praise of Toadstools', preceding the present Hundredth Anniversary Volume for the Royal Miniature Society.

Her work covers detailed pictures of plants and flowers and in 1985 she founded the Society of Botanical Artists of which she is the Founder President.

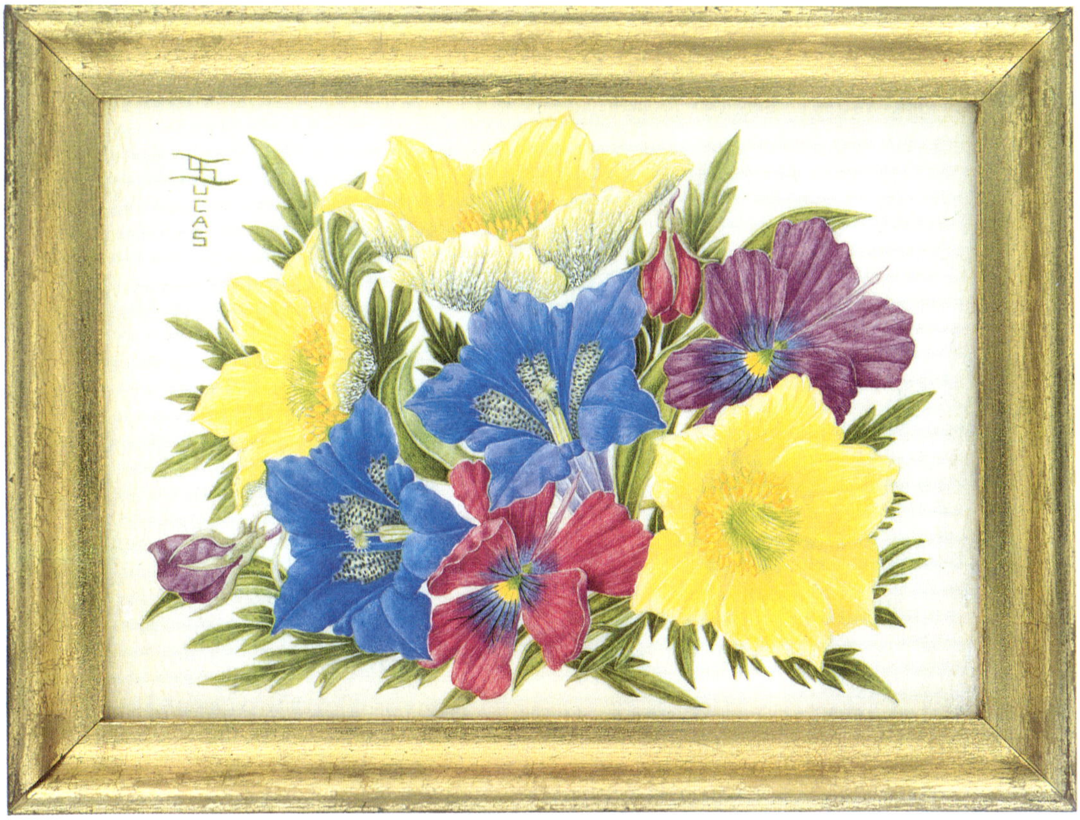
LUCAS

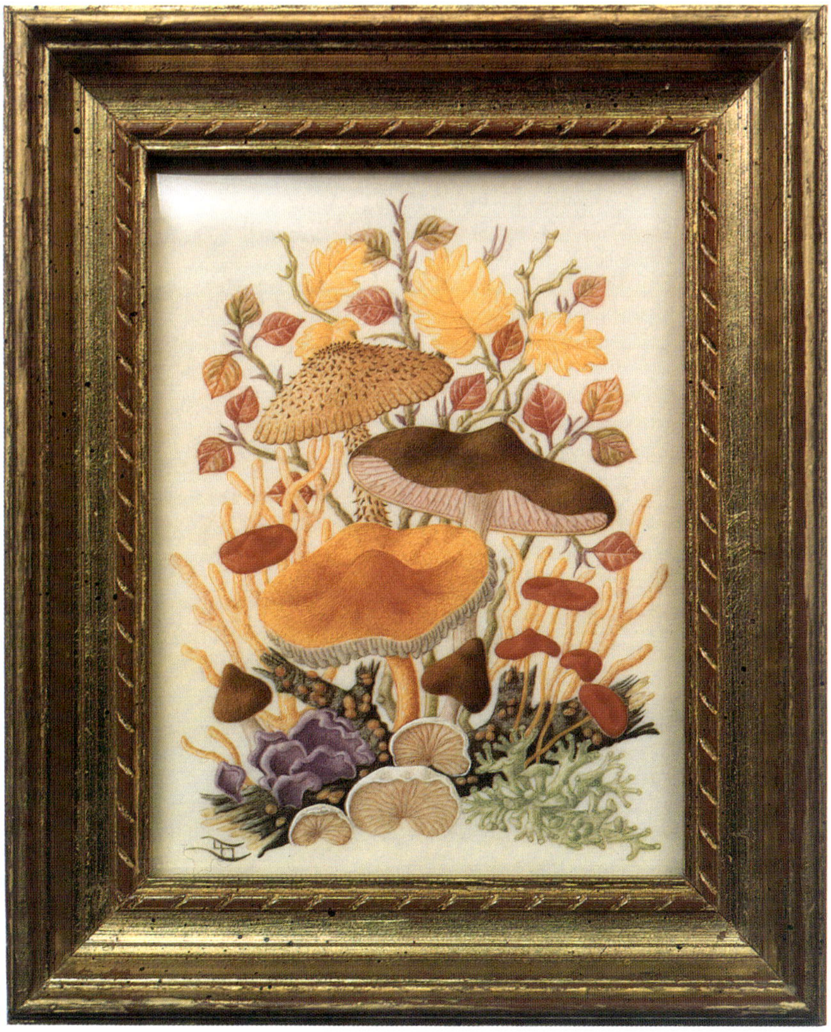

Peter Dreiser

VPRMS FGE FDC BAG

"Stagnation"

(glass worked in high relief)

this pictures the sad plight of fish in polluted waters and speaks of the artist's deep concern for the world of nature and its protection and conservation

view from above

side view

He was born in Cologne, but after his early years life there became unbearable and in 1943 the family left the ruined city for Bavaria, where the Allgäu valley became home for the next three years. The locals treated them with hostility and life at school was strained, but outside were the mountains and forests and the meandering trout stream flowing through aromatic alpine meadows. A child from an industrial city thought this was paradise and cherished memories are the foundation of his love for the countryside. On expulsion from paradise in 1946, when the authorities enforced their return to Cologne, the twin spires of the cathedral, stretching above the frozen November mist, greeted them after a twelve day journey in a cattle truck.

School days finished, he was advised to study arts or crafts and visited the glass college at Rheinbach, run by Bohemian refugees following Czechoslovakian glass-making traditions. Training was thorough, covering all aspects from stained glass to cutting and engraving. Engraved glass won his admiration and he enrolled for a three year course, discovering that to learn was fun.

Aged eighteen he worked as a glass cutter, but the drudgery of conveyor belt methods was a slavery he endured for only a few weeks before moving to a family firm, cutting and engraving. In 1955 he took a position with a London glass company, expanding into luxury glass, and so left Germany.

In 1958 he built an engraving lathe from metal scraps, so could use his spare time engraving artistic pieces. In 1962 Thomas Goode & Co. offered him a permanent position, but after eight years he became a freelance craftsman having joined the Society of Designer Craftsmen in the sixties. After exhibiting with the Royal Miniature Society several times he was elected an Associate in 1972 and a Member in 1978. In 1993 he won a Gold Memorial Bowl Honourable Mention and the Bidder and Borne – Royal Miniature Society Sculpture Award. In 1975 he was a Founder Member of the Guild of Glass Engravers and a Craftsman in the Crafts Council Index. In 1977, with a Crafts Council Bursary, he toured Czechoslovakia and Germany to study collections and visit a glass school in Bohemia. On his return he collaborated in writing 'The Techniques of Glass Engraving', now a text-book.

He accepts commissions, but it is work done for exhibitions that expresses his love of nature and despair at its destruction. Collectors and museums buy these pieces. He works with the traditional wheel-engraving lathe using copper, stone and diamond wheels and, when necessary, a combination of wheels, dental burrs and tungsten tips.

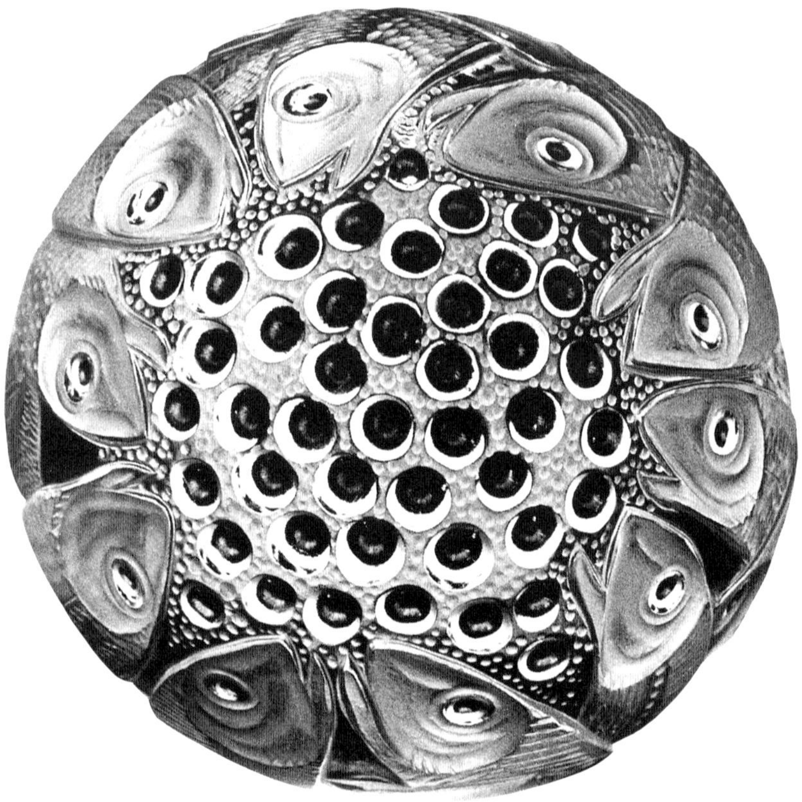

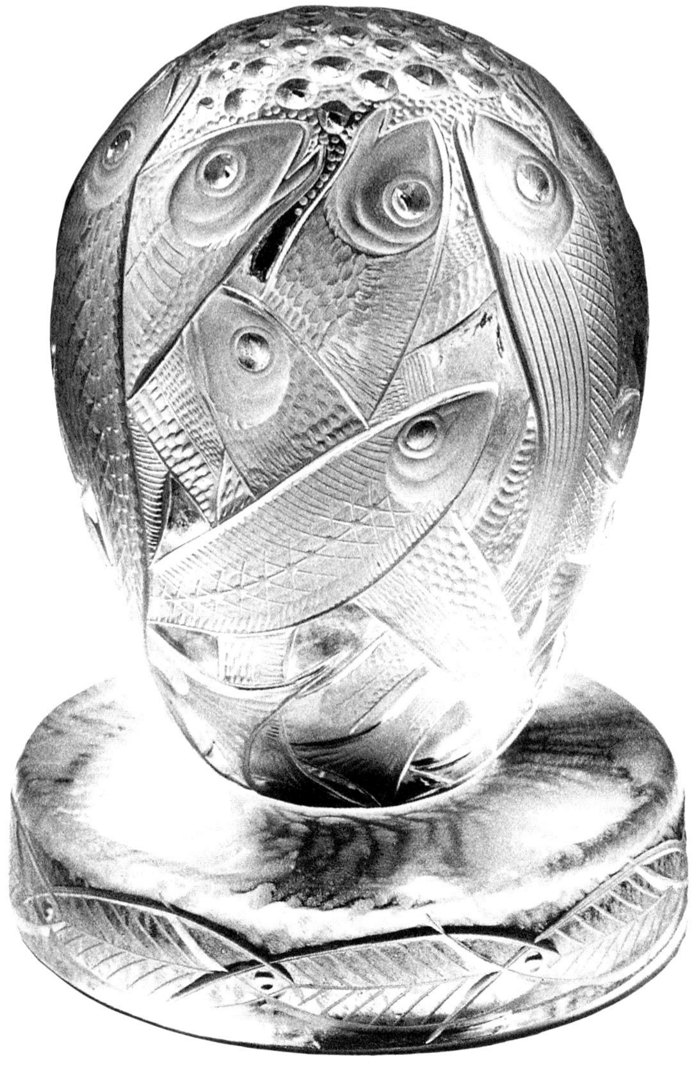

G. Sydney Shorthouse

VPRMS MASF HS MAA

Johan Ten-Houten
(water-colour on ivory)

Vivienne Cawson
(water-colour on Ivorine)

Alice Shorthouse
(water-colour on ivory)

Harold Larwood
(water-colour on ivory)

He was born in Leicestershire and the early art influences on him as a boy were from the family and especially from an art teacher who wrote and illustrated wildlife books. Growing up in the countryside meant that he chose his subjects from the nature around him which he saw and loved. Almost unconsciously this became a challenge to paint things in the finest detail possible.

After war-time flying service in the Royal Air Force he followed a career in commercial design in the Gas Industry, heading a design team at the East Midlands Gas Board Headquarters. At the age of forty he joined the Board of a Leicester Company and founded City Design, which served the broadly based design needs in retail and manufacturing of the footwear industry, both in Britain and Europe.

He began miniature painting when he retired in 1983 and is now a Vice President of the Royal Miniature Society, a Council Member of the Hilliard Society and a Signature Member of the Miniature Artists of America. He belongs to the Miniature Art Society of Florida and has exhibited there and in Washington D.C. for a number of years.

His awards include several Gold Memorial Bowl Honourable Mention Diplomas, the Mundy Sovereign Portrait Award, the Bell Portrait Award and others from the Hilliard Society, with various prizes in the United States.

Among his many commissions are portraits of several well-known cricketers painted for the Nottinghamshire County Cricket Club.

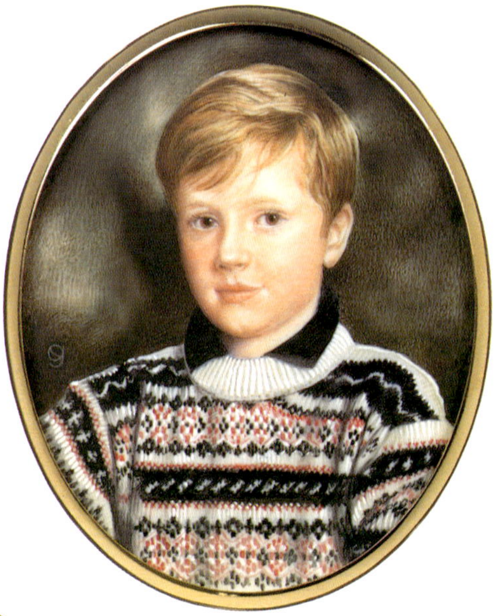

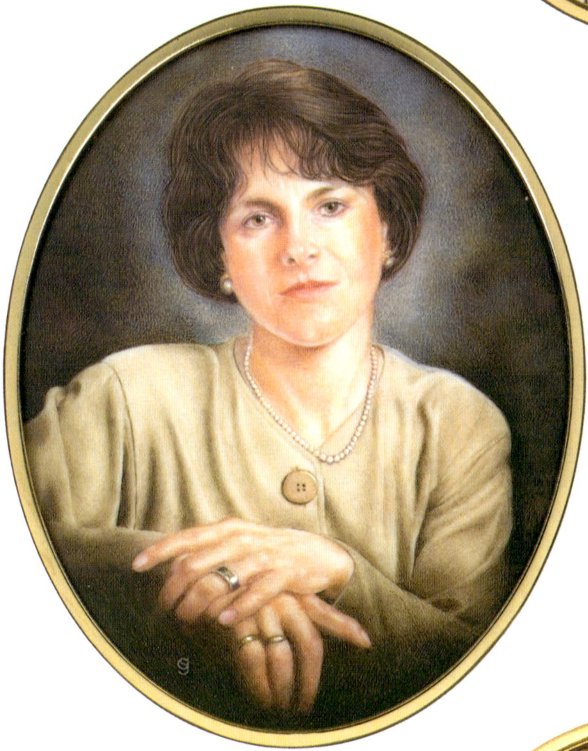

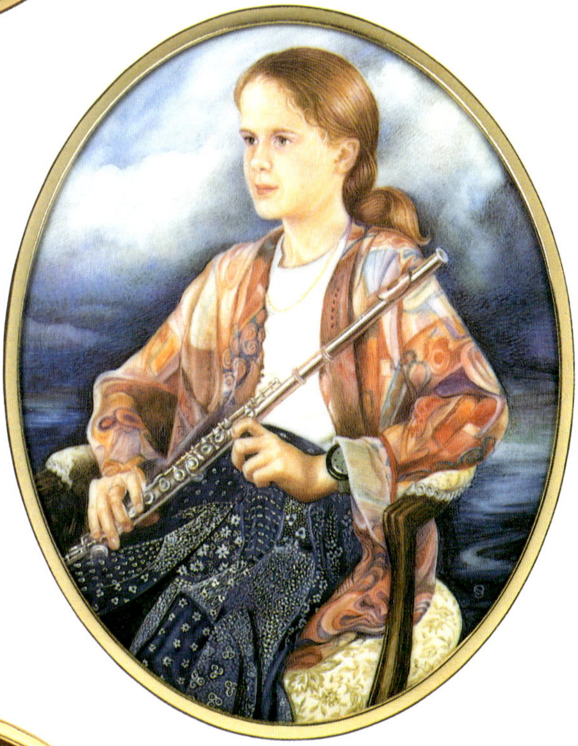

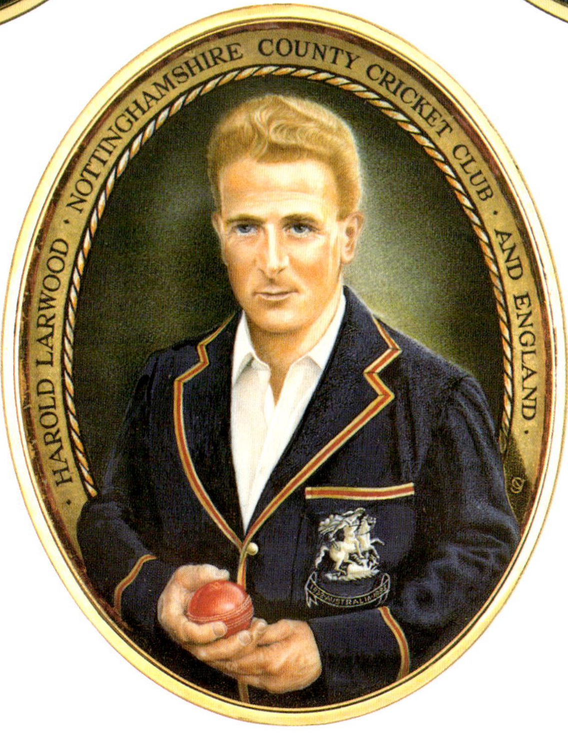
HAROLD LARWOOD · NOTTINGHAMSHIRE COUNTY CRICKET CLUB · AND ENGLAND

Alastair MacDonald

RMS Hon.UA FRSA

Late October
(gouache on card)
kindly lent by Brigitte Helmich-Kemp

Waterend, Mymms
(gouache on card)
kindly lent by the President

Alastair was born in Tighnabruaich in the Kyles of Bute in 1934. Educated in south-east London during the Second World War he won a scholarship to the Woolwich Polytechnic School of Arts and Crafts. His main interests were fabric design, heraldry and cartoons, the latter inspired by the comic sections of the New York Herald Tribune sent with food parcels by an uncle living in Key West.

He served with the Royal Engineers in Germany and was in Holland during the flood disaster of 1953/54, assisting with bridging and clearing up operations. He learned sign-writing from displaced people, painted a series of murals on Regimental activities and another set for the NAAFI in Osnabruck, for the Coronation. Having a flair for humorous illustration he drew cartoons for the Regimental magazine and worked as Sportspresserzeichner for the Osnabrucker Tageblatt. Convalescence after a serious operation led to training as a telephonist with Army Movement Control based in London's Royal Docks.

He first exhibited with the Royal Society of Miniature Painters, Sculptors and Gravers in 1966. Elected an Associate in 1968, and a Member in 1969, he was a regular member of Council between 1972 and 1981 when he became Honorary Treasurer.

He has exhibited at national level for many years and awards include three Gold Memorial Bowl Honourable Mentions, the Prix du Souvenir Jossett Bossez, Chaville, Paris (International Award), the Llewellyn Alexander Commendation of Excellence and the Masters Award in 1995. He was also a Hunting Group Finalist.

Apart from painting miniatures, he spent over thirty years as a Senior Artist and Display Supervisor in the field of lettering and serigraphics. Designing sales promotion and point of sale material meant that, although based at Head Office, he travelled throughout Britain to superstore openings and refurbishments and trained display staff. He designed badges, logos and sign-written boards for major art societies and other organizations.

He is an Honorary Member of the United Society of Artists, a Life Fellow of the Royal Society of Arts and Founder Vice President and programme secretary of the Hatfield Art Society. A keen member of the Royal British Legion he is Treasurer of his local branch and the Barnet Borough Branches Association. He serves on the management committee of Breaks Manor Youth and Community Centre dealing with publicity.

Alastair and his wife Anne celebrated their thirty-eighth wedding anniversary recently and have two sons, three daughters and six grand-children.

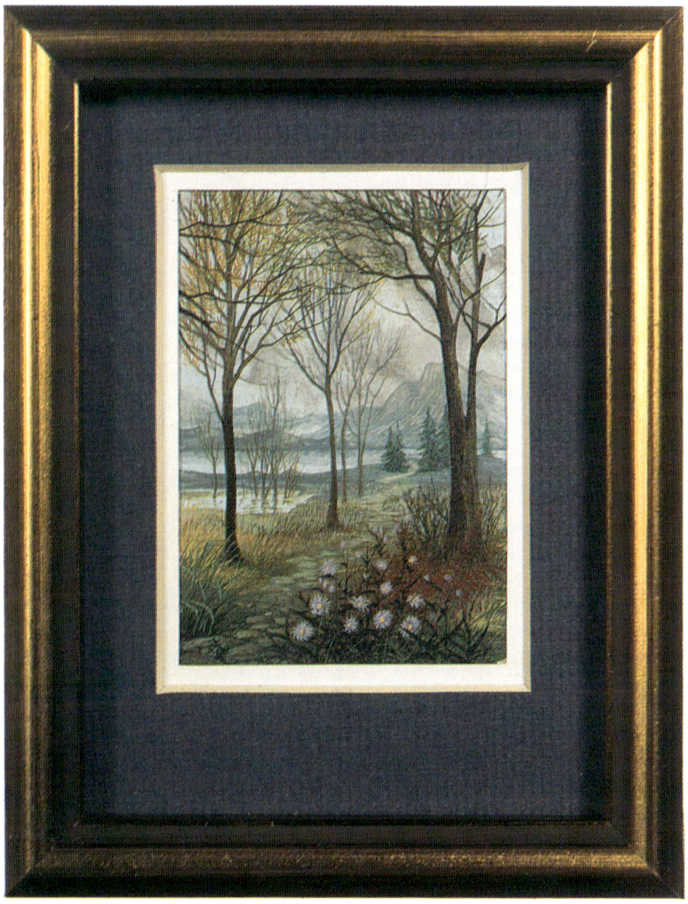

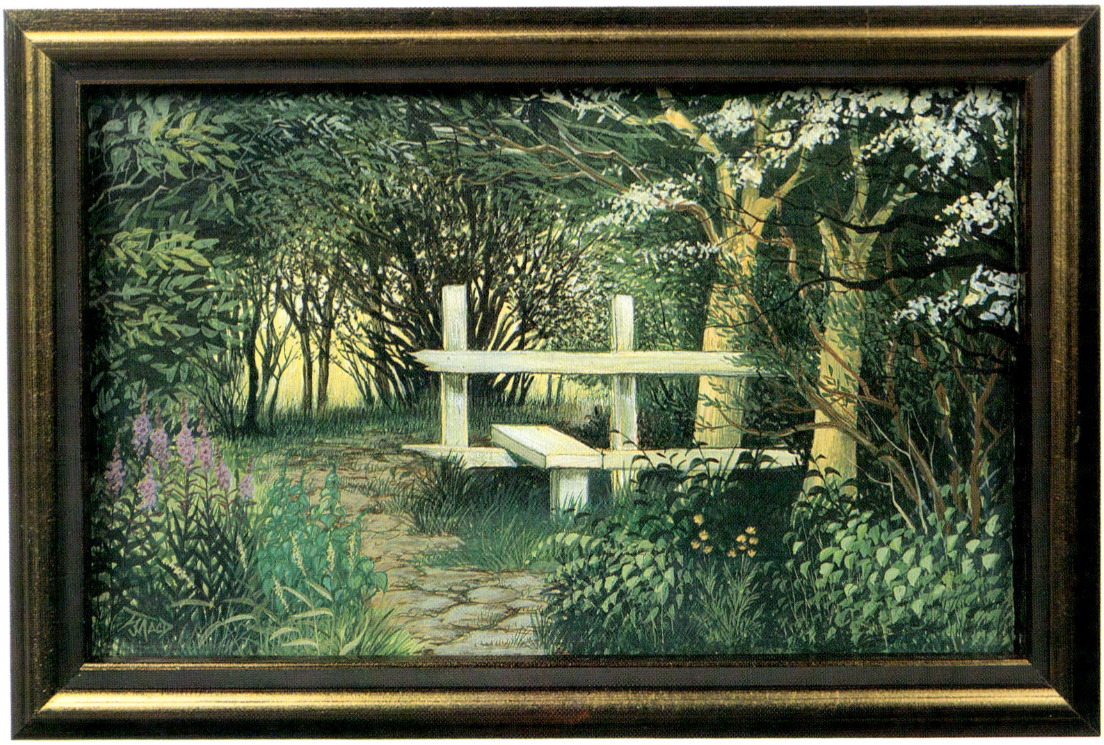

Phoebe Sholto Douglas

RMS SWA HS

One Day Old
(Rotring Artist's colour on paper)

Children Playing
(Rotring Artist's colour on paper)

She is a portrait and subject miniature painter in water-colour on ivory or vellum.

Born in Chiswick on December 27th 1906, the daughter of the humorous artist Lawson Wood, she was the fourth generation of artists in the family and started drawing at a very early age, always with the ambition to follow in her father's footsteps.

Educated privately she studied art at Eastbourne School of Art under Reeves Fowkes.

Out into the world to earn a living, not always in art, she drew and studied constantly, when time allowed, and wrote children's stories for Dean and Son and the Oxford University Press, including pen and ink illustrations. She married Keith Sholto Douglas.

Four years in the display department of Plummer Roddis in Brighton was followed by another four as advertising manager with William McIlroy in Reading. The same time was spent with Gilbert Adams, a photographer in Reading, retouching and colouring photographs including miniatures on ivory. These were done on a photographic base not acceptable, of course, as originals. This work sparked off the idea of painting miniatures. Copious studies on techniques and visits to museums followed and miniature painting became her main interest. She moved to Kent to become Head of the Art Department at Bethany School, an independent boarding school for boys, for seventeen and a half years.

In the fifties she began exhibiting miniatures and was elected an Associate of the Royal Miniature Society in 1970 and a Member two years later. She is a Member of the Society of Women Artists, the Hilliard Society and of the former Artist Enamellers of Great Britain. She exhibited at the Royal Institute, the Royal Society of British Artists, The Royal Academy and had several one-man exhibitions. She painted twenty-five bird miniatures in enamel on copper for the Nottingham Court Press, to be incorporated in the binding of a special edition of poetry and prose.

In 1983 her series of articles on miniature painting appeared in the Artist magazine. Her honours include the Mundy Sovereign Portrait Award and a Gold Memorial Bowl Honourable Mention in the Royal Miniature Society Exhibition of 1985.

Her work is represented in Daphne Foskett's book 'Collecting Miniatures', but apart from miniatures she paints imaginative water-colours and oil portraits. One of her father is with a collection of his own work in the Sunderland Art Gallery and she has miniatures in a private collection in Toronto.

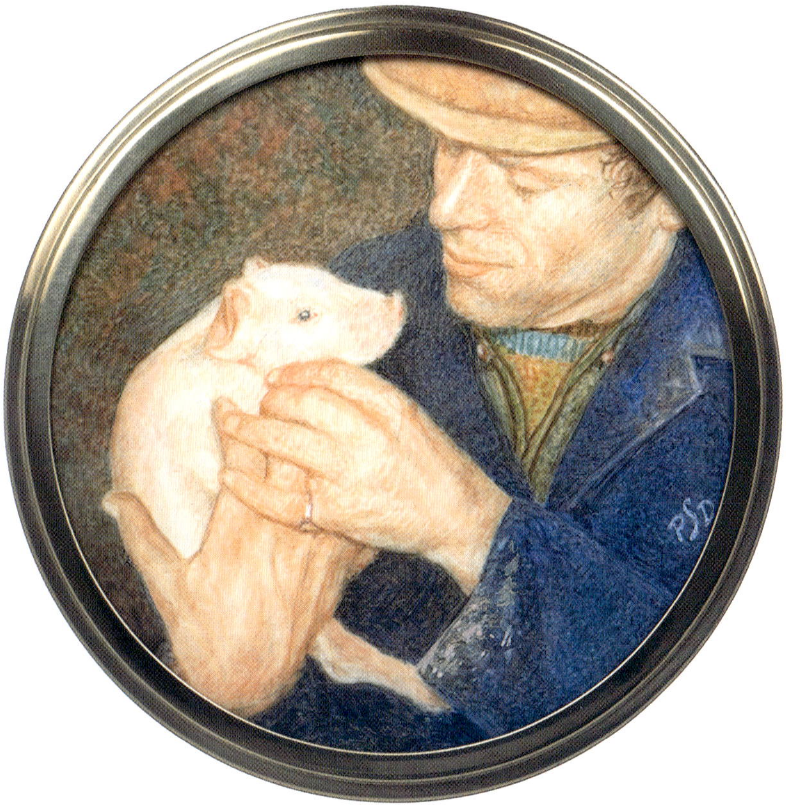
PSD

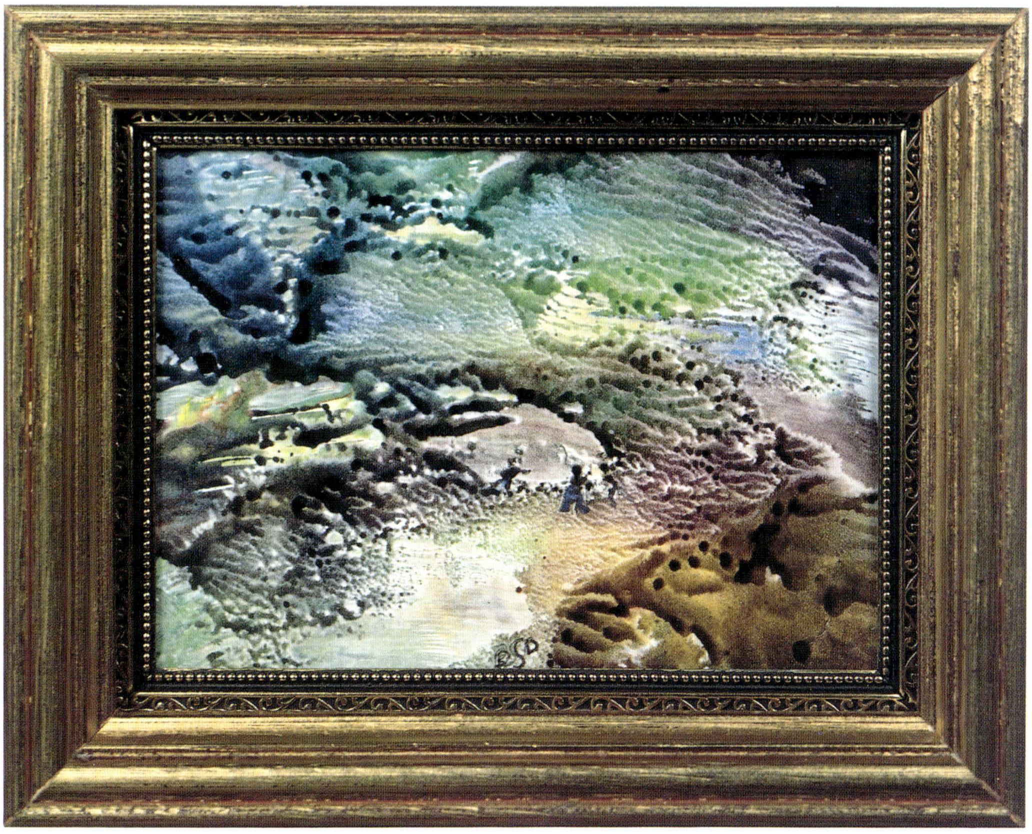

Patricia Nichols *RMS SWA*

Charlotte Franks
(oil on ivory)

Wing Commander
E.T. Carpenter AFC
(oil on ivory)

Patricia Nichols studied at the Central School of Art in London. She began painting miniatures in 1963 and was elected to full Membership of the Royal Miniature Society three years later. She served for many years on the Council and hanging committees of the Society. In 1986 she won the Mundy Sovereign Portrait Award for the most outstanding portrait in the Royal Miniature Society exhibition.

Her work has been exhibited widely and she is now one of the leading portrait miniaturists in the country, gaining particular acclaim for her portraits of children. Notable commissions have included Prince William and Prince Harry, Princess Haya, daughter of King Hussein of Jordan, and a series of portraits for The Franklin Mint. Patricia Nichols is also a member of the Society of Women Artists.

Although commissions have taken her as far afield as Los Angeles and Cape Town, normally she works and teaches in London and at her home in Norfolk.

Maureen Pearson *ARMS HS*

Trim Bridge, Bath
(water-colour and gouache on card)

Maureen was born in Cornwall in 1933 and attended the local Art School, learned to play the 'cello and piano, and was a member of the Cornwall Schools Orchestra. She became a State Registered Occupational Therapist at St Loyes School in Exeter and later was the Head Occupational Therapist for Birmingham City Council Social Services. In 1956 she married an architect and had a son and two daughters. In 1984 she moved to Bath becoming a general manager for Social Services Community Care Implementation in 1992.

During training as an occupational therapist she met a tutor, living in exile from Hungary, whose knowledge of art stemmed from her father's library in Budapest destroyed during World War Two, who gave her the most valuable tuition she had ever known. Her main subject has been architecture and commissioned work included her picture framer's shop in Bath.

She began painting miniatures seriously in 1989 and her first miniature in the Hilliard Society exhibition in 1990 won the Suzanne Lucas Best in Exhibition Award and five paintings were accepted by the Royal Miniature Society. In 1991 she received an Honourable Mention as the runner-up for the Gold Memorial Bowl at the Society's exhibition in London.

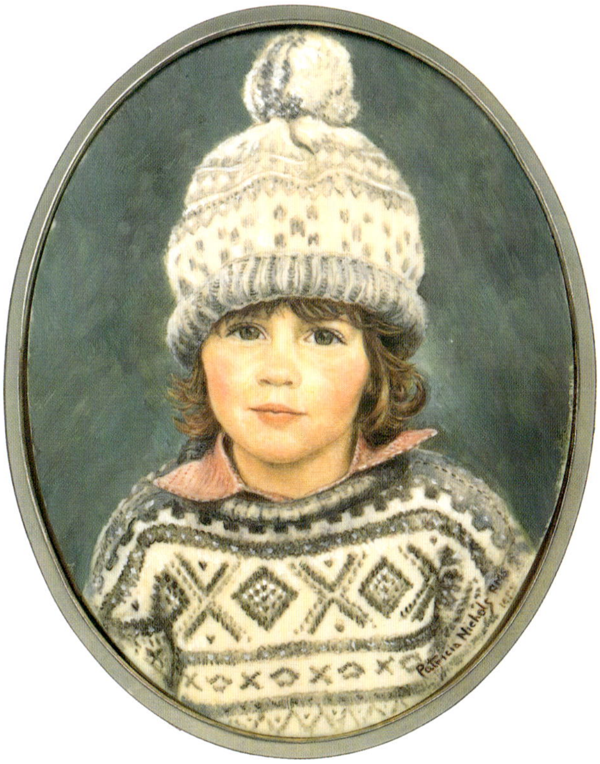

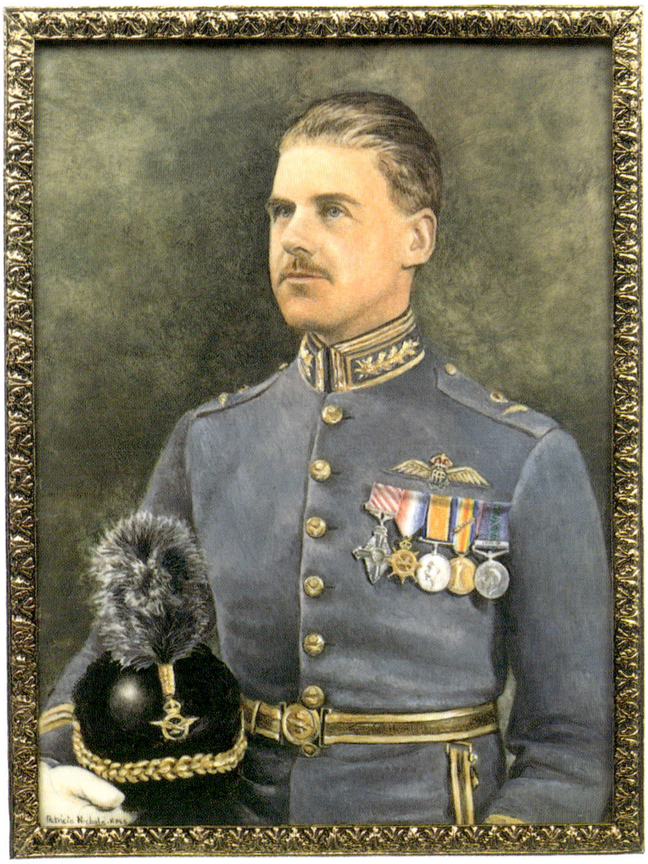

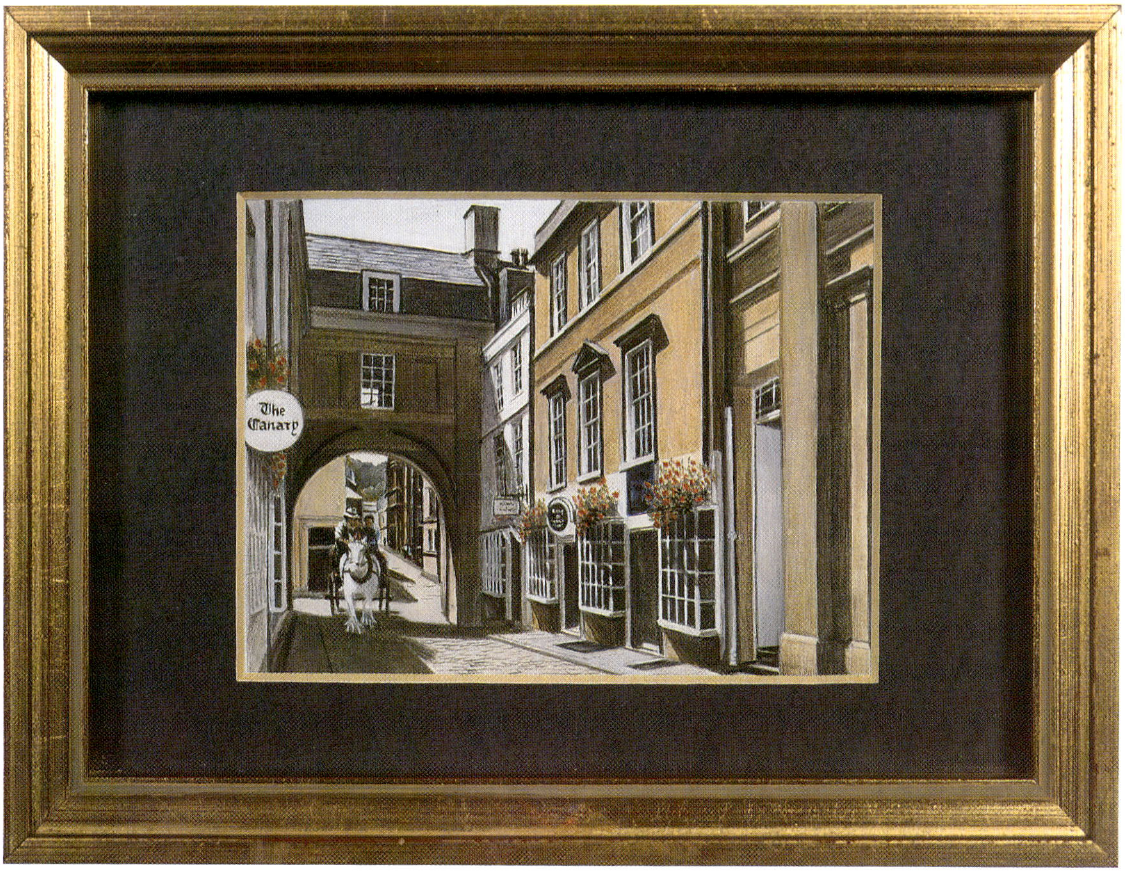
The Canary

Dorothy Bushell *RMS SWA HS*

Peter
(water-colour on Ivorine)

Jane
(water-colour on Ivorine)

She studied at the Halifax School of Art and at Reigate School of Art, working mainly on portraits in oil, then eventually developing an interest in painting miniatures in water-colour. After exhibiting at the Royal Academy of Arts Summer Exhibition and at the Mall Galleries with the Royal Miniature Society, she was elected a Member of the Society, showing thereafter at the Westminster Gallery to which the Society had moved.

She received the Mundy Sovereign Portrait Award in 1983, twice won a Gold Memorial Bowl Honourable Mention and also a Llewellyn Alexander Special Mention at their exhibition in 1993 with their Most Outstanding Miniature Award in 1994.

Her work is in the private collections of The Society of Apothecaries of London, The Royal Anglian Regiment, Le Comte le Moyne de Martigny and Major Sandys of Graythwaite.

Jonathan Halbert *RMS*

Golden Eagle Calling
(water-colour on Ivorine)
kindly lent by the President

Terriers Waiting
(water-colour on Ivorine)

He was born in the isolated splendour of the Scottish Lowlands, amid rolling hills and woodland, to the call of the curlew and the bleating of sheep. At the age of six he sculpted a little boot, four inches high and five long, out of papier-maché, painted it bright scarlet with a black sole and lining, then proudly presented it to his mother who kept and treasured the gift. Now, some forty years on, that little boot lives to-day as a loving keepsake, instilling the belief that artists are born, not made.

From that early age his skill developed, as surely and steadily as his passionate and earnest belief that there was no other course in life for him but to paint. By the age of eleven he had won his first National Art Prize, by combining painting and a country boy's enquiring interest in wildlife.

When a group of exotic wax-wings landed in the shrubbery outside the classroom window, stopping the maths lesson short, it was he who could tell his teacher and classmates the birds' identity and origin. To-day little has changed in that philosophy, and his work continues to convey a gentle, informed knowledge which charms and delights.

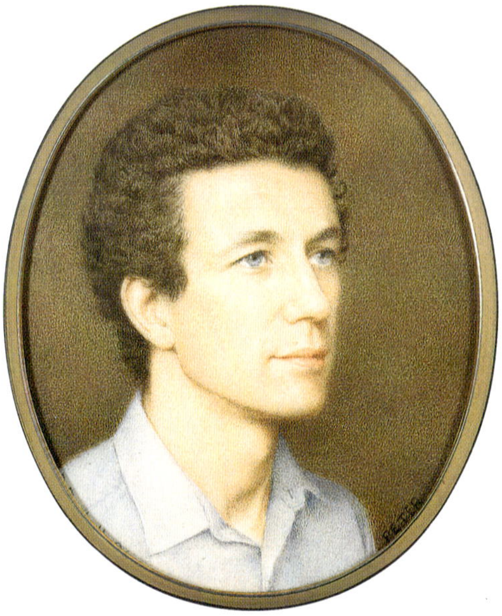

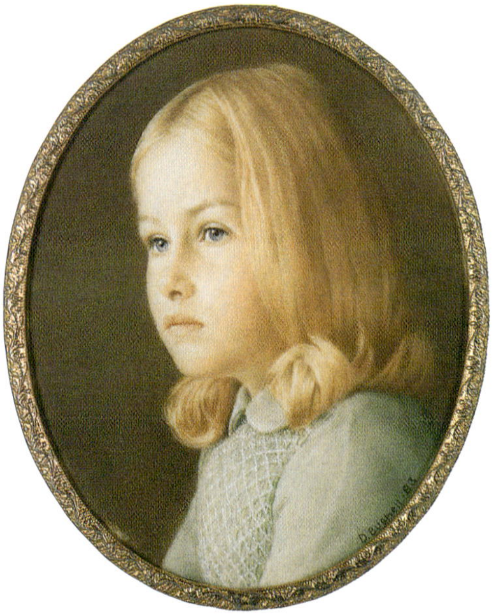

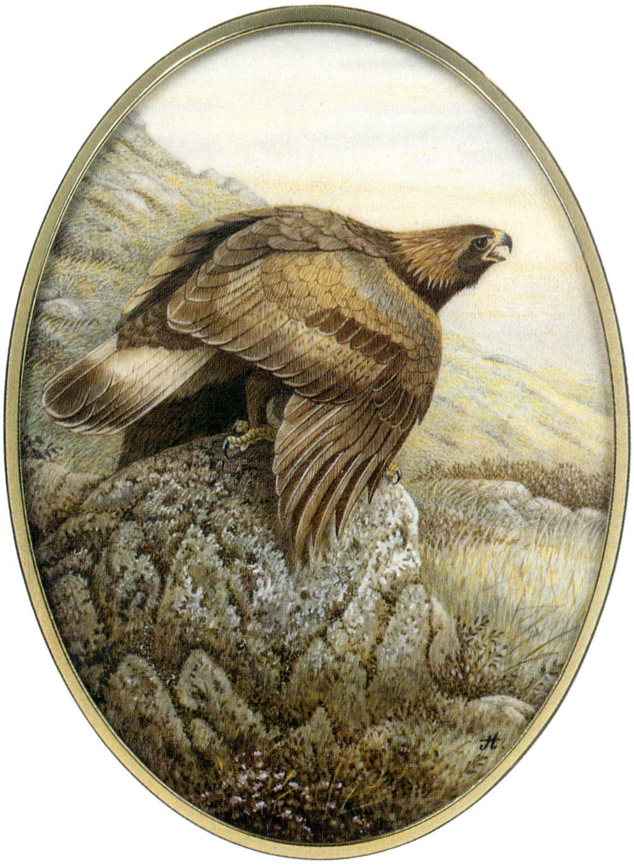

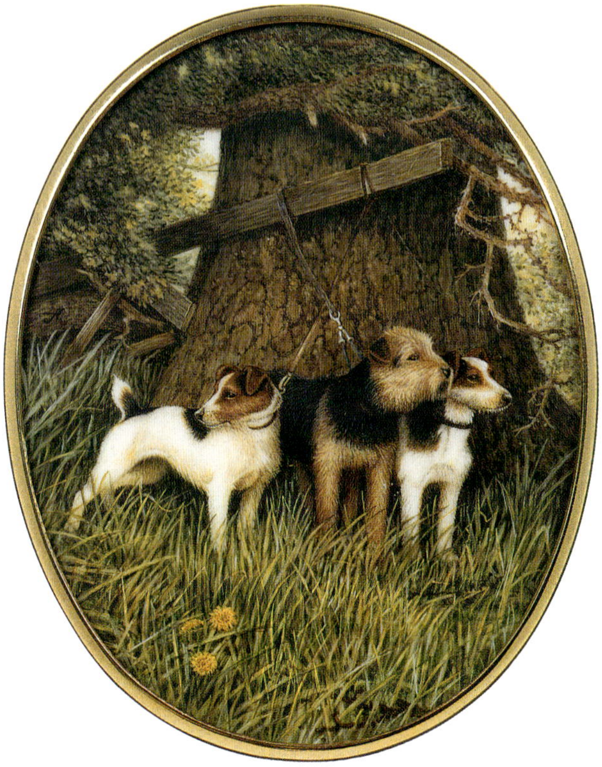

Jean Moore *RMS*

Ducks on the Pond
(water-colour on Arches paper)

Guardians of the Way
(water-colour on Arches paper)

Jean, who was born in Valletta, Malta in 1928, showed her interest in painting when very young and sketched scenes of the Broads where the family lived from 1935. She was educated privately and then attended the Lowestoft School of Art.

She valued deeply the help given to her by her father, the late Captain R.E.C. Dunbar RN, who instilled in her the importance of perspective, light and shade and the handling of water-colours.

Twice married, with three sons and five grand-children, she is now living on her own in St. Leonards in Sussex. Over the years she has had many exhibitions and recently has taken up writing.

Jean feels she may be a little eccentric in preferring to live alone with her cats and the tame seagulls which visit her windowsill.

But she loves the countryside, lonely places, flowers and wildlife and is at present working on a series of large tree studies in oils.

Stephanie Harrison *NDD RMS FSBA HS*

Foaming Cow Parsley
(gouache on Court board)
kindly lent by the President

Born in 1939 in King's Lynn, Norfolk, she studied for the National Diploma in Design at the Medway College of Art. She spent time as an illustrator and graphic designer in industry, science and at the British Museum for the Natural History Department. Since 1979 she has been a freelance artist concentrating on painting and illustration. As well as one-woman exhibitions in London and Kent, she is both a gallery artist and a regular exhibitor at a number of London galleries. A Member of the Royal Miniature Society, she has won a Gold Bowl Honourable Mention and a First Prize Fairman Award in 1990. She belongs to the Society of Botanical Artists and the Hilliard Society of Miniaturists and exhibits regularly at Society annual exhibitions. Her published work includes illustrations for a number of books and greetings cards. Her subjects are wide-ranging and take in botanical, house, landscape and still life studies; also meticulous paintings of aircraft and motor transport. She has work in many private collections in Britain and abroad.

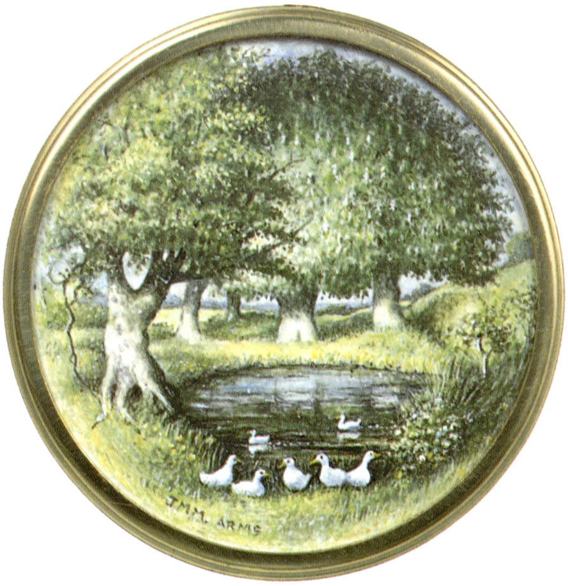

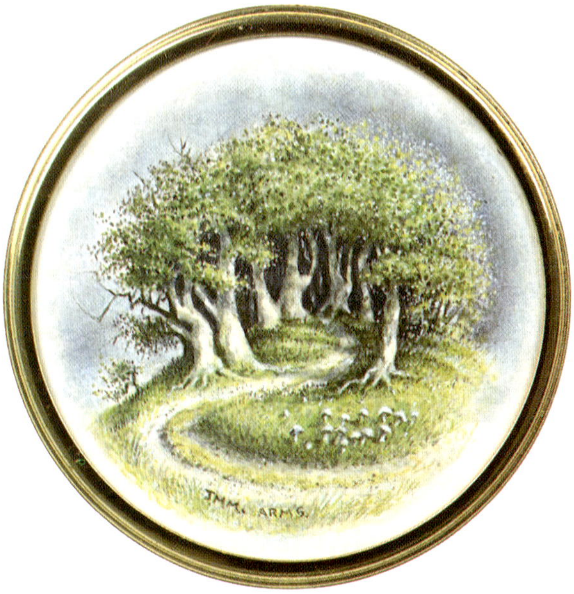

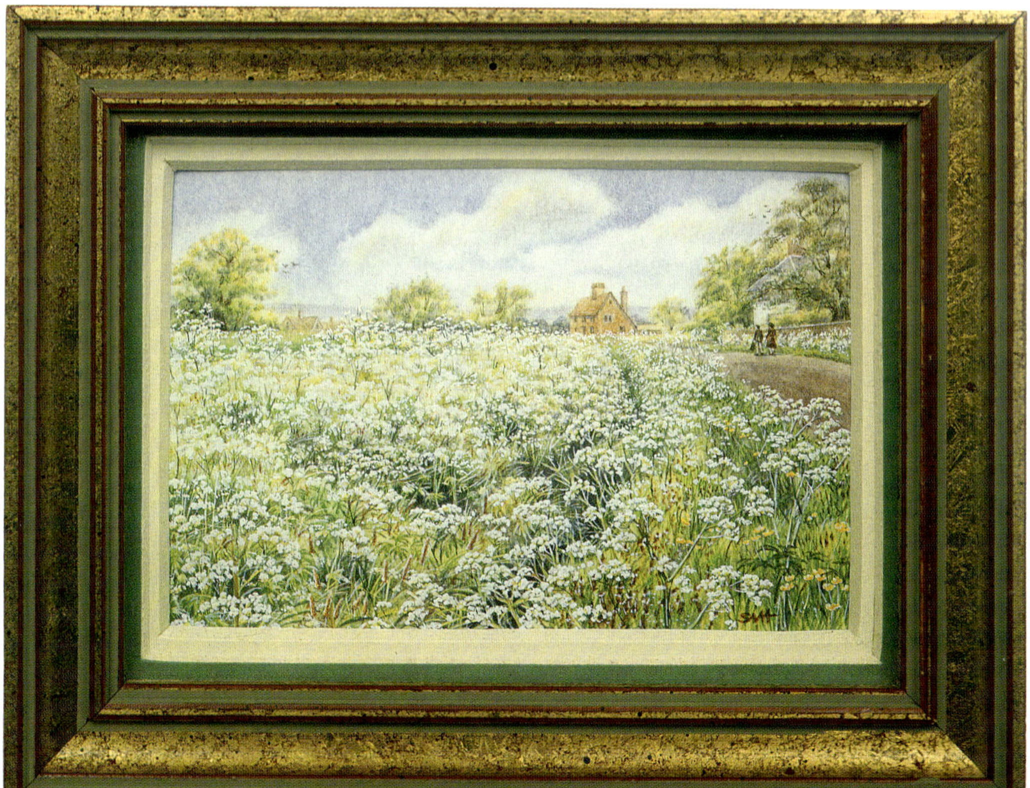

Jan Markut

BA MA (Fine Arts) RMS MASF UPA HS GMAS MAA

Portrait of Krystyna Markut
(oil on Ivorine)
kindly lent by Krystyna Markut

Self Portrait
(oil on Ivorine)
kindly lent by Krystyna Markut

Born to Polish parents in Ars-sur-Moselle, France in 1928, Jan Markut returned with his family, before World War II, to Poland where he obtained his Bachelor of Arts Degree at Poznan University in 1949 and his Master of Fine Arts at the Poznan Academy of Fine Arts in 1954.

A prolific artist, Jan mastered many media in Poland and after his emigration to the United States in 1972. Among his creative studies were mosaics, murals, icons, calligraphy, illuminated texts, sculpture, fabric design and miniature painting.

Miniature art took up most of Jan's energy and dedication. His sensitive style gained him many awards, Membership of the Royal Miniature Society in 1983, where he won the Gold Memorial Bowl Honourable Mention twice, and Signature Membership of the Miniature Artists of America. He sustained Memberships of the Miniature Art Societies of Florida and Georgia, the Union of Polish Artists and in 1989 was listed in Men of Achievement, published in Cambridge, England.

Jan's masterpiece in miniatures was the portrait collection of the Presidents of the United States which took eleven years to accomplish. It conveyed most eloquently his love of the country which afforded him artistic freedom.

Jane Blake *RMS MASF HS MAA*

The Flautist
(oil on ivory)
kindly lent by the Artist's Family

Myra, The Bride
(oil on ivory)
kindly lent by the Artist's Family

Born in Burgaw, North Carolina, in 1933, Jane Blake went to Florida in 1967 with her three sons in hopes of supporting them by her art. Adept in portraiture, sculpture, stained glass and photography, with a Photographic Craftsmen's degree, she wrote 'How to Retouch Color Photographs for Fun and Profit.' Extending her love of detail to miniature painting, she joined a class in 1973 which became the nucleus of the Miniature Art Society of Florida.

As the Society's International Receiver, Jane formed ties with artists all over the world, travelling and sharing her philosophy of the miniature's rightful place in contemporary art combined with its historical importance.

In 1987 Jane Blake became a Member of the Miniature Artists of America and the first American to achieve Membership of the Royal Society of Miniature Painters, Sculptors and Gravers, winning later a Gold Memorial Bowl Honourable Mention.

Among the masterpieces she created before she died in 1993 were the official portraits of the Governors' Wives of Florida, displayed in the Governor's Mansion, and the Jane Blake Birthday Book, a hand-bound collection of works donated by artists from sixteen countries. It is an appropriate symbol of the artistic unity she worked tirelessly to achieve.

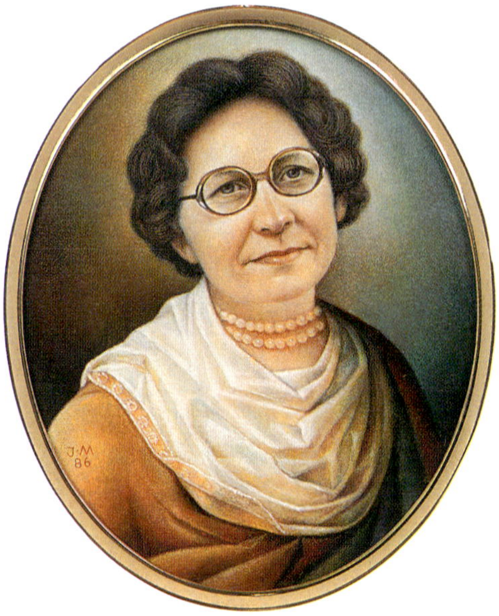
J.M
86
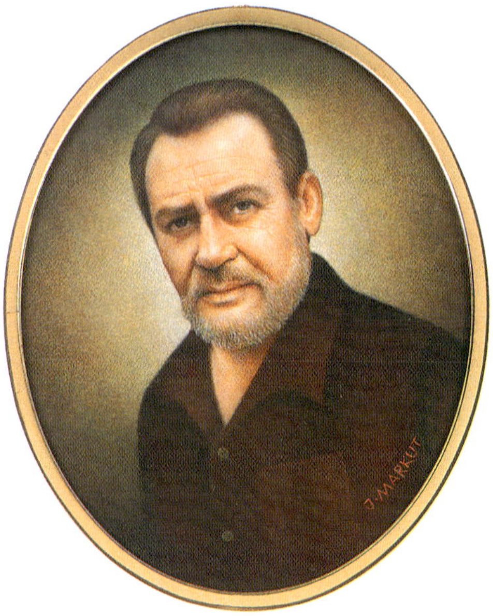
J.MARKUT
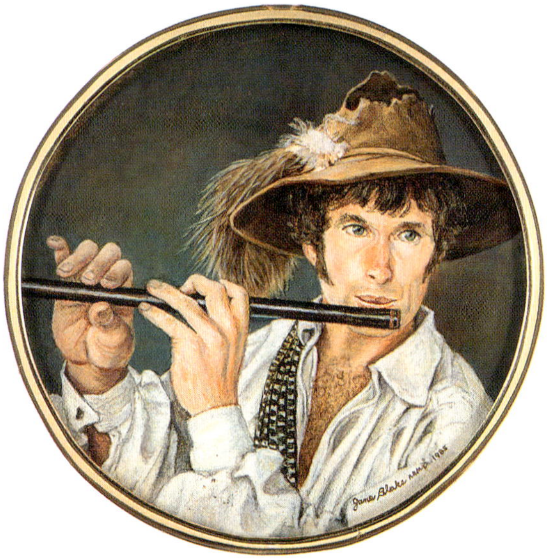
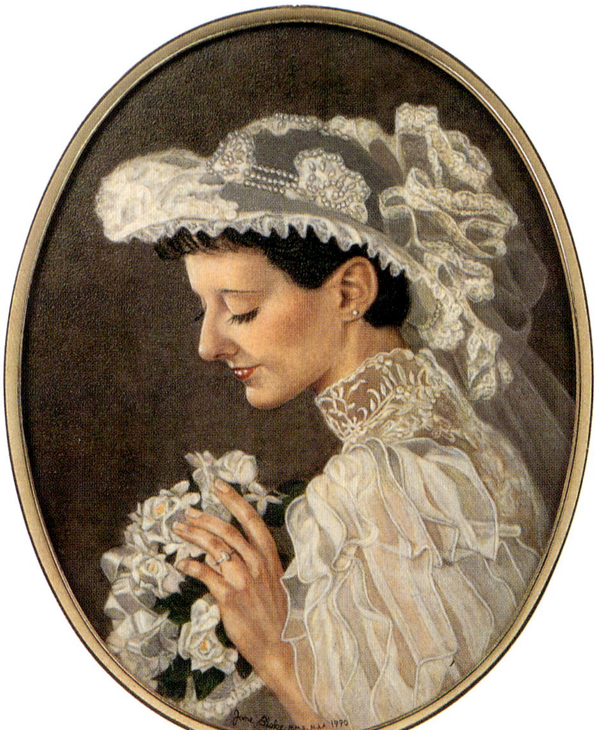

Cathy Simpson *RMS ARBSA HS*

The Hare and the Tortoise
(gouache on Arches paper)

She was born on November 15th 1959, a Scorpio with Scorpio rising, and says she has been rising ever since.

She left Leicester University in 1980, with a degree in Art History; however, it was her happy years spent as a student at St Martin's School of Art which equipped her for a career as a children's illustrator. She has worked for Methuen, Blackie, George Philip, Corgi and the BBC, amongst others, her latest published works being two books of nursery rhymes which show her miniature technique to perfection.

She exhibited with the Royal Miniature Society in 1988, was elected an Associate in 1989, received a Gold Memorial Bowl Honourable Mention in 1990 and was elected a Member in 1992. She has won awards from the MASF, GMAS and the RBSA and exhibited with many other art societies, including the RI, RBA, SWA, SWLA and the Hilliard.

Now her illustrations and paintings are possible only when she is not submerged in the Art Department of Bromsgrove School. She guides fourteen to eighteen year-olds to 'A' level, encouraging them to develop their own careers in the Arts. Usually she teaches them to paint pictures which are somewhat larger than her own!

Rita Whitaker *RMS MASF SM (London)*

A Victorian Farm Kitchen
(low stoving enamel on copper)
from the Diploma Collection

A most gifted artist, unique in that she enamels her paintings on copper in a manner known only to herself.

She studied at the Regent Street Polytechnic under Stuart Tresilian, then later, during a long stay in the United States, she began experimenting with enamelling for paintings, having worked previously for London jewellers.

Rita, who paints mostly in miniature, is a Member of the Royal Miniature Society, the Miniature Art Society of Florida and the Society of Miniaturists. Her favourite subjects are wildlife and architecturally fine, or historical, buildings. Going back over the generations is one of her delights and she can make street scenes live as they did long ago. Much of her work is from sketches in the field, as of an Egyptian bazaar, Somalis in Somalia, cable cars in San Francisco, or landscapes in Wales and the wildlife which abounds near her home, on the slopes of the Preseli mountains, in the Pembrokeshire National Park.

She exhibits with the Royal Miniature Society, the Society of Miniaturists, at the Medici and Llewellyn Alexander Galleries, and has had work accepted for the Royal Academy Summer Exhibition. In the United States she has won top awards in Florida and Georgia. The Llewellyn Alexander Gallery awarded her a Commendation of Excellence in 1995.

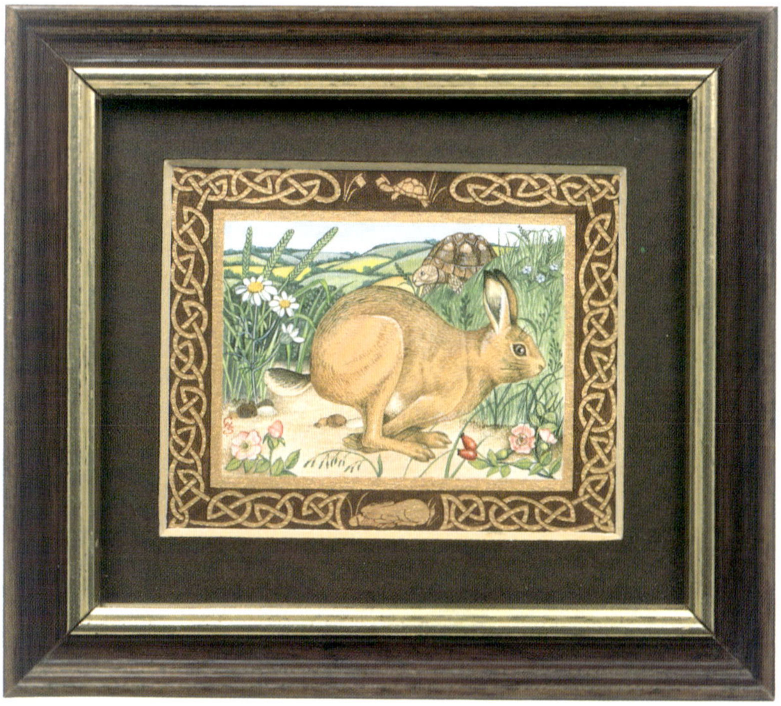

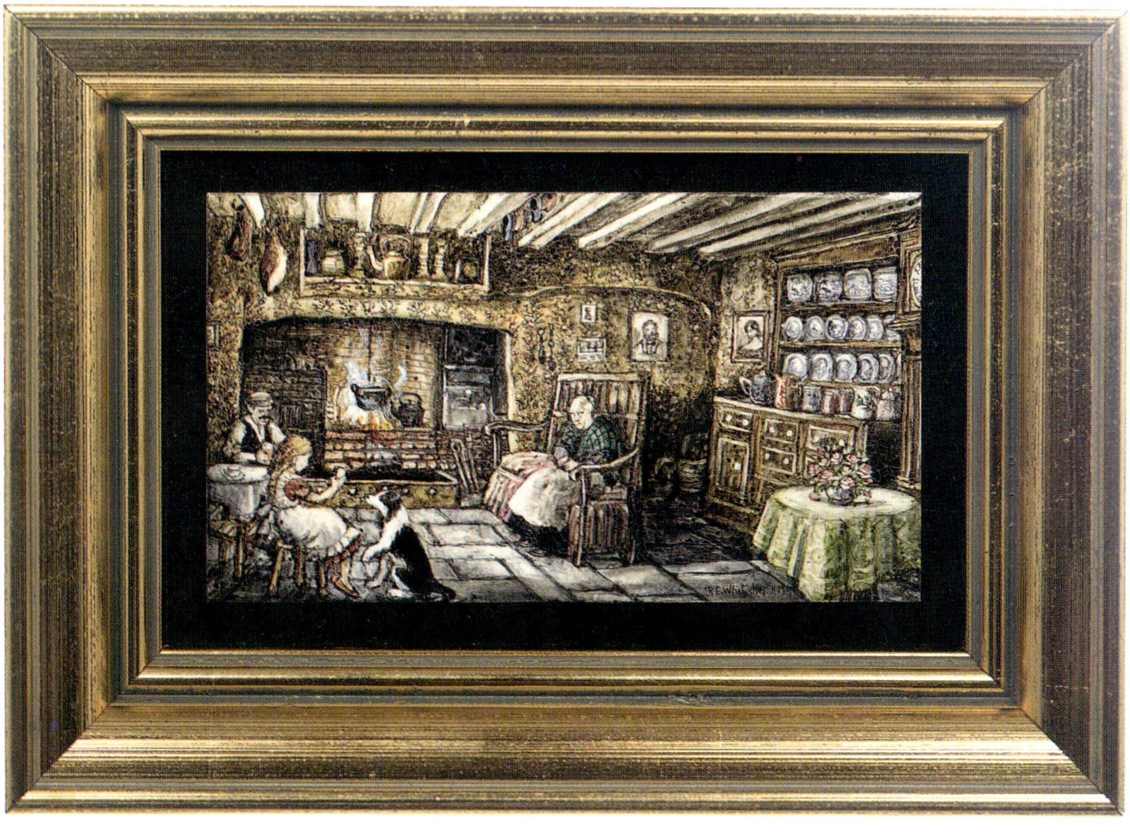

Julian Bernard Macey *ARMS*

The Tas Valley at Shotesham
(oil on Ivorine)

The Black Mill
(oil on Ivorine)
kindly lent by Dr. R.T. Davies

Hassingham Church, Norfolk
(oil on Ivorine)

Autumn at Fritton, Norfolk
(oil on Ivorine)

Julian was born in Minehead, Somerset in 1920 and educated at the Duke of York's Royal Military School, Dover.

A career in Youth and Community work in Norfolk brought him into contact with the local artists from which an interest in art developed, but it was not until retirement in 1980 that he was able to devote more time to painting.

He is entirely self-taught and his paintings in pastels, oils and water-colours are developed from pencil sketches done on location. His miniatures, mainly of Norfolk scenes, are painted in oil on Ivorine.

He was made an Honorary Life Member of the Great Yarmouth and District Society of Artists for long and dedicated service to art. He also has a great interest in promoting art projects in hospitals and serves on the James Paget Hospital Arts Committee.

Elected an Associate Member of the Royal Miniature Society in 1990, he exhibits his admirable small works annually with the Society, as well as widely in Norfolk.

Sylvia Cave *MA (Hons.) ARMS HS*

Toad
(water-colour on vellum)

Sylvia lives on the Quantock Hills, West Somerset, where her subjects are local plants and wildlife. Her particular interest is in the jewel-like qualities of insects and reptiles which she combines with the surreal shapes of mosses, toadstools and lichens.

She paints in water-colour on manuscript vellum, occasionally using body colour to emphasize, for example, warts on a toad's skin. Sylvia paints larger water-colours on paper and, combined with Chinese ink, on silk. Another favourite subject is cats, of which she often paints portraits, both miniature and full size.

Her work has been exhibited in London and West Country galleries. It is frequently commissioned for private collections in Britain and abroad, as also for greetings cards. In 1991 she won the Suzanne Lucas Best in Exhibition Award at the Hilliard Society.

After studying at the Byam Shaw School of Art, in London, Sylvia attended Edinburgh University and graduated with an MA (Honours) in Fine Art and Archaeology. She worked in art publishing in New York before becoming a freelance professional artist. She gives adult education courses in botanical illustration and lectures on a variety of topics, with particular interest in illuminated manuscripts and tapestries of the Middle Ages.

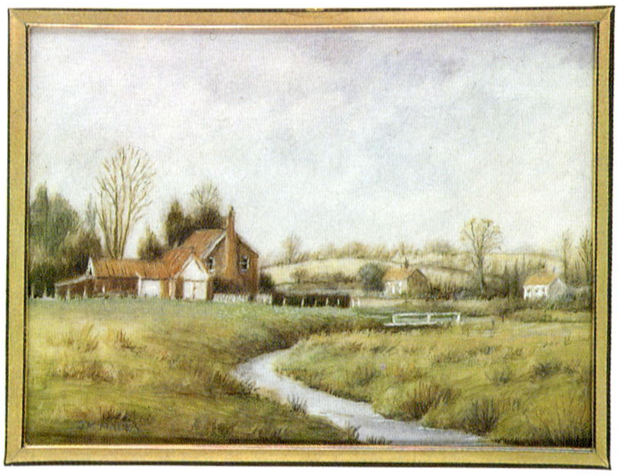

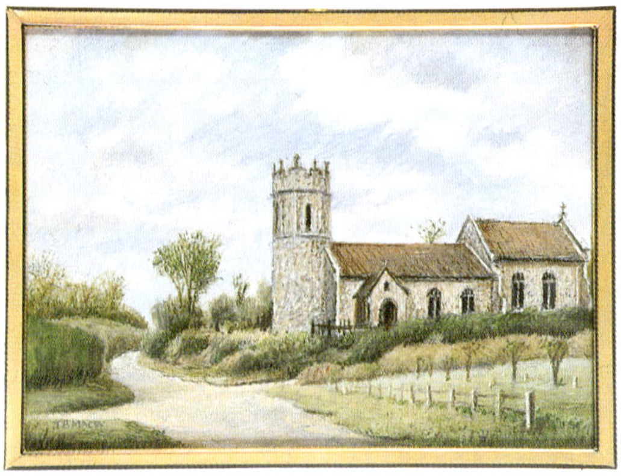

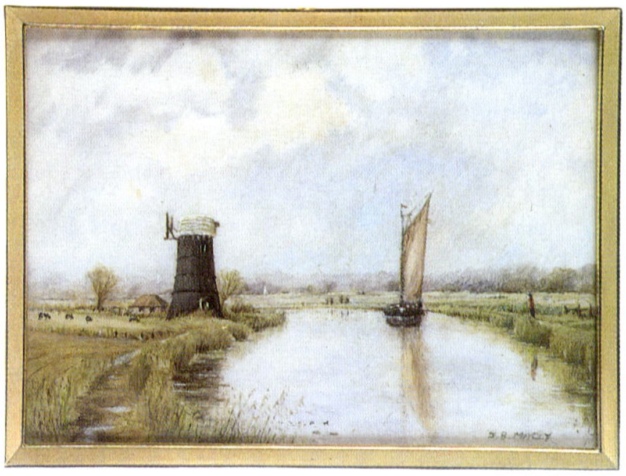

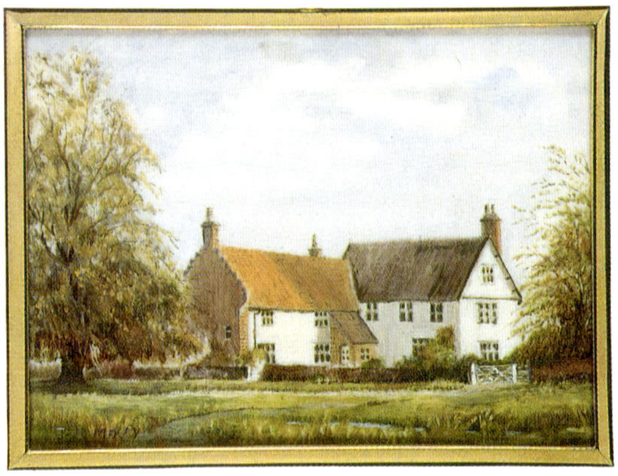

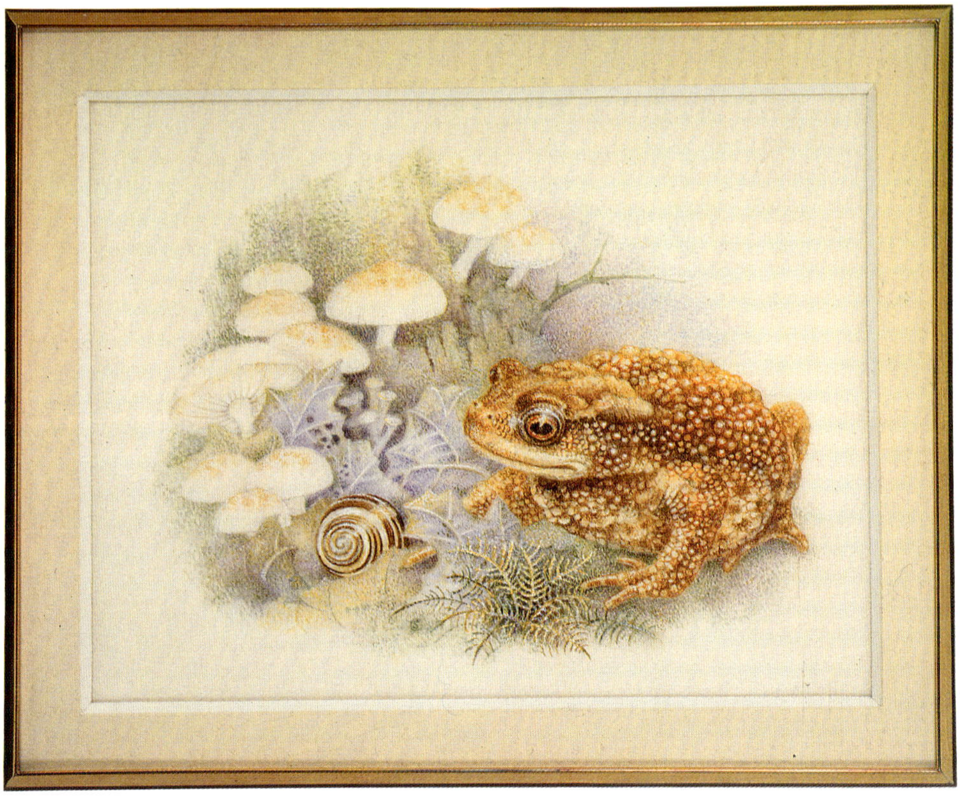

Marcelle D. Shears

RMS PVPSWA SM (London) HSF

The Worshipful the Mayor of Fareham, Mrs H.M. Joyce OBE
(water-colour on vellum)

The President, Suzanne Lucas FLS PRMS FPSBA SWA HSF
(water-colour on vellum)

Born in Croydon, Surrey in 1926 of artistic parents, she walked home from school through fields of orchids alive with the gentle sound of bees. Later she worked in war-torn London where land-mines, flames and flying bombs never interrupted the teaching she had from George H. Tozer. But not until 1970, after running away to marry a Royal Marine and bring up Rebecca and Juanita, could she practice profile portraiture from life.

Loving encouragement from her family helped her to become a leading profilist. She opened a silhouette studio in Fareham, painting from life, updating ancestral collections and designing for the gift trade.

She paints on vellum and antique ivory, framed in precious settings, with work in private collections world-wide. She has exhibited in Britain, including the Royal Academy of Arts, and the United States, winning many awards in Florida and Georgia. She has been a Hunting Group finalist, received the Suzanne Lucas Award at the Hilliard Society, a Gold Memorial Bowl Honourable Mention and a Llewellyn Alexander Masters Award in 1995. In 1988 she and her mother moved to Dartmoor where her mother died, aged a hundred and two. Marcelle broke her back, recovered and has a studio, surrounded by the magic of Dartmoor.

Jenny Brooks *ATC ARMS HS*

In Pensive Mood
(pencil)

Jenny Brooks began miniatures in 1987, but has been painting and drawing since childhood. She studied Fine Art at the Bath Academy of Art and obtained her postgraduate Art Teacher's Certificate at Goldsmiths' College, London. After teaching art in a south-east London comprehensive school and at Riddlesworth Hall, Norfolk, she now combines freelance work with lecturing on Fine Art in north-west Bristol.

At the Hilliard Society's exhibition in 1990 she won the Suzanne Lucas Best Novice Award and in 1994 the Bell Portrait Award. In 1991 she became a Council Member of the Society. She exhibited in Montelimar, France, at the London Barbican Tenth Anniversary Exhibition in 1992 and with the Miniature Art Society of Florida where, in 1993, she won the First in Portrait Award.

Having shown with the Royal Miniature Society since 1989 she was elected an Associate in 1993 and awarded a Gold Memorial Bowl Honourable Mention.

She draws in faint outline before tones are developed in layers of short diagonal hatching with a 9H pencil. This is repeated painstakingly using softer pencils for darker tones.

She is a perfectionist whose work needs a quiet atmosphere to achieve miniatures renowned for careful execution and beautiful quality of detail.

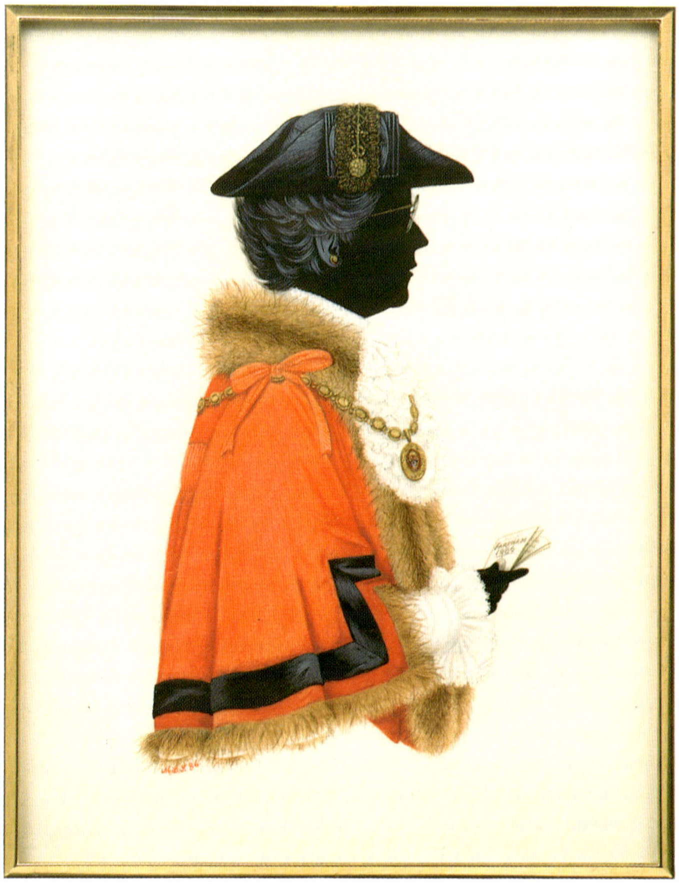

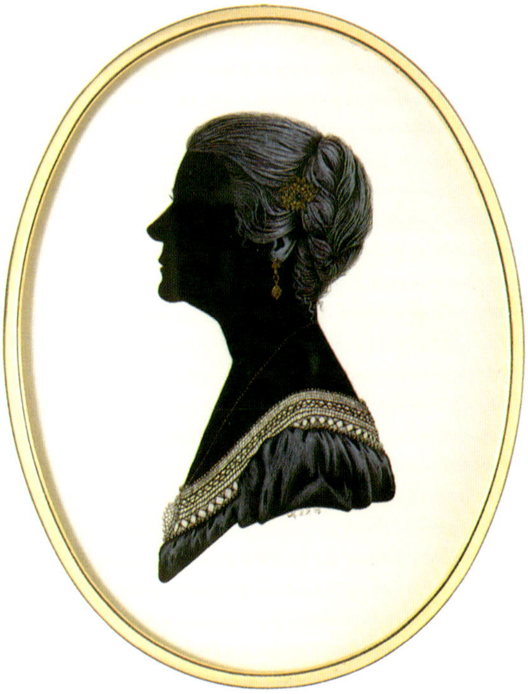

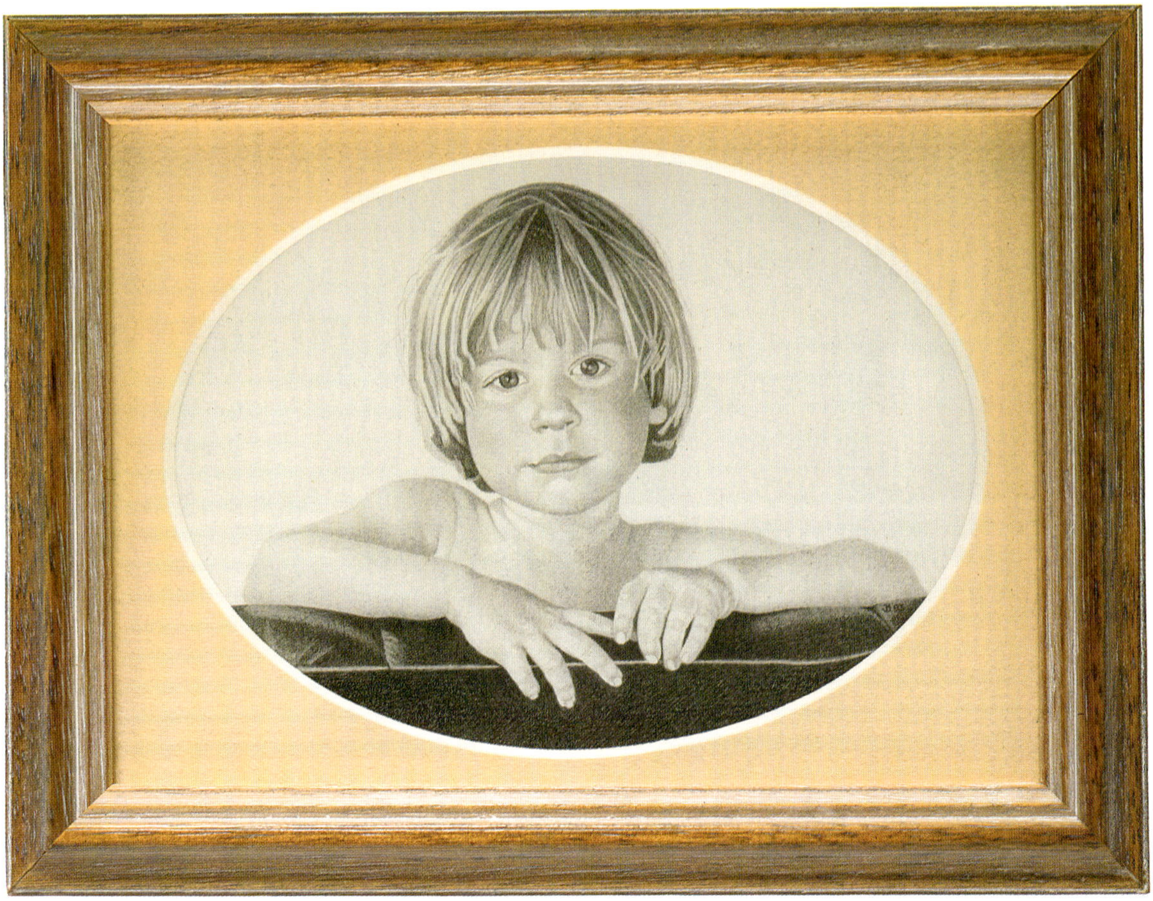

Catherine Ogden *RMS ARBSA SWA*

Sun and Shadows
(water-colour on paper)

Boats and Floats
(water-colour on paper)

She is a London-born artist who has always enjoyed drawing and painting but did not take the decision to paint full-time until 1985. Working in water-colour, for both miniatures and larger size works, she features pretty harbours or boats in river and coastal settings of Britain and Brittany.

Several paintings have been published by greetings card companies and work was commissioned for a collectors' plate. She was elected an Associate of the Royal Society of Miniature Painters, Sculptors and Gravers in 1990, a Member in 1993 and is also a Member of the Society of Women Artists since 1988 and an Associate Member of The Royal Birmingham Society of Artists since 1992. She has exhibited with the Royal Institute of Painters in Water Colours, the Royal Water Colour Society and The Royal Society of Marine Artists. Her work received an award from The Birmingham and Midland Institute in 1992, a Commendation from the Royal Birmingham Society of Artists and a Commendation of Excellence from the Llewellyn Alexander Gallery in 1995.

Barbara Valentine *NDD ARMS MASF HS*

Lovebird with Lilies
(water-colour on Ivorine)

Cockatiel with Grapes
(water-colour on Ivorine)

Still Life with Cockatoos
(water-colour on Ivorine)
kindly lent by Mrs. Jane Hume

Barbara Valentine was trained under Betty Swanwick at Goldsmiths' College School of Art and was awarded the National Diploma of Design in Illustration in 1964. Her career has covered various branches of art including glass engraving, fabric design, architectural clay work, water-colours and life-size oils. Finally this all led up to a pivotal point in 1986 when a sculptress friend showed her two miniature paintings. From that moment miniatures became her obsession, as well as profession.

Her work has won the Suzanne Lucas Novice Award at the Hilliard Society, the First in Floral at the Miniature Art Society of Florida, further awards from the Ulster Society of Miniaturists and the Llewellyn Alexander Miniature Exhibition and her miniatures have been hung in the Royal Academy Summer Exhibition four years in succession from 1990 to 1993.

She lectures on the history and techniques of miniature art and teaches adult classes in water-colours and miniature painting at Claverham Community College.

She and her husband, leading marine painter Louis Dodd, share their purpose-built studio block with their sculptress daughter and their son, who is a photographer. She devotes time to her deep interest in pastel teaching for the disabled.

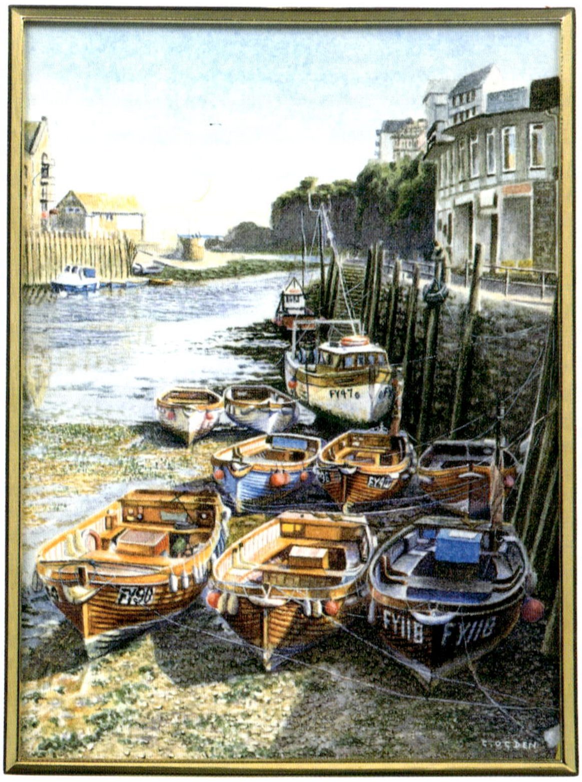
FY90
FY118
C.OGDEN

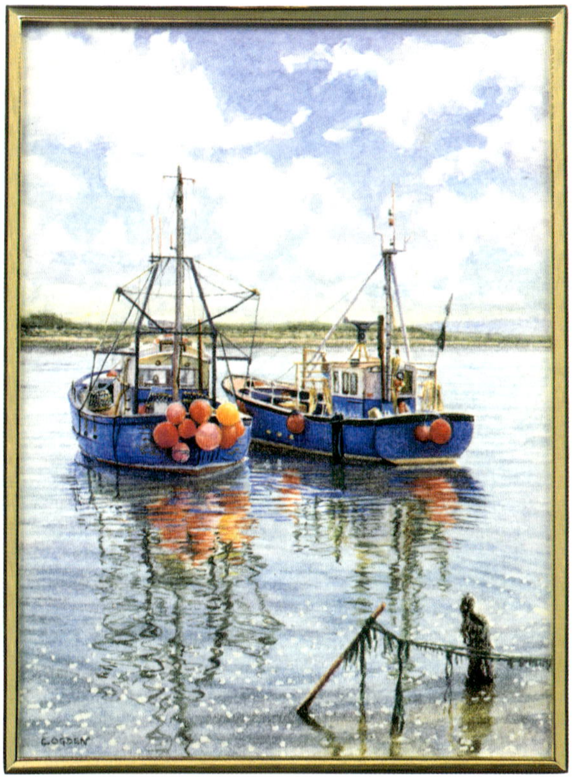
C.OGDEN

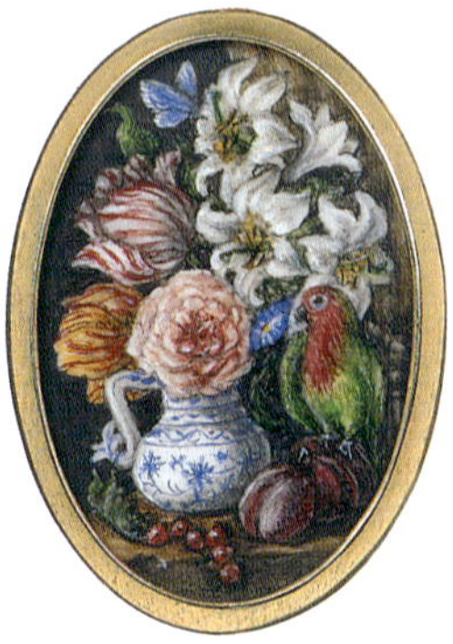

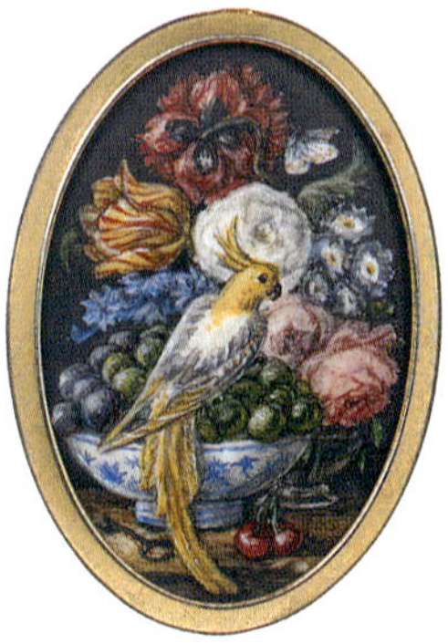

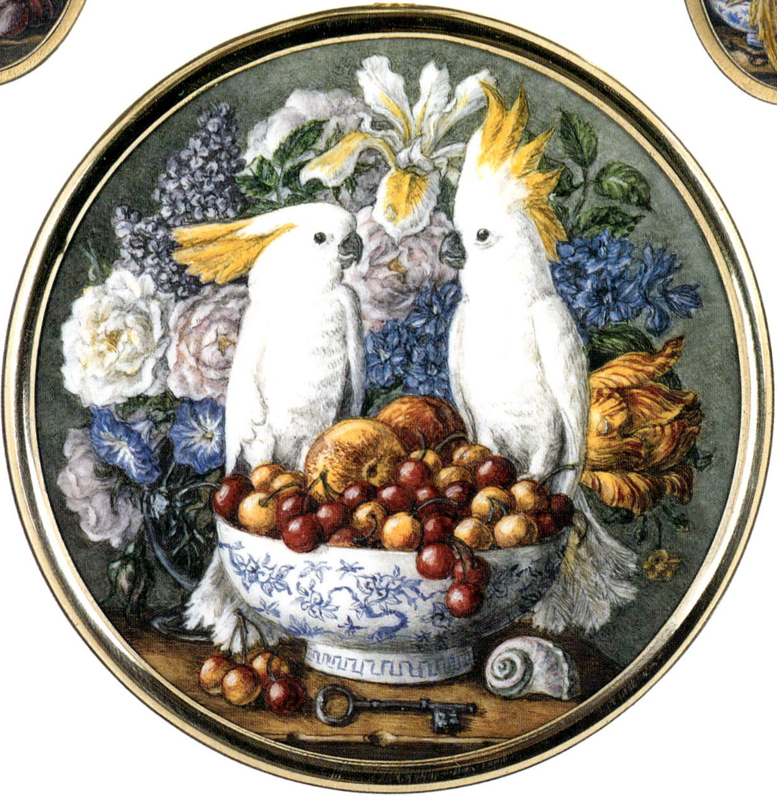

Sheila Sanford *RI RMS MASF HS*

The White Hunter
(water-colour on vellum)

She studied at St. Martin's School of Art, Charing Cross Road, London. After several years of freelance work in advertising and for publishers, illustrating magazines and book jackets, and bringing up a family, Sheila Sanford started painting to please herself. She found that the disciplines of publishing stood her in good stead and she was able to produce representational work of any subject she tried.

Intricate detail fascinated her and led to the study of painting in miniature. She became a full Member of the Royal Society of Miniature Painters in 1986. Before that she had become a Member of The Royal Institute of Painters in Water Colours. A visit to friends in Florida brought her into contact with the international Miniature Art Society of Florida where she exhibited for many years, receiving numerous awards. She was honoured to be asked to judge the 1994 exhibition.

She and her husband are in partnership with a fine art publishing company, Skittle Prints, which reproduces many of her paintings as cards and prints. She exhibits at several galleries amongst which are the Llewellyn Alexander, the Edwin Pollard (now the Kingsmead in Great Bookham) and the Blakesley Gallery, Northamptonshire.

Eric Eustace *ARMS HS*

Canterbury
(water-colour on Arches paper)

He began working life in a print factory and, called up at eighteen, served with the R.A.F. as a photographer for four years, mainly in the Far East. Returning to his previous job, and increasingly dissatisfied with unfulfilling work, he left and enrolled in a full-time course at Luton College of Art, later incorporated with Luton University. He lived on savings for two years, but then had to find employment as grants were not easily come by in those times. He managed an Art and Design studio for an engineering firm until 1979, then took the plunge, began painting full-time and sold at several local galleries, with water-colours accepted by the Royal Institute of Painters in Water Colours and the National Society.

In 1989, as his paintings became much smaller, he began working in miniature and had two paintings accepted by the Royal Miniature Society. In 1990 five were accepted by both the Royal Miniature Society and the Hilliard Society.

Fully committed to miniature painting, and with increasing pleasure and satisfaction from it, he wishes only to improve his technique and extend his range.

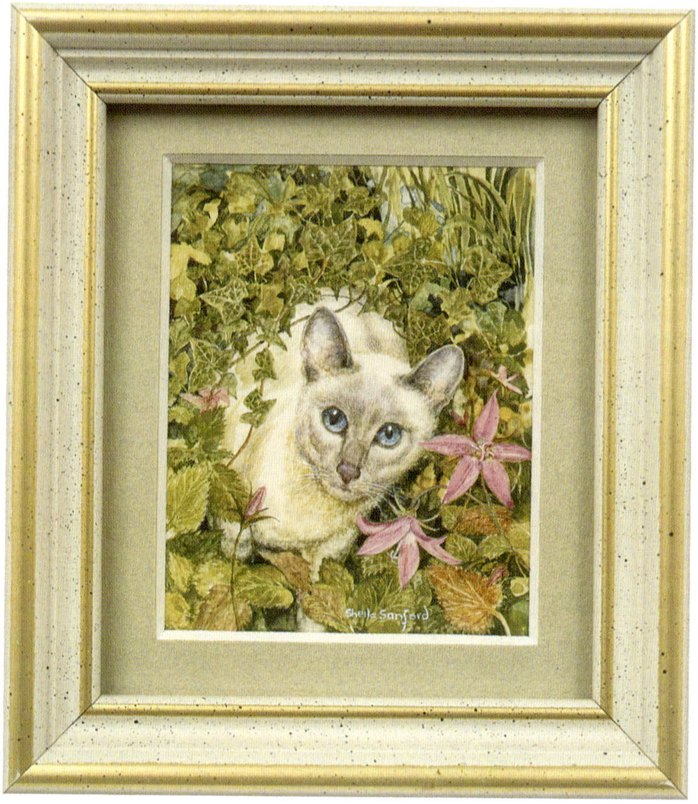
Sheila Sanford

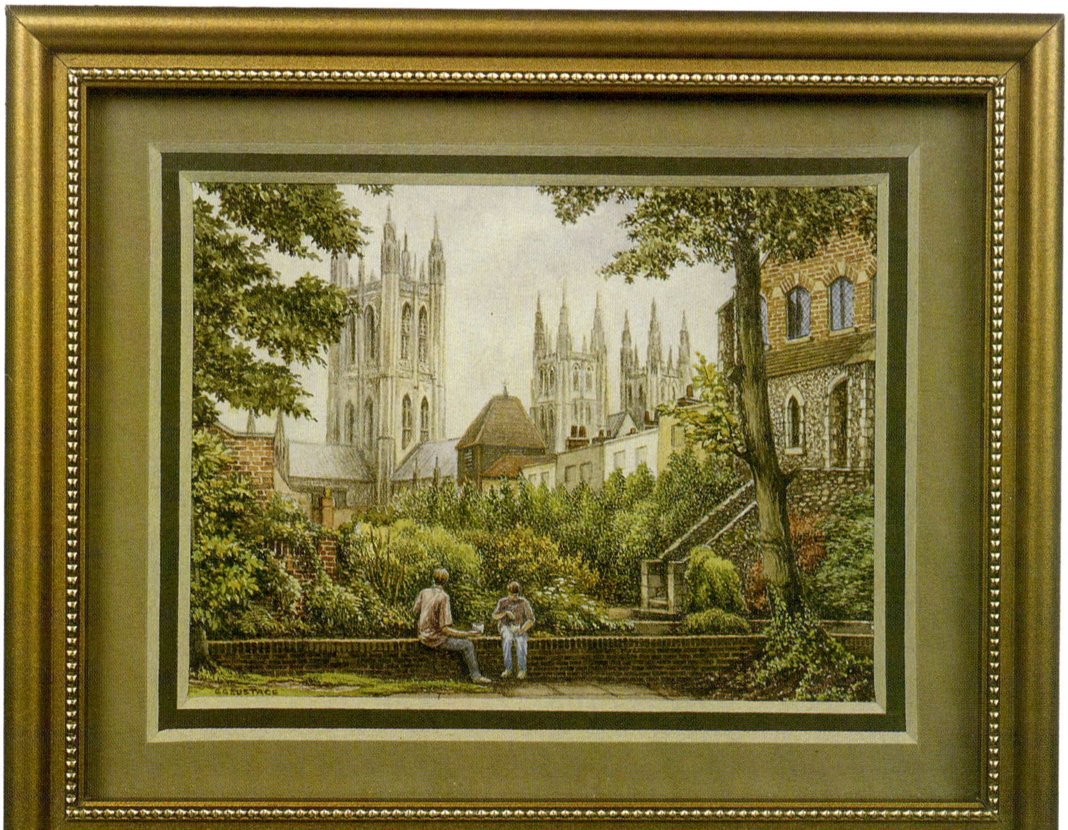

Joan Campbell *RMS SWA MASF*

Palace of Westminster
(water-colour on Ivorine)

Tower of London
(water-colour on Ivorine)

She was born in Essex and educated at Loughton County High School for Girls where she matriculated in Art with Distinction. The outbreak of war terminated her further studies until she resumed painting, at forty years of age, in Adult Education classes.

A painter in oils and acrylics, she used careful observation of nature for landscapes and flowers, also miniatures in water-colour of birds and animals. She is a Member of the Royal Miniature Society, the Society of Women Artists and the Miniature Art Society of Florida with which she has exhibited since 1969 in the United States.

She had work shown in the Paris Salon in 1973 and 1974 and one-woman exhibitions at Weybridge, Starston Grange, in Norfolk and Chichester. There is a permanent collection of her work in Barclays Bank, Hillingdon, and in 1981 she was commissioned by the Franklin Mint of America to paint the 'Birds of the World' miniature porcelain plate collection.

She has taught miniature painting at Frays College, Uxbridge, Tresham College, Kettering and currently from her studio at home. Joan is a keen ornithologist and loves gardening and travel.

Margaret Carver *ARMS HS*

Sunshine and Shadows
(oil on Ivorine)

High Summer, River Thurne, Norfolk
(oil on Ivorine)

Breydon Water, Great Yarmouth
(oil on Ivorine)

Spring at Shotesham, Norfolk
(oil on Ivorine)

Margaret Carver, married with two sons, was born in 1941 at West Caister, Norfolk where she lives still.

She started painting in 1971 as a hobby, but soon this casual interest in art developed into a serious commitment. After ten years studying on her own she gave up her work in accountancy and became a full-time artist in 1982. She specialized in landscapes, working in oil, water-colour and pastel. Five successful one-man exhibitions followed and in 1986 she was elected an Associate Member of the Royal Society of Miniature Painters, Sculptors and Gravers.

Persevering in all weathers, she makes preparatory sketches on location for her miniature landscapes, inspired by the wide skies and subtle greens of the Norfolk country. She works to capture the changing moods of Broadland on the smallest possible scale and her love of the marshy meadows, with windmills and dykes, has always influenced her and does so to this day.

Margaret is also in her seventh year as Chairman of the Great Yarmouth and District Society of Artists and is a Founder Member of the James Paget Hospital Arts Committee, with joint responsibility for organizing exhibitions and promoting art projects within the hospital.

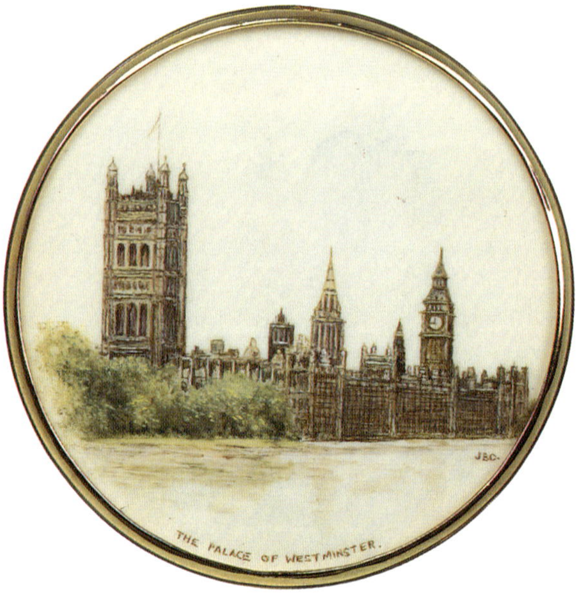
JBC.
THE PALACE OF WESTMINSTER.

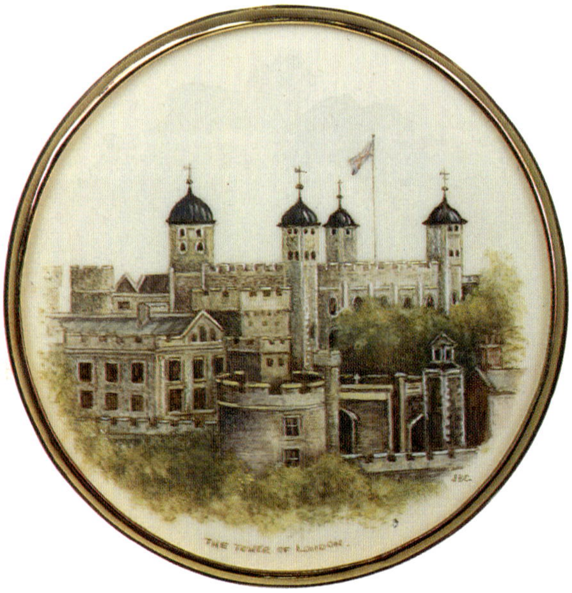
JBC.
THE TOWER OF LONDON.

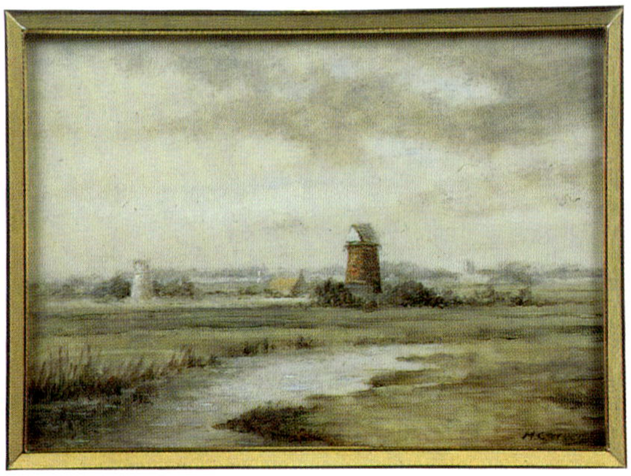

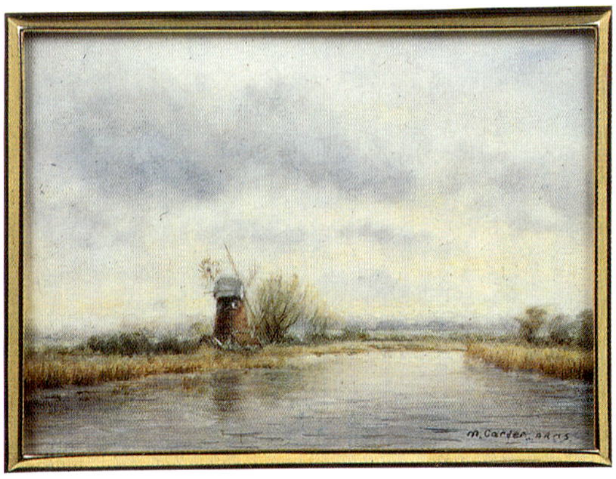

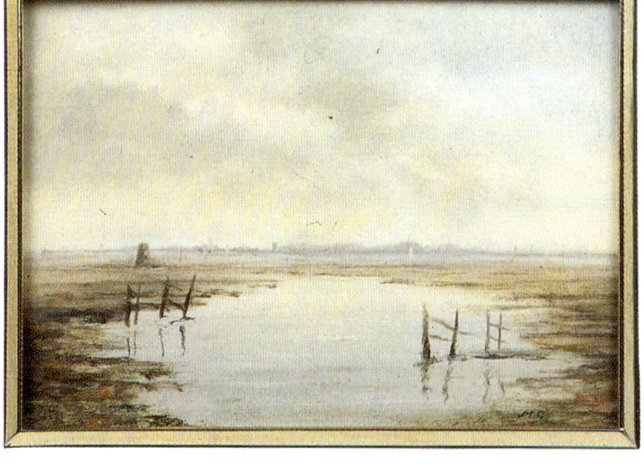

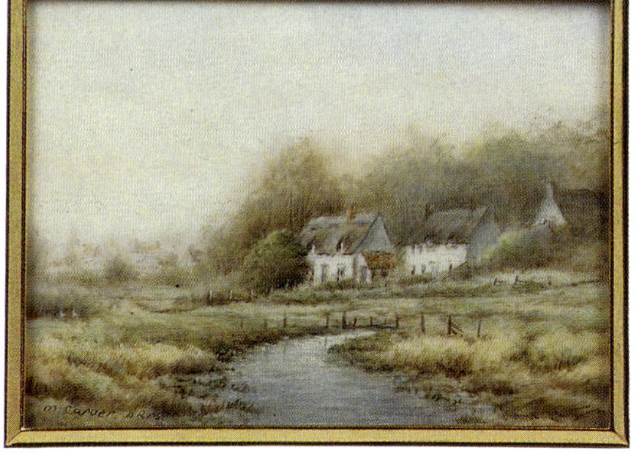

Joan M. Horsman ARMS

Ring O'Roses
(oil on Ivorine)

The Rocking Horse
(oil on Ivorine)

Joan Horsman has been painting for thirty years after training at Chichester and also Guildford for Portrait and General Drawing and Painting.

Her particular interest is in painting miniatures in oil and she was elected in 1990 as an Associate Member of the Royal Society of Miniature Painters. Her subjects include birds, butterflies, flowers and occasional portraits, but she specializes in painting period costume. For this she studied by drawing at the Victoria and Albert Museum and the Bath Museum of Costume.

She has exhibited regularly with the Royal Society of Miniature Painters and the Society of Women Artists, first at the Mall Galleries and then at the Westminster Gallery. Her miniatures have been accepted several times at the Royal Academy Summer Exhibition.

Her work is on show with galleries in Sussex, Wales and London.

Brenda Carole Rayment ARMS

Susan
(oil on Ivorine)

Little Sweetheart
(oil on Ivorine)

She was born on the fifth of May in 1951 at Paddock Wood, Kent and attended Kidbrooke Comprehensive School in South London. She lived in the London Borough of Bexley for twenty years and is married with one son and one daughter.

She took up art as a hobby, after the birth of her daughter in 1980, and in the same year joined Bexley Adult Education Classes where fellow Royal Miniature Society Member Barry Shiraishi was teaching the painting and drawing class. Meeting other miniature painters in the class inspired her interest in miniature art.

Brenda went on attending classes until 1990 and exhibited work with the Royal Miniature Society for several years, achieving election to Associate Membership in 1991. She has shown work at the Society of Women Artists Exhibition.

In November 1990 she moved to Mullion in Cornwall where her interests include antique collecting, gardening and reading.

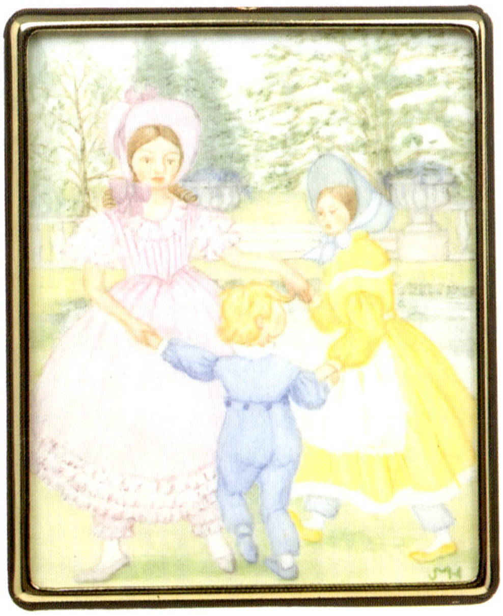
JMH

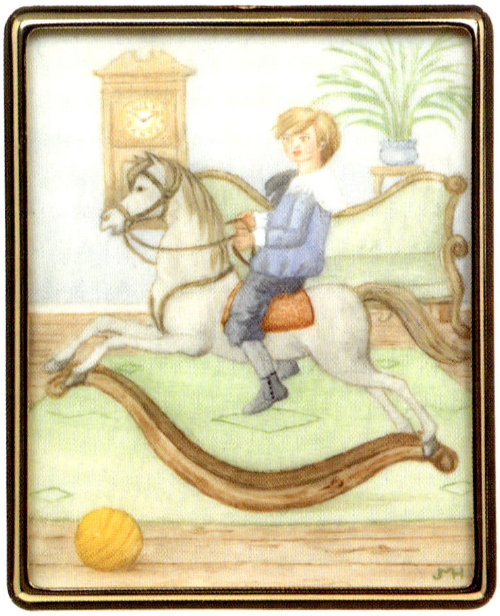
JMH

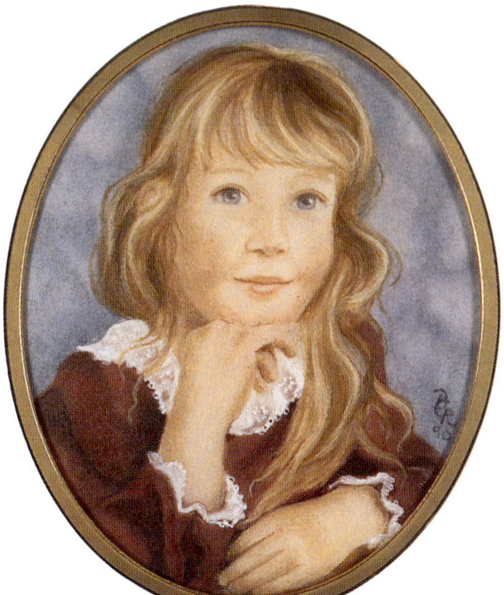

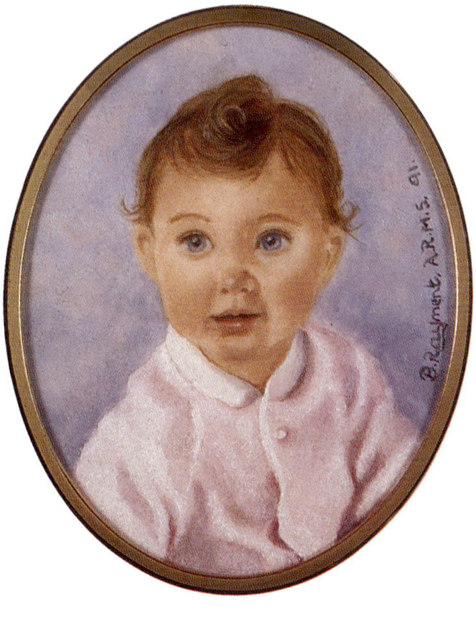
B.Rayment, A.R.M.S. 91

David Weston *ARMS UA BWS SM FRSA*

Freshening Near the Bar, Chichester Estuary
(water-colour on board)

David has shown at the Royal Institute of Painters in Water Colours, the New English Art Club, the Royal Society of British Artists, the Royal Society of Marine Artists, the British Watercolour Society, the United Society of Artists of which he was a Council Member, the National Society and the Pastel Society. Formerly a Member of the Royal Water Colour Society's Art Club, in 1985 he became a Founder Member of the British Watercolour Society and belonged to its Membership and Selection Committee.

He has exhibited in Paris, Geneva, Stockholm, Malmö, Lundt and with the Ulster Miniature Society in Northern Ireland.

He has shown as well at the William Wyllie, the Llewellyn Alexander and the New Academy Galleries in London, also in provincial galleries throughout the country.

His work is in the collections of the National Westminster and Barclays Banks and commissioned work has been presented to Richard Branson.

Heather Watson *ARMS HS*

The Gatehouse to Coverham Abbey
(water-colour on Arches paper)

Heather became interested in miniature painting in the mid nineteen-eighties when she saw some contemporary miniature work for the first time. Having seen only historical portrait miniatures previously, she was fascinated by the variety of subject matter covered by the modern miniaturist and felt that her own detailed style would adapt well to miniature painting.

By 1989 her work was accepted for exhibition by the Royal Miniature Society and in 1992 she was elected an Associate Member. She has exhibited annually with the Hilliard Society since 1990 and in 1993 she had work shown at the Royal Academy of Arts Summer Exhibition.

She uses water-colour on vellum or on fine water-colour paper, specializing in garden landscapes. She is particularly interested in the beauty of light shining through foliage and on water, exploring lovely effects through painting river and woodland scenes. Most recently she has added still life to her subjects and especially enjoys painting glassware.

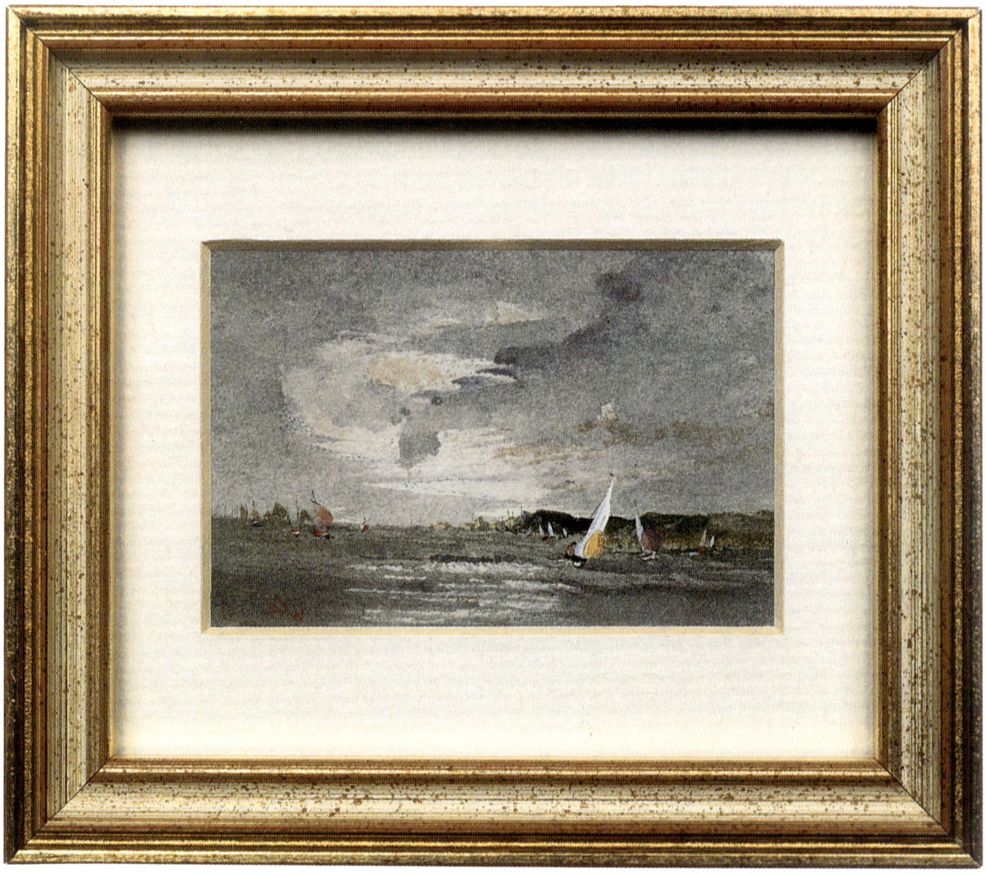

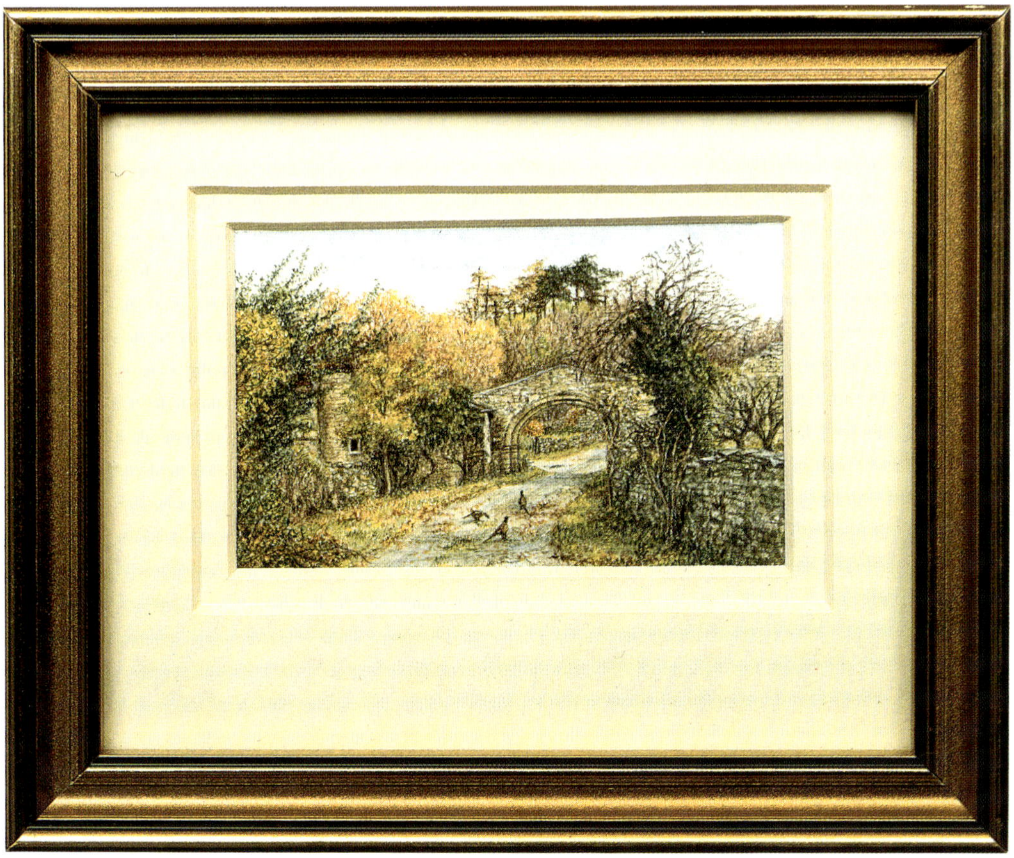

Rosmar Booth

ARMS MPSG MASF HSF GMAS MMAS MASNJ

French Clown
(mixed media on card)

Fantasy Clown
(mixed media on card)

Carnival Clown
(mixed media on card)

Rosmar Booth, married and living in the county of Essex, England, with her husband Peter, was born in Olot, a Catalan town in Northern Spain.

A former fashion designer and language tutor, Rosmar studied art privately and at college while living in Spain, France and England.

She has participated in many art exhibitions in England, the United States of America, Spain, France, Sweden, Northern Ireland and Canada. She had miniatures selected for showing in the Royal Academy of Arts Summer Exhibitions of 1987 and 1993.

Her work is included in numerous private collections in several countries. Winner of seventeen awards, she is an Associate Member of the Royal Society of Miniature Painters, Sculptors and Gravers, a Founder Member of the Hilliard Society of Miniaturists and also a member of the many Societies noted after her name.

This artist works in oil, acrylic and water-colour, using a personal and untraditional self-taught technique.

Sheila M. Slicer

ARMS MASF ASMA (Victoria)

Self Portrait
(water-colour on Ivorine)

Sarah
(water-colour on Ivorine)

Born in England in 1930 she studied at Bradford Regional College of Art where she was awarded a Diploma of Commercial Art, with Distinction in Fashion Drawing, and worked in England and Canada as a freelance fashion artist.

She began painting miniatures in 1970, specializing in portraits and using transparent water-colour on ivory or Ivorine, in the traditional manner. She exhibited with the Royal Society of Miniature Painters in 1970, was elected an Associate, then showed with the Miniature Art Society of Florida in 1978 becoming a Member and winning three first prizes.

A Founder Member of the Yorkshire Watercolour Society, as Exhibition Secretary she organized three exhibitions a year. It was the first Society allowed to exhibit in the Palace of Westminster in the gallery between the Lords and Commons.

She has made a film for Yorkshire Television, painting a miniature from start to finish, given demonstrations and lectures and worked restoring 18th century miniatures.

Sheila has exhibited in England, Andorra, America and Sweden with work in collections there and in Bermuda, Australia, Japan and Singapore. A Founder Member of the Australian Society of Miniature Art in Victoria she foresees a great future for societies in Australia.

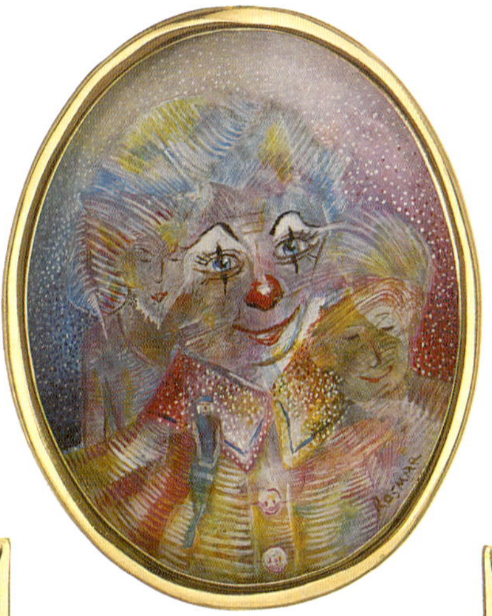

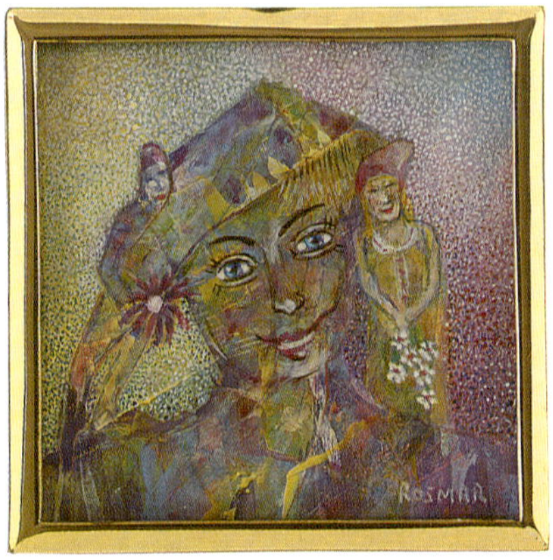
ROSMAR

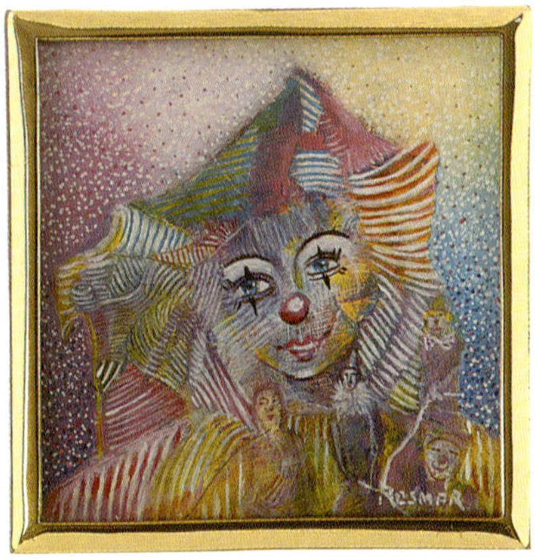
ROSMAR

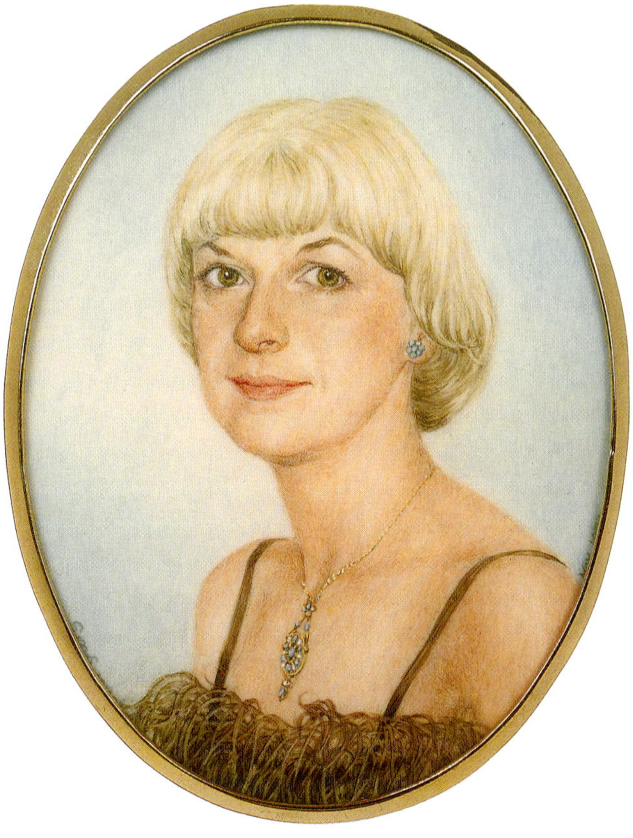

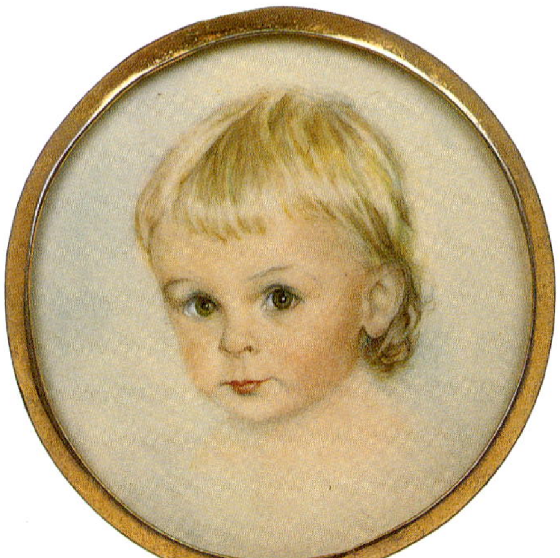

R. Anne Upson NDD RMS

Pampas
(water-colour on paper)
kindly lent by
Mrs. Rosalind Martin

Aledan
(water-colour on paper)
kindly lent by
R. Mair Esq.

Anne was born in Wigan and her father was a vicar. Her mother was a florist and a Member of the Cathedral Guild of Embroidery at Canterbury. School-days were spent at Sleep Hall School, St. Ives, Huntingdon, followed by four years at Maidstone Art College, studying graphic art, where she was awarded the National Diploma of Design. In 1960 she married Peter, a jockey, and later had two children, Tony and Deirdre. Anne has had an interest in equine physiotherapy for fifteen years and was a Founder Member of the National Association of Animal Therapists. She lives with her husband in an attractive part of Kent under the South Downs. Her main artistic interest is in painting animals and their welfare is of great importance to her.

Rex Trayhorne RMS

Down a Hampshire Lane
(water-colour on paper)
kindly lent by the President

He is a professional water-colour artist and a Member of the Royal Miniature Society. Having trained as a Technical Illustrator in airbrushing and highly finished techniques he paints emphasizing drawing and design with minute attention to detail.

As a freelance he prepared architectural impressions, cartoons, photo-retouching, models and graphic designs, but in 1981 he turned to water-colour painting. He moved to an old cottage in Romsey, which is home, studio and a gallery for his paintings.

Member of four local Art Societies, he became the Exhibition Secretary of Romsey Art Group and tutored at Southampton College of Higher Education. Lectures, demonstrations, exhibiting and writing for art magazines, are all part of his life and he organizes the Wessex Artists Exhibitions in Salisbury.

Prints of his work and cards have been reproduced by Fine Art publishers and he has won many competitions including the National First Prize in the Saunders Waterford Water-colour Competition. He exhibited at the Royal Institute, was highly commended at the Royal Water Colour Society's Exhibition and was a finalist in the BBC's Summertime Exhibition at the Tate Gallery.

He appeared on the BBC2 programme 'Painters', painting Salisbury Cathedral, and has produced his own video 'Adventure into Water-colour'.

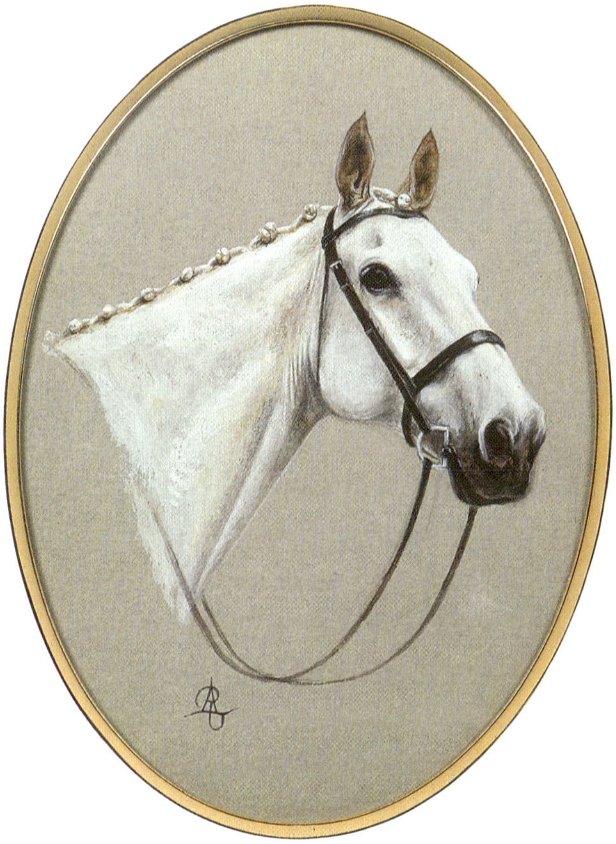
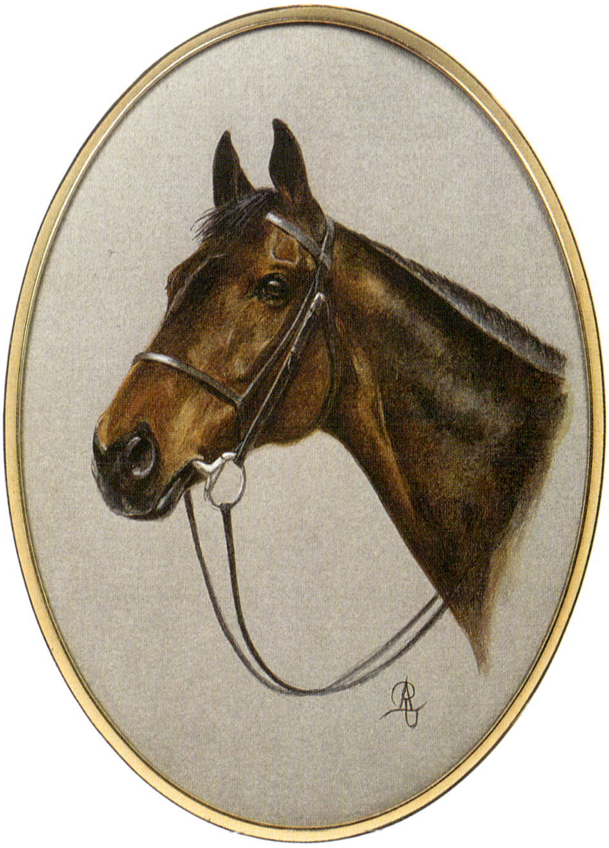
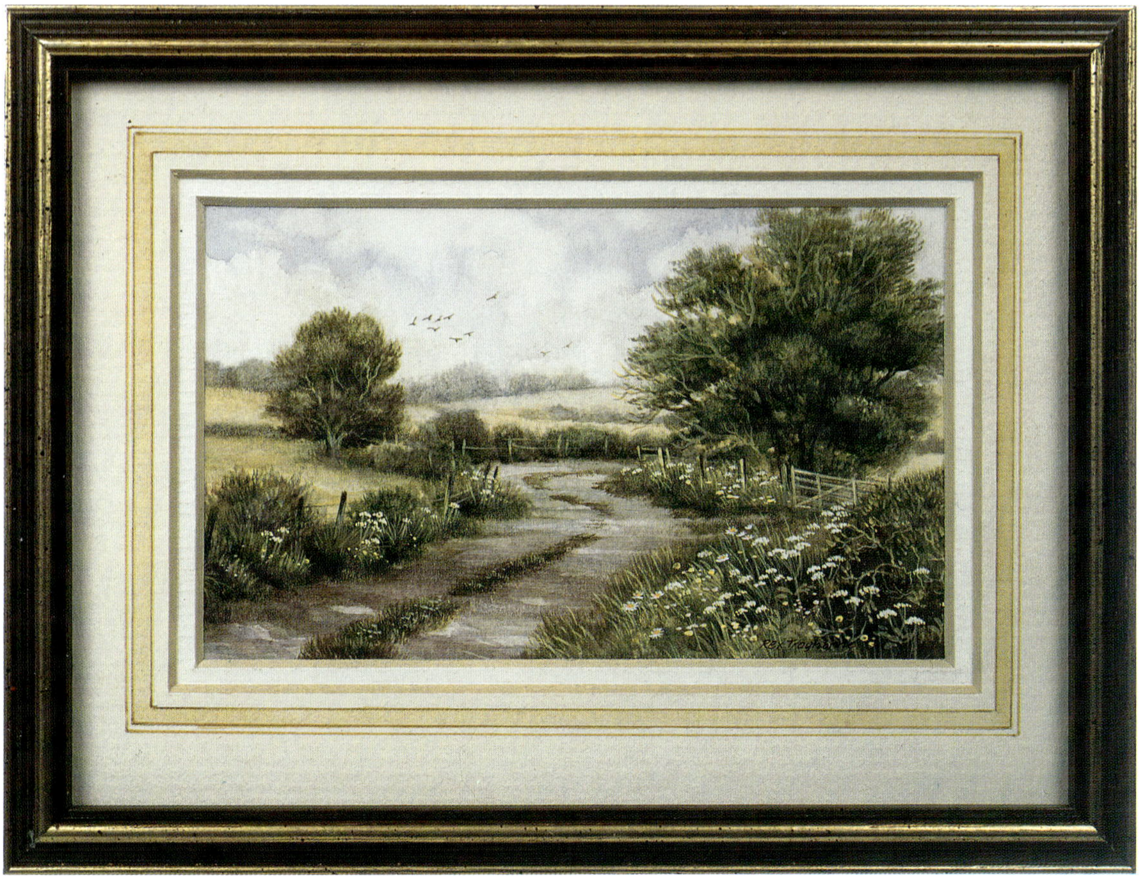

Gladys Hayton *ARMS SM (London) HS*

Fred
(water-colour on Ivorine)
kindly lent by the President

Chester
(water-colour on Ivorine)
kindly lent by the President

Gladys was born in Poole, Dorset and began painting when she was ten.

She attended Poole School of Art and her certificates qualified her to paint at Poole Pottery. Work entailed decorating pots with stylised traditional patterns and other elaborate designs. Painters were disciplined and work examined twice daily. A lower standard was fined one penny a small pot and two pence a larger one, good training indeed! Her pots were chosen by the Pottery for exhibition at the British Industries Fair in Buenos Aires. The ware she painted is highly collectable and auctioned at Christie's alongside Doulton ceramics.

She loves cats and has painted animals for over twenty years. Exhibiting at many exhibitions she is commissioned to paint people's pets.

She discovered water-colour miniatures and enjoys painting in this medium. Eager to learn, she attended courses teaching valuable techniques, which she uses to good effect.

She has exhibited with the Royal Miniature Society since 1982 and is an Associate Member; also a Member of the Hilliard Society and Society of Miniaturists. Her miniatures are found world-wide in Alaska, Australia, New Zealand, Europe and the Far East. They are collected because of their appealing subjects and delicate, sympathetic treatment.

Alan Farrell *MIEE ARMS*

Chalybeate Spring, the Pantiles, Tunbridge Wells
(water-colour on Fabriano paper)

Alan Farrell was born in London in 1932 and after spending a few years in the Royal Air Force he trained as a Chartered Engineer, becoming a Member of the Institution of Electrical Engineers.

He always had an interest in painting, mainly in water-colour, but had no formal training. He joined the Estuary Group of painters based in Pitsea, Essex, in 1963, which influenced him significantly and from which his liking for marine subjects arose.

He started exhibiting seriously in 1981 and was elected an Associate Member of the Royal Miniature Society in 1984. He has exhibited widely with the Royal Society of Marine Artists, the Royal Institute of Painters in Water Colours, the Royal Society of British Artists, Britain in Water Colour and at the International Boat Show.

He belongs to several groups of artists in Sussex, including the Association of Sussex Artists, and gives demonstrations and talks on aspects of painting.

Due to work as an engineer he travelled widely at home and abroad and in his spare time built several houses. He lives in a listed building, which was the village store and post office at Whitesmith in Sussex, and runs a business dealing in antiques and paintings.

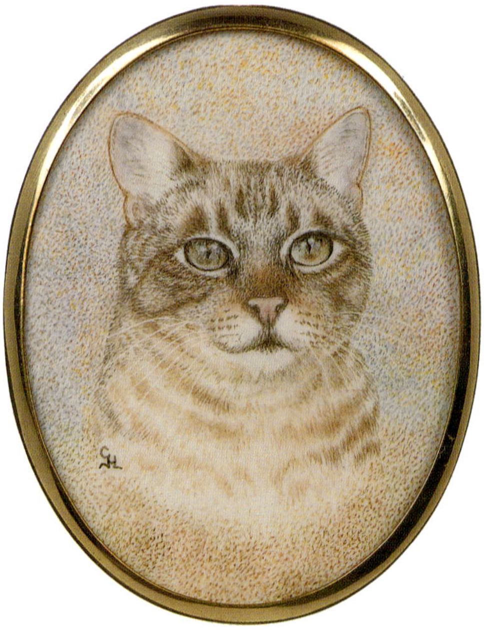

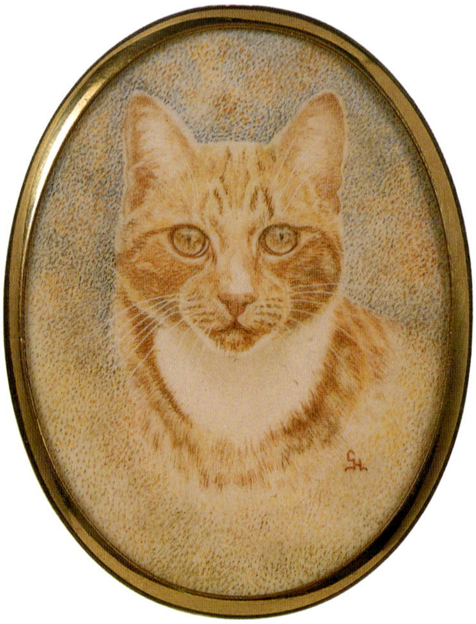

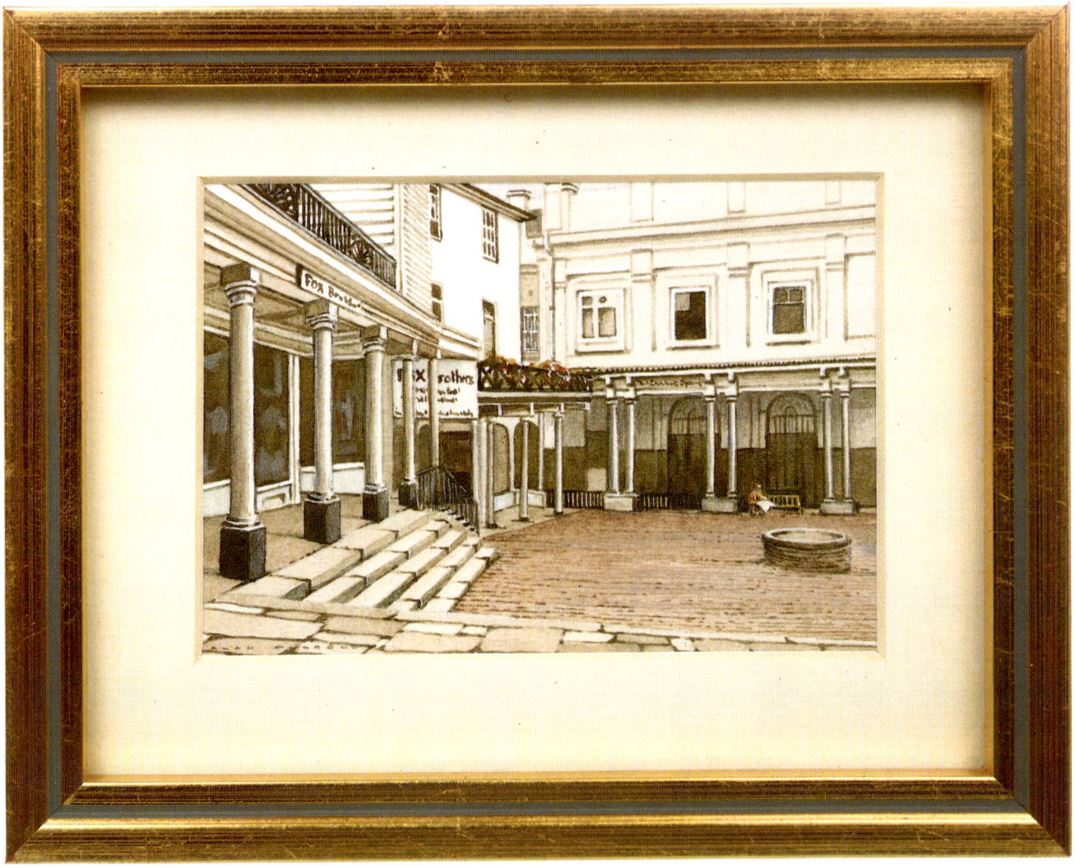

William Bennett

LLB (Lond.) RMS HS ASMA (Victoria)

Joe
(water-colour on ivory)
from the Diploma Collection

Mrs. Joan Miller
(water-colour on ivory)
from the Diploma Collection

He is a painter of miniature portraits, still life and marine subjects in oil and water-colour. Born in London in 1917, he studied there at the Sir John Cass College. He has exhibited at the Royal Academy of Arts, with the Federation of British Artists, the City of London Art Exhibitions, the Gallery Americana in Carmel, California and the Winters Gallery, St. Louis, Illinois. His one-man exhibitions include three in the United States of America; Geslong, Victoria, Australia in 1986, 1987, 1988 and two in Melbourne, Victoria in 1989, 1990. He is a member of the Royal Society of Miniature Painters, Sculptors and Gravers and the Victoria Society of Artists in Melbourne, Australia.

William Bennett has work in many private collections, including that of Her Majesty the Queen.

Iris Huckvale *RMS SWA SBA*

Tawny Owl
(oil on Ivorine)

Still Life with Red Rose
(oil on Ivorine)

Iris Huckvale was born into an artistic and musical family and has been painting and drawing from a very early age. Not seeking a formal training, she has developed her work through observation and experimentation. After a period of large still life and landscape painting, a visit to the Royal Miniature Society's exhibition at the Mall Galleries in 1970 provided inspiration to develop her already strong interest in small-scale and detailed work. She has been painting in oil in the miniature style almost exclusively since then, her subjects including wildlife, still life, landscape and botanical studies.

After she was elected a Member of the Royal Miniature Society in 1983, Membership of the Society of Women Artists and the Society of Botanical Artists followed and she has shown in the annual exhibitions held by these Societies for many years. Her paintings have also been accepted by the Society of Wildlife Artists and at the Royal Academy Summer Exhibition. The Medici Society has published reproductions of her work as greetings cards.

She exhibits in various galleries in London and throughout the country, as also in the United States with the Miniature Art Society of Florida.

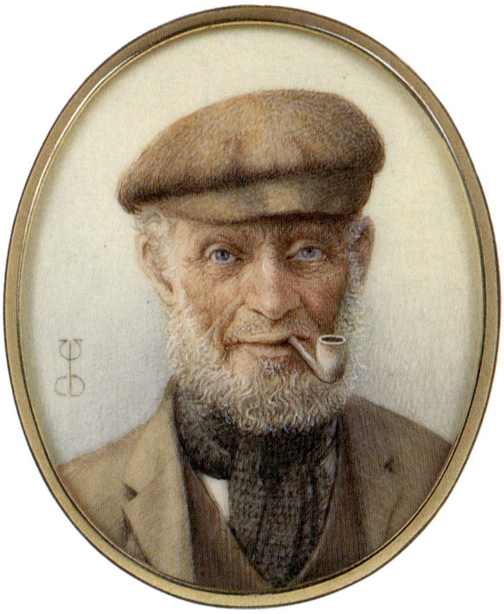

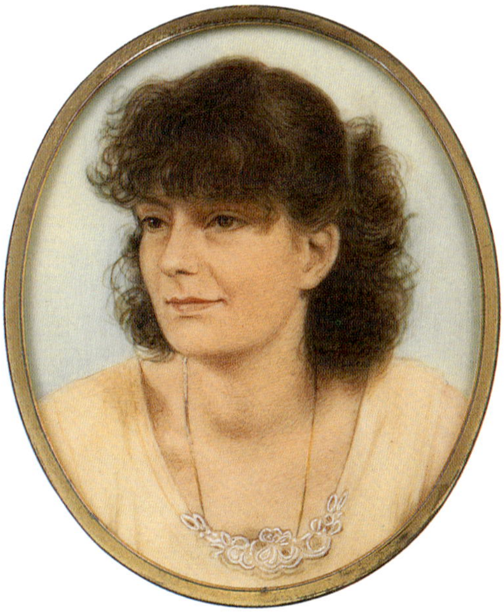

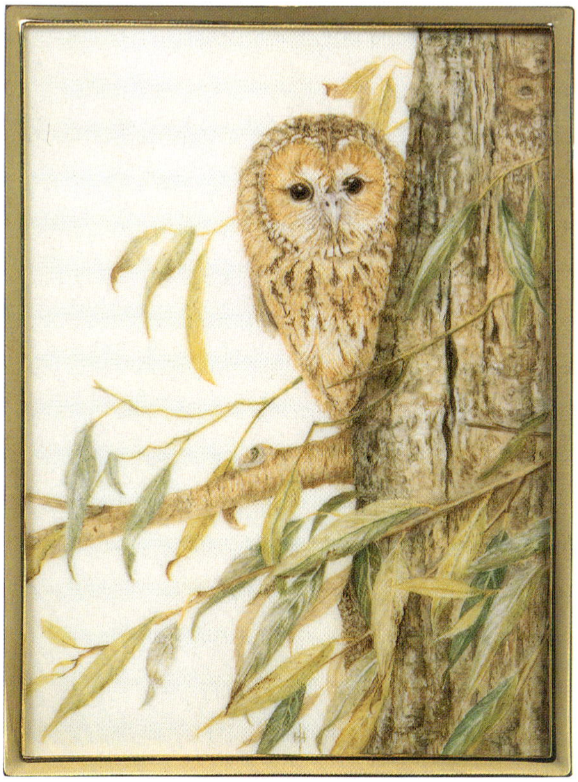

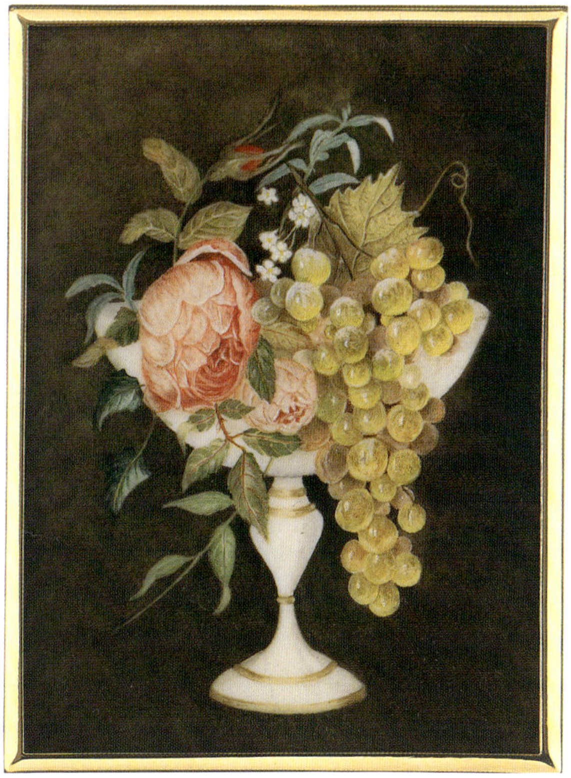

Valerie Baines *FLS ARMS FSBA*

Small Coppers on Ragwort
(water-colour on Bristol board)

Common Blues on Trefoil
(water-colour on Bristol board)

When she was very young Valerie Baines was already interested in art and music. She trained at Harrow Art School, then studied the piano and singing at the Royal College of Music for three years. When about to leave she saw an exhibition of flower paintings by Sanderson's bursary students, so she applied for a bursary and was offered a job as a designer in their studio, where she stayed for five years until leaving to get married.

For some time painting took second place to looking after her family. In later years, with more time to paint, she exhibited at the Royal Academy Summer exhibition, the Mall Galleries, and regularly with the Royal Society of Miniature Painters and the Society of Botanical Artists. She exhibited also in Canada, America and France.

She has illustrated several natural history books including 'The Naturalist's Garden,' 'The Story of Silk,' 'Meadows' and others by John Feltwell, FLS; also educational books for Collins and 'Glorious Butterflies and their Flora', with paintings of nearly seventy British butterflies and their caterpillars' food plants, for the Silver Jubilee of the Butterfly Conservation Society.

In 1991 she was elected a Fellow of the Linnean Society of London.

Alois Majzlik *BA (Hons.) RMS HS*

The Angler
(oil on copper)
kindly lent by Alastair C. Twort Esq.

Alois was born on January 31, 1913 in Czechoslovakia. He received art tuition at an early age from a well-known Czech artist. Later he worked on the interior restoration of old churches and monasteries before turning to stage design.

At eighteen he held his first exhibition, then exhibiting in various European countries and North Africa.

He arrived in England with the Free Czech Army, formed in France in 1940, and worked, mostly as an artist, for both the army and the exiled Czech Government. The army gave him permission to finish his studies at the then Oxford based London University Slade School under Professor Schwabe. He gained an Honours Degree and a Special Prize for Lithography.

Married, he returned to his country in 1946 but was forced back to England for political reasons in 1947. At first he lived in Hampstead but eventually settled with his family in Kent and obtained British Nationality.

He exhibits in several galleries in England, Canada, the United States and has had commissions for Australia.

Elected a Member of the Royal Miniature Society in 1983, he also belongs to the Hilliard Society. His miniatures are painted in oil on copper.

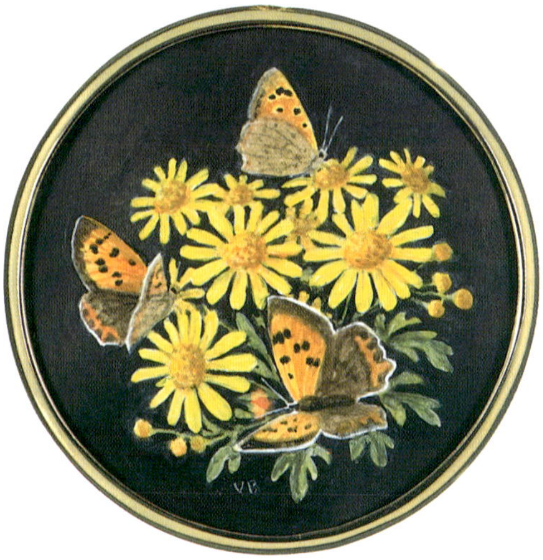
VB

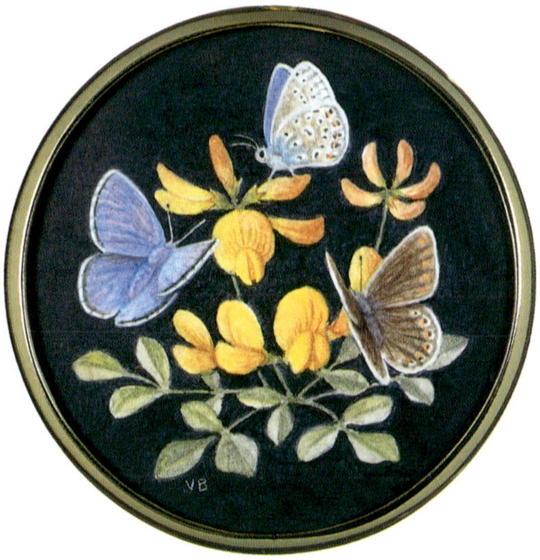
VB

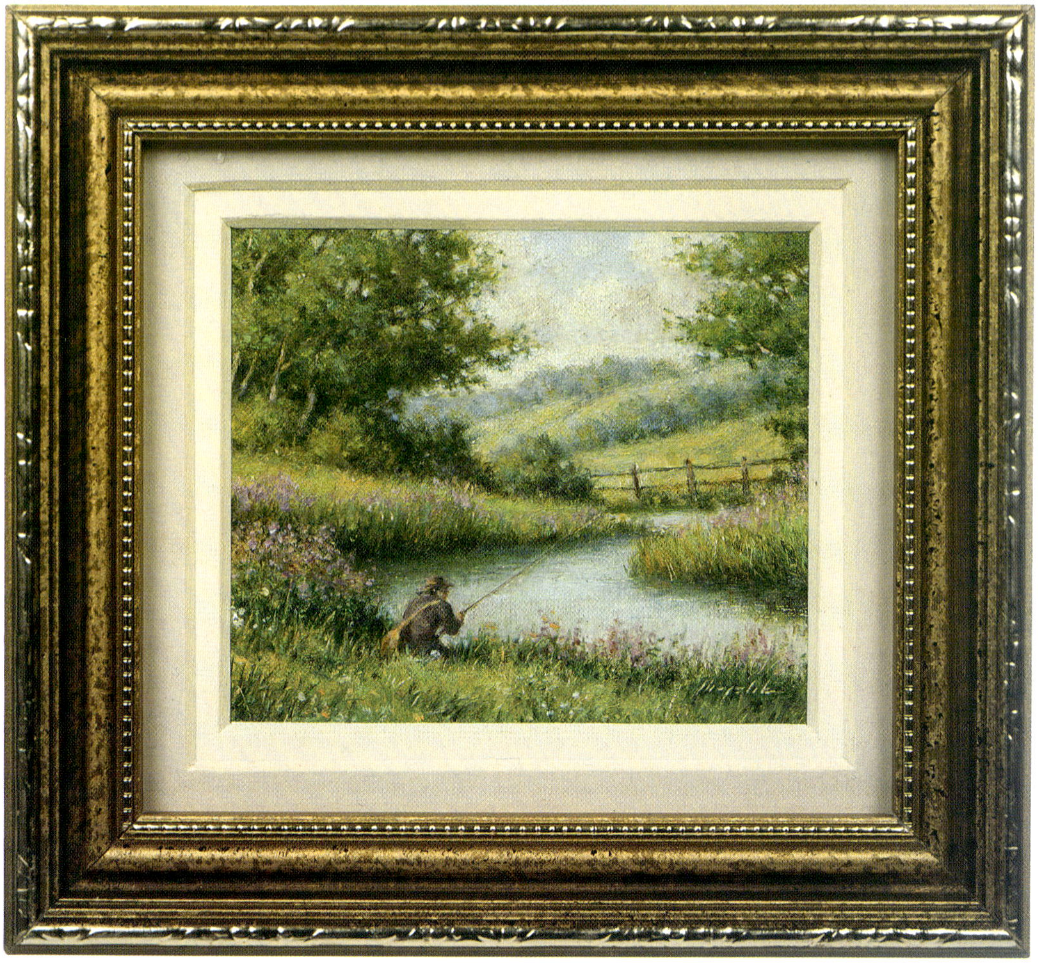

Anita Emmerich

RMS SWA MASF HSF GMAS ASMA (Queensland)

Georgian Lady Wearing a Mob Cap - late 1780's
(oil on vellum)

Georgian Lady Wearing a Balloon Hat - late 1780's
(oil on vellum)

Anita is a miniature painter in oils and specializes in shade portraits. From large oil pictures she turned to the fascinating art of the miniature in 1979. She is now a well-established shade profile portraitist of contemporary and historical subjects. Her work is unusual as she paints deep colours into the sitter's hair and clothing, yet still keeps within classical traditions. Using the finest layers of oil, and sometimes ink, she works on vellum or old ivory.

In 1990 she was elected an Associate of the Royal Miniature Society followed by Membership in 1993. She is a Founder Member of the Hilliard Society and belongs to several societies in the United States and Australia where she has won awards and an Honourable Mention from the Society of Miniature Painters, Sculptors and Gravers in Washington DC, with a Llewellyn Alexander Commendation of Excellence in 1995. She has shown at the Royal Academy Summer Exhibition, with the National Society at the Mall Galleries and other London galleries.

In 1993 she was Contemporary Art Consultant to the Rochester Diocese Advisory Committee, but resigned to give herself more time for painting. She hopes to develop her profile miniatures and her dream is to establish a permanent gallery for contemporary miniaturists.

Claudia Myatt *ARMS SWA MASF HS*

After the Race
(water-colour on Bristol board)

Claudia had no formal art training but began painting in water-colours twelve years ago, specializing in miniature landscapes. In 1991 she gave up a career in London and moved to Suffolk to paint full-time.

Her work material comes from sketches and photographs taken on location, concentrating in particular on marine landscapes and traditional sailing craft. Many paintings are commissioned, covering a wide range of subjects from landscapes to yachts.

She has exhibited in Britain, France and the United States where she won first prize in 1991, and second in 1994, for Marine Art at the Miniature Art Society of Florida. At the Georgia Miniature Art Society in 1993 she was awarded first prize for 'Six square inches or less.'

She is an Associate of the Royal Miniature Society, a Member of the Society of Women Artists, the East Anglian Group of Marine Artists, the Hilliard Society of Miniaturists and the Miniature Art Society of Florida.

For two years her twenty-four foot gaff cutter was her home and studio, sailing to galleries and events around the coast, including the British Pavilion at the Brest '92 Festival of Sail and the Dutch Classic Yacht Regatta in 1993.

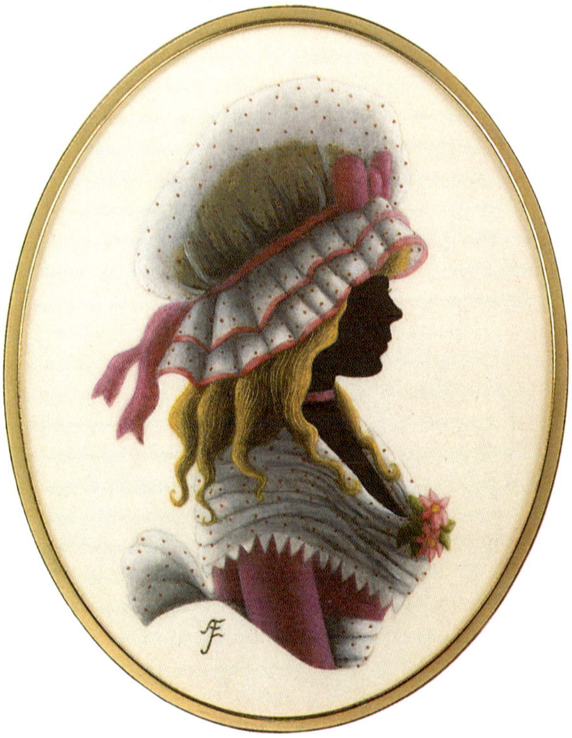

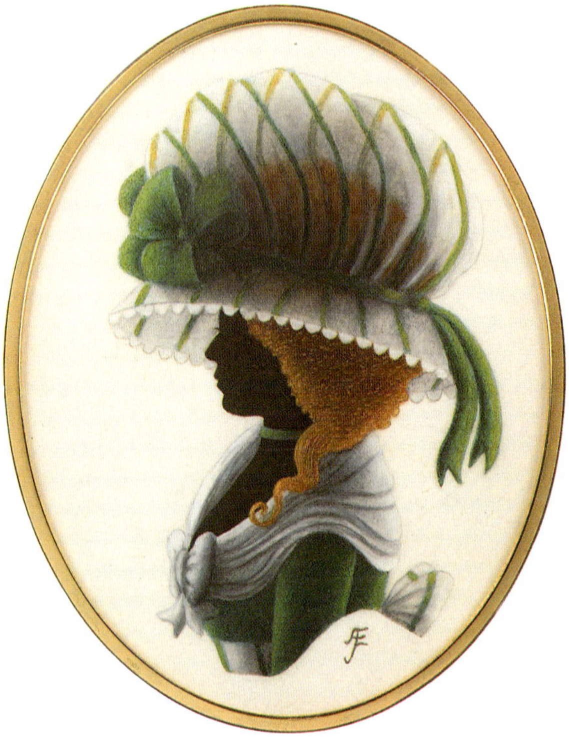

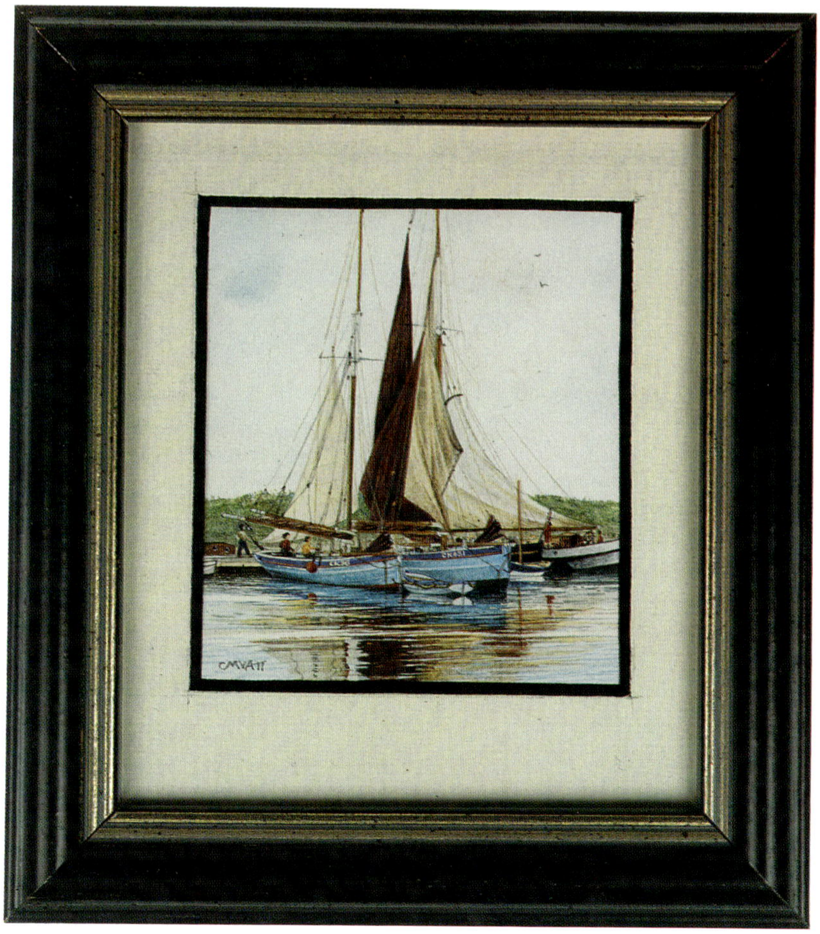

Margaret Elaine Ryder

PVPRMS SWA FSBA MASF SM (London) HS

Wild Flowers of August
(water-colour on vellum)

Wild Flowers of Spring
(water-colour on vellum)

She was born Margaret Elaine Wordsworth in Sheffield in 1908 and studied at the Sheffield College of Art, winning many scholarships. She married Norman Vint Ryder and had two children, Peter Darrell and Angela who was a Member of the Bluebell Girls and on the stage for a number of years.

Margaret worked in London and Manchester as a freelance commercial artist for twenty years. She is a portrait, flower and landscape painter, in oil, pastel and water-colour, and a miniature painter using ivory or vellum as the base for her work.

She is a Member of the Royal Society of Miniature Painters, Sculptors and Gravers, the Society of Women Artists, the Society of Miniaturists, a Founder Member of the Society of Botanical Artists and the Hilliard Society of Miniaturists and she is the President of the Sheffield Society of Women Artists.

She has exhibited at the Royal Academy, the Paris Salon; the Pastel Society, Royal Institute and RWS Flower Painters Exhibitions; the Manchester Academy, the Aberdeen Society of Artists, Perth in Australia and the United States. Apart from this busy routine she has had five one-man shows and four shared with other artists.

Colin Scott-Kestin *ARMS ASEqA HS*

Tittle-tattle
(water-colour on paper)
kindly lent by Mrs. Mary Scott-Kestin

He attended Beckenham School of Art in 1938. During war service with the Royal Signals he did paintings of life in the Forces, one of which was purchased by the Ministry of Information and others are at the Royal Signals Museum at Blandford in Dorset.

After the war circumstances did not allow him to spend much time on art, but later short periods of study with the late Dr. Eric Ennion proved invaluable in teaching him to paint moving animals.

Now a full-time artist, his main interests are landscapes and animal subjects, especially horses. He has fulfilled a number of private commissions and he is a regular exhibitor with the Society of Equestrian Artists of which he is an Associate Member. His work has also been shown at the Royal Bath and West Show, galleries in the provinces and in London at the Llewellyn Alexander Gallery where he was awarded a Commendation of Excellence in 1995.

Recently he has taken up miniature painting, working mainly in water-colours or gouache on hot-pressed paper and card. His pictures are composed from his own photographs and sketches. He is a Member of the Hilliard Society of Miniaturists and was elected an Associate Member of the Royal Miniature Society in 1992.

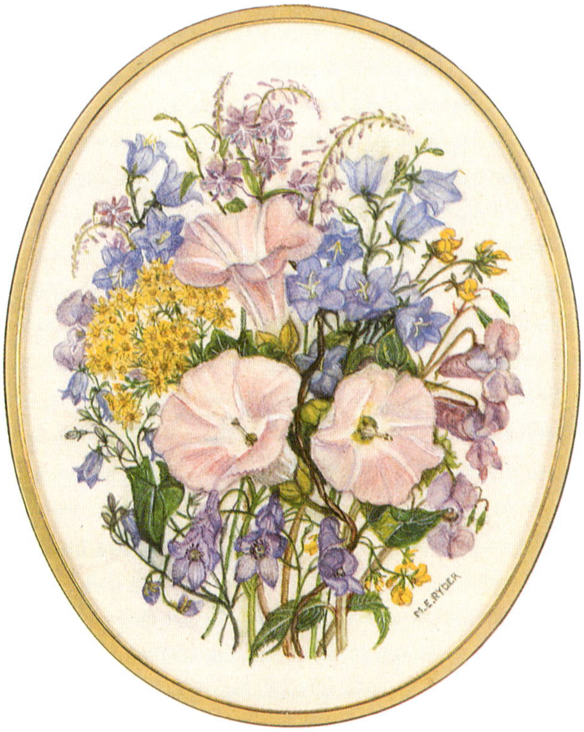
M.E.RYDER

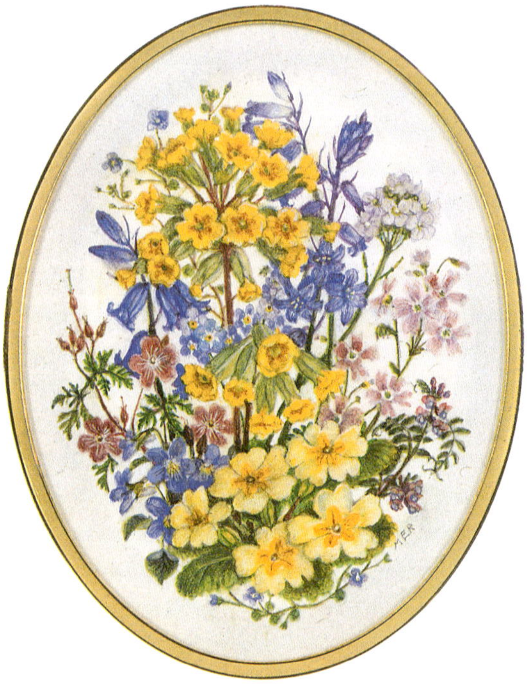

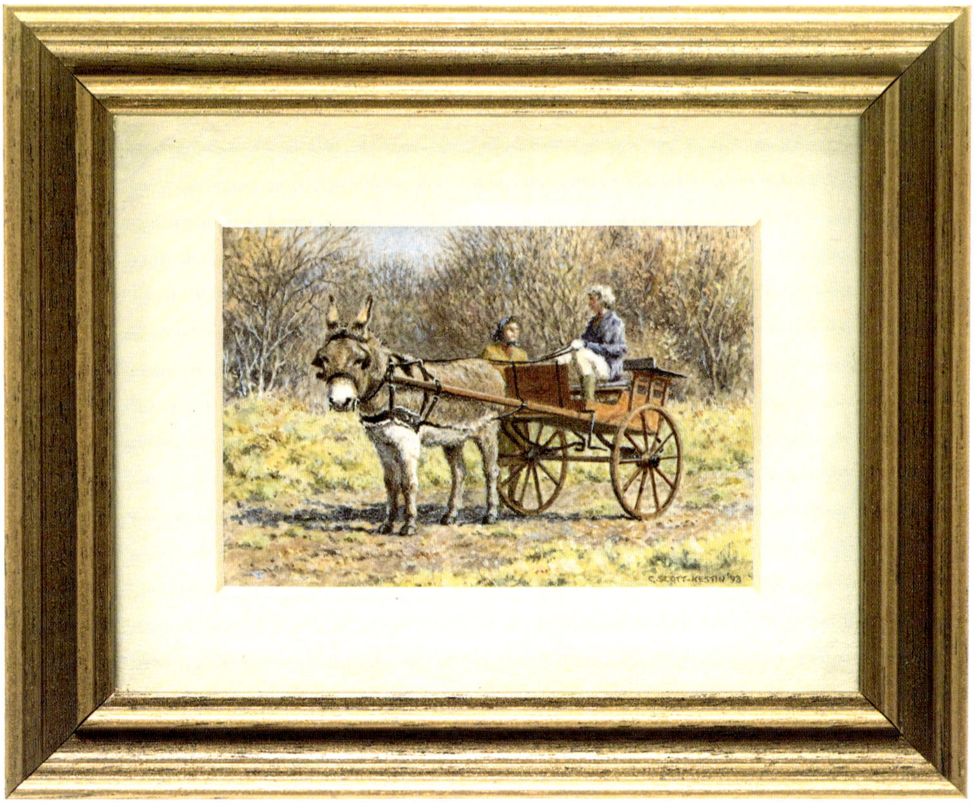
C.SCOTT-KESTIN '93

Glenys R. Caldicott *ARMS SWA SM*

Irish Setter - Mike
(gouache on Canford card)

Harvey C. Caldicott
(gouache on Canford card)

Born on August 20th, 1941 in Nottingham she was educated in Mablethorpe, Lincolnshire, in Grimsby at Highfield College and then at Grimsby School of Art. She moved to London in 1960 and followed various occupations including silk-screen printer, stage costumier and assistant interior decorator.

She married, had one son and moved to Birmingham in 1972 where she restored and sold antique costume. She studied fashion at Bournville College of Art, taught fashion history and sewing skills in the Birmingham area until her illness in 1984, then turned to miniature painting as a full time occupation.

She exhibited annually with the Royal Miniature Society from 1988. In 1989 she won the Margaret Ryder Award and in 1990 was elected an Associate Member.

In 1991 she was elected a Member of the Society of Women Artists and exhibited with the British Watercolour Society in Ilkley, becoming a Member of the Society of Miniaturists. She received a Llewellyn Alexander Award in 1992 and has won the Dartington Rose Bowl. Glenys works in gouache, painting portraits, but she specializes in animal miniatures which are mostly of dogs and cats. Her work is in a number of private collections.

Alice C. Butler *RMS*

High Summer
(water-colour on vellum)
from the Diploma Collection

Catkin
(water-colour on vellum)

She was born in Kent but moved later to Redbourne in Hertfordshire and afterwards to Malmesbury, where she had a studio-shop near the Abbey. She exhibited at the Royal West of England Academy and the Royal Academy of Arts.

In 1938 she married Maurice Bizley, a Wiltshire man, and came to Cornwall where she lives at Perranporth. Her husband died in 1967. She has a daughter and two grandsons.

In 1955 she was made a Bard of the Cornish Gorsedd for services to Cornwall and her book 'The Slate Figures of Cornwall,' recording the unique carved memorials of the County, which she illustrated with line drawings.

She has been a Member of the St. Ives Society of Artists for over forty years and in 1957 was elected an Associate Member of the Royal Miniature Society followed in 1961 by Membership. This year she has presented work to the Society's Diploma Collection. She has a deep love of Cornwall and its history, living in the Perranzabuloi which claims St. Piran as Patron Saint. She has been, for many years, the curator of Perranzabuloi Folk Museum and the Recorder of the Old Cornwall Society's local branch.

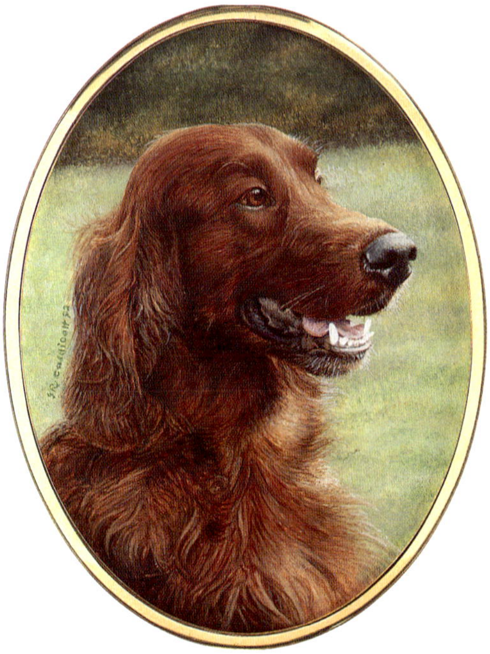

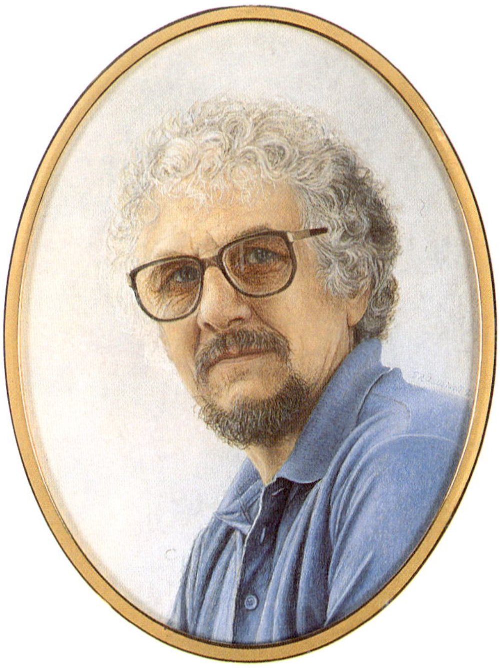

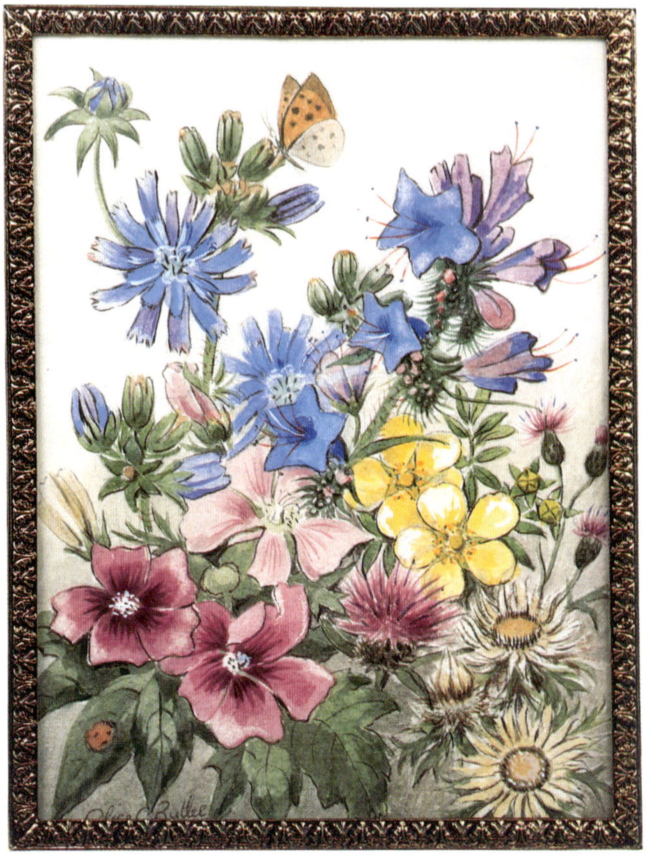

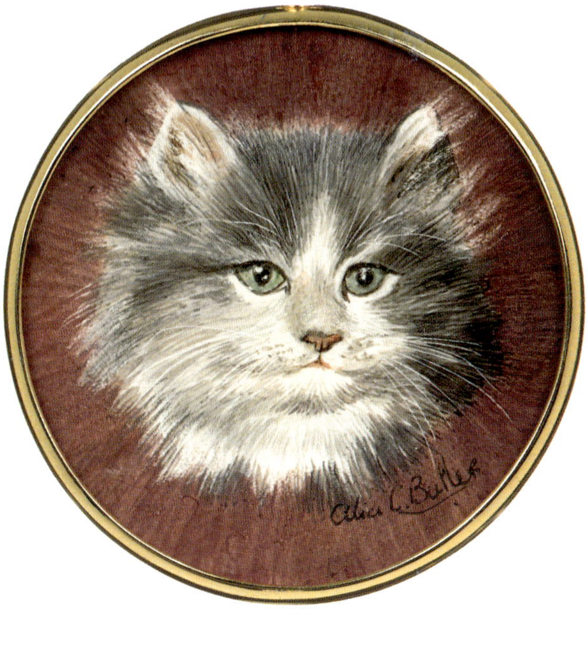

Peter Toms *ARMS HS*

Marine Group
(water-colour on paper)

Born in 1940 he has had a life-long interest in art. He started painting in 1981 and was so successful that he gave up an engineering career in 1982 to paint full-time. He exhibited at the Royal Institute of Painters in Water Colours, the Royal Society of British Artists and the Royal Society of Marine Artists.

In 1991 he was elected an Associate of the Royal Miniature Society and a Member of the Hilliard Society.

His works are collected world-wide and by political and television celebrities. Other collections which include his pictures are British Aerospace, Link Publications, H.M. Land Registry, The Astrid Trust, N.V. Amev Group of the Netherlands, Royal Hampshire Regiment, National Mutual Life Assurance Society, Royal Navy, Brittany Ferries (presented by Poole Harbour Commissioners) and twelve marine paintings were commissioned by a London Bank in 1987.

He was featured in an article in the Classic Boat Magazine and a programme on the BBC's South To-day. With over twenty-five one-man exhibitions to his credit he is also a tutor and speaker on water-colour techniques and the President of the Dorchester Art Club.

Elisabeth Norman *ARMS SBA HS*

Two Auriculas "Fanny Marbeck" and "Haffner"
(water-colour on paper)

She trained as a dress designer at Nottingham Art School but did not start painting seriously until her husband's retirement.

Although she enjoys working with all plant life, she specializes in auriculas which, usually, she grows herself before painting them. Fruits are also much-loved subjects. She finds it helps accuracy if she paints life-size, botanically correct pictures before translating them into miniatures with their specialized quality and techniques. Using water-colour on paper she will, on occasion, add a little body colour where necessary.

She exhibits regularly with the Society of Botanical Artists, where she has been a Member of Council, and with them has taken part in special exhibitions at the Linnean Society of London, Hampton Court Flower Show and Rufford, Nottingham. She shows annually with the Hilliard Society in Wells and took part in their special exhibitions in Montelimar, France and at the Barbican, London as part of their tenth anniversary celebrations. She has exhibited paintings at the Royal Horticultural Society's Flower Shows and won the Silver Grenfell Medal with a Commendation of Excellence from the Llewellyn Alexander Gallery in 1995.

Elisabeth is a dedicated gardener which clashes sometimes with the possession of five cats: a Burmese, a Siamese and three of the Devon Rex breed. These she paints as well.

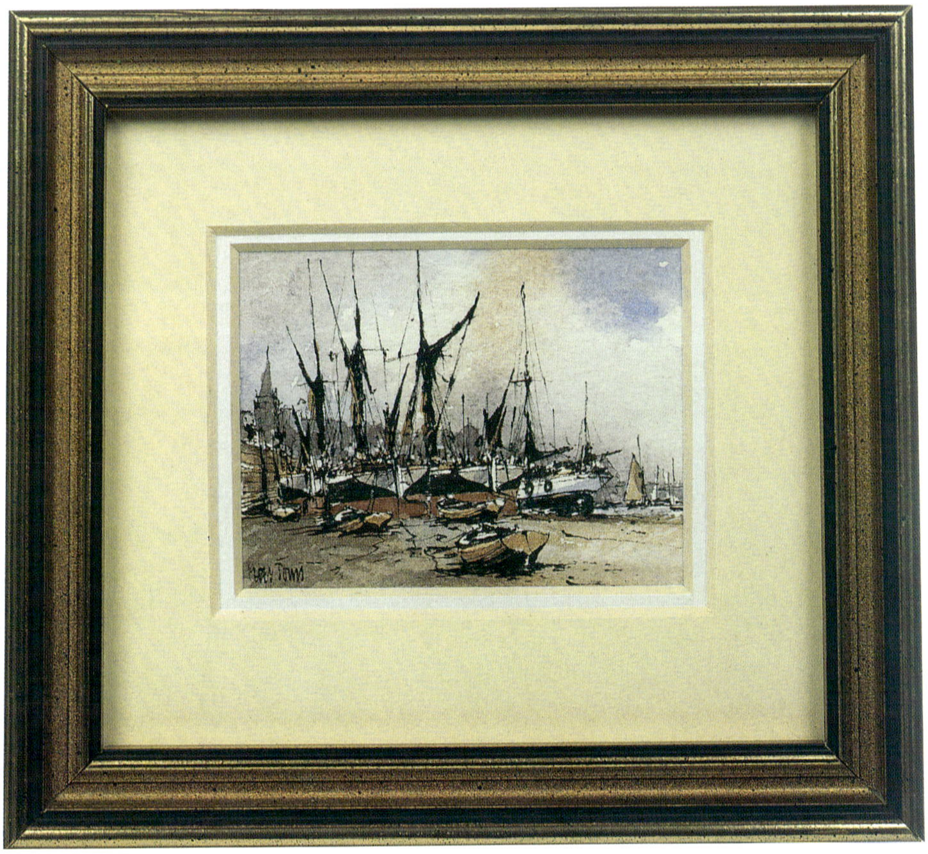

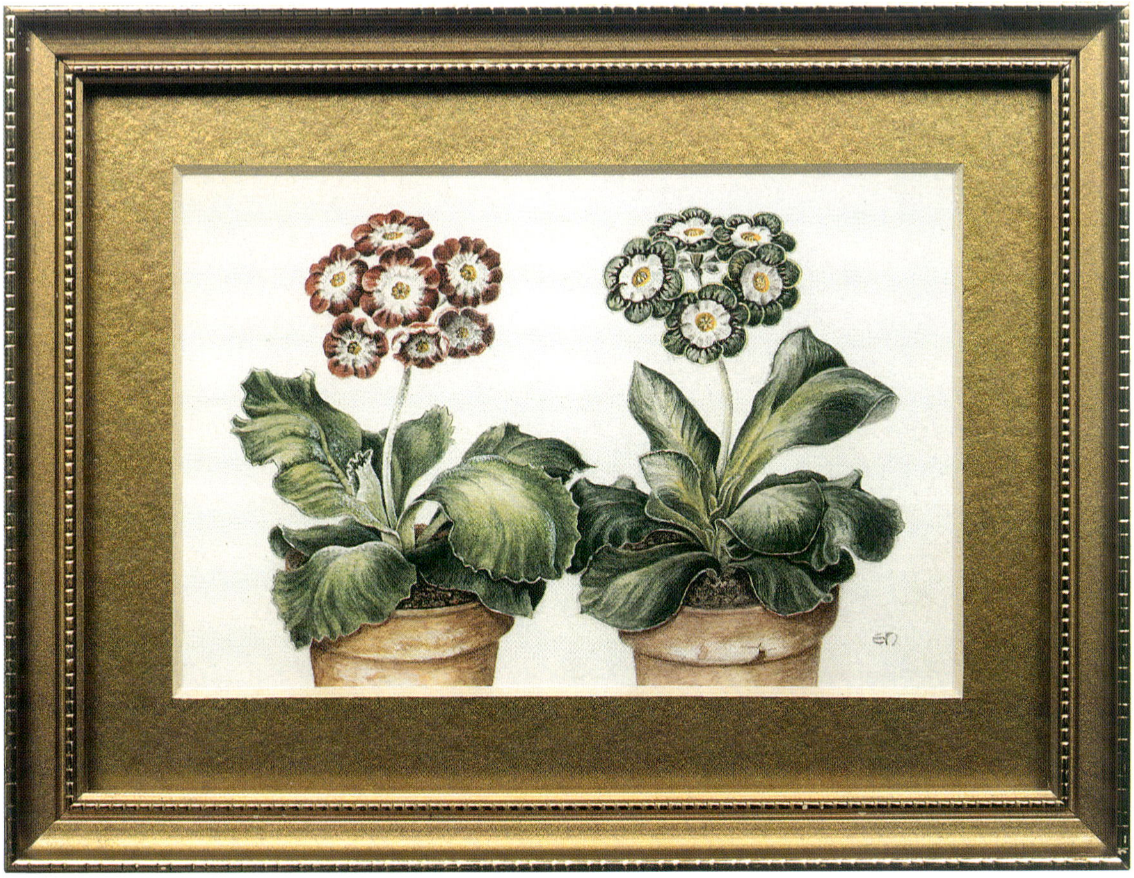

Gillie Hoyte Byrom *RMS BSOE HS*

Mia with Leo
(hand-painted vitreous enamel on copper)

Mrs. Gordon Hamilton
(hand-painted vitreous enamel on copper)

She began enamelling in 1977 and during ten years made hand-painted enamel jewellery set in silver or gold, but now specializes in enamel portrait miniatures.

Gillie has been a member of the Devon Guild of Craftsmen since 1979 and Chairman from 1989 to 1992. She exhibits annually with the Royal Miniature Society becoming an Associate Member in 1991. The Hilliard Society elected her to membership in 1992 and she is a Member of the British Society of Enamellers since 1986. In 1990 she received the Margaret Ryder Award and two portraits won prizes from the Florida Miniature Art Society.

That same year she studied enamel painting at the Llotja School in Barcelona with Andreu Vilasis and Nuria Lopez Ribalta, taking master classes with Marie Angeles Cera de Derch on the fine eighteenth century techniques.

Enamelling requires intense concentration, preparing the base by fusing vitreous enamel onto copper sheet which has been shaped carefully for a frame or box. Each miniature is fired at about 900°C at least a dozen times, gradually modelling the head in vitreous enamel paint using the finest miniaturist's brushes. The finished piece will never fade, can be polished like glass and would survive a fire!

Marian Tumelty *ARMS SBA*

Springtime
(water-colour on vellum)

Narcissi
(water-colour on vellum)

Marian Tumelty was born in Norwich, Norfolk and studied at the Bath Academy of Art in Corsham, Wiltshire. She is married with two children and now lives and works in Stevenage, Hertfordshire.

She has always loved drawing and painting and from an early age found that working in fine detail gave her the greatest of pleasure and satisfaction. However, it is only comparatively recently that she has been able to develop her work in this way. Her inspiration comes from the wealth of beauty to be seen in flowers, fruits and plants of all kinds. She has been a member of the Society of Botanical Artists since 1988 and in 1993 was one of the first artists to be awarded the Society's Certificate of Botanical Merit.

Miniature painting has always held a fascination for her, but it was not until 1992 that she had time to try her hand at it! Her very first miniatures were accepted for exhibition by the Royal Society of Miniature Painters, Sculptors and Gravers and a year later she was made an Associate Member of the Society.

She continues to exhibit widely and her work is in many private collections at home and abroad.

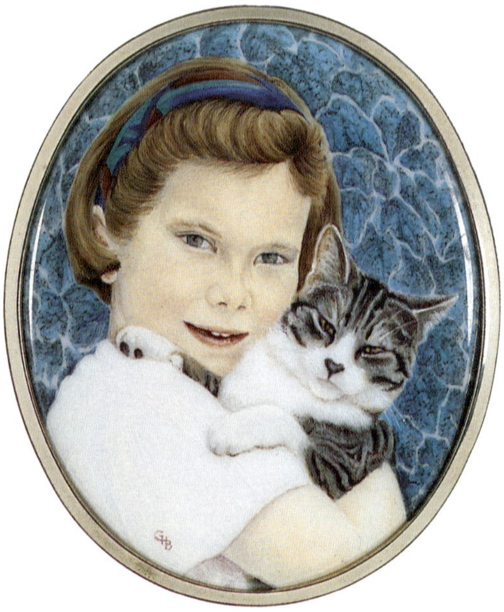

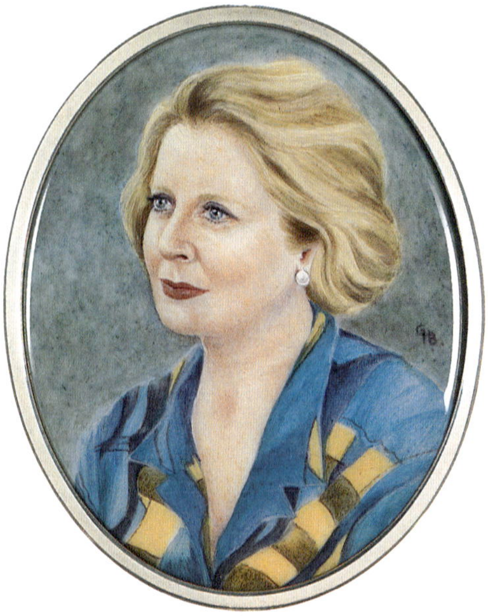

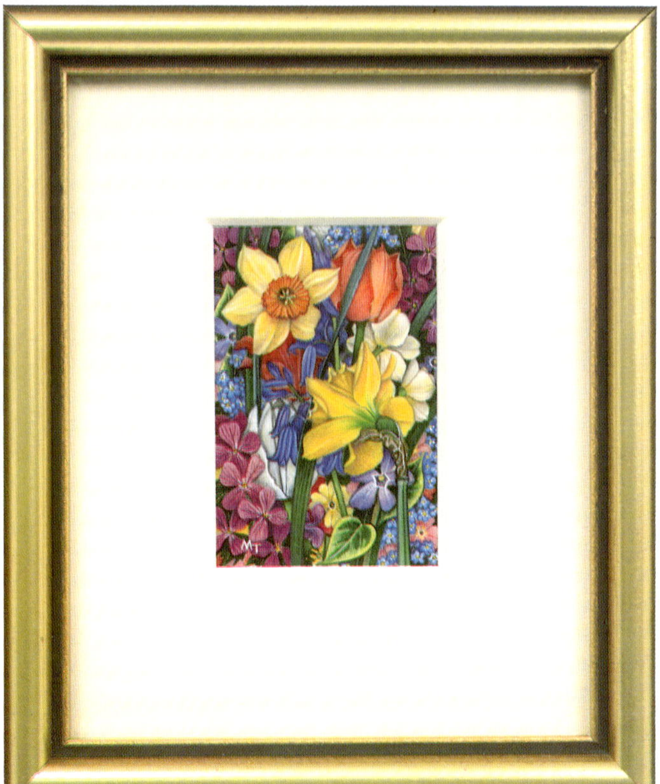

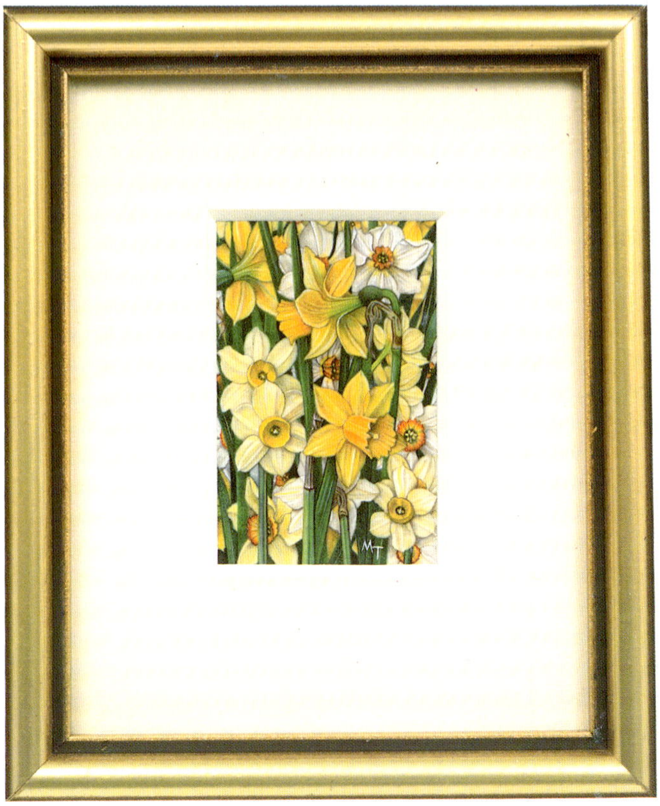

Kathleen Nelson *RMS HSF*

Mouse in Spring
(water-colour on vellum)

Robin
(water-colour on vellum)
from the Diploma Collection

She was born in 1956 and, self-taught, has been painting professionally since 1975. Her wide range of interests are reflected in her paintings of British birds and animals, natural history in general and portraits of domestic pets and farm animals. She has always kept a number of animals which are models for her pictures - everything from poultry, which she loves and paints with inimitable skill, to ponies and a variety of waifs, strays and casualties brought to her for care.

She likes to set her subjects in their own landscapes: they must look at home, as if living where they belong. She works in pencil, water-colour and oil, excelling in finest detail and jewel-like colours, and enjoys painting larger work as well as miniatures.

She exhibits regularly with the Royal Miniature Society and the Hilliard Society.

In 1981 she was a finalist in the Hunting Group Art Prizes, with a miniature of a wren; in 1984 she was given the Drummond award; in 1985 a Gold Memorial Bowl Honourable Mention and in 1993 the second prize Fairman Award. In 1994 she won another Gold Memorial Bowl Honourable Mention and a Commendation of Excellence from the Llewellyn Alexander Gallery with a second Commendation in 1995.

Margaret Burton *RMS SWA*

Christmas Woods
(water-colour on Ivorine)

Born in Harrow, Middlesex, Margaret Burton trained as a commercial artist at Ealing Art College.

During the course of her training she spent valuable and memorable times travelling throughout the English countryside, accumulating a wealth of material which would surface later in her career when she started painting full-time.

In the early 1960's, with her training complete, she found an opportunity to further her skills in the production of detailed artwork when she was employed by a large international glass company.

In the meantime she moved from Middlesex to Berkshire, committing herself to a career as a painter in 1968. This commitment was rewarded when she became an Associate Member of the Royal Miniature Society in 1989 and was elected as a Member in 1992. Her achievement was emphasized by winning a Gold Memorial Bowl Honourable Mention in 1994 having already received the first prize of the distinguished Fairman Members' Subject Miniature Award. Recognition continued when she was elected a Member of the Society of Women Artists in 1994.

A figurative painter, she specializes now in water-colour miniatures, still remaining faithful to her vision of the English countryside which she shares with us in soft, gentle colours.

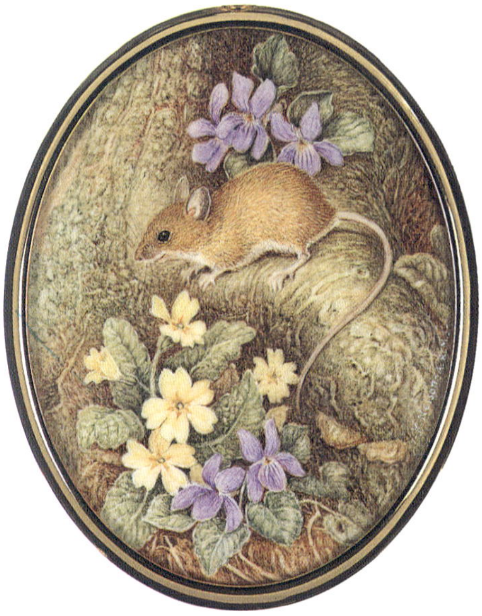

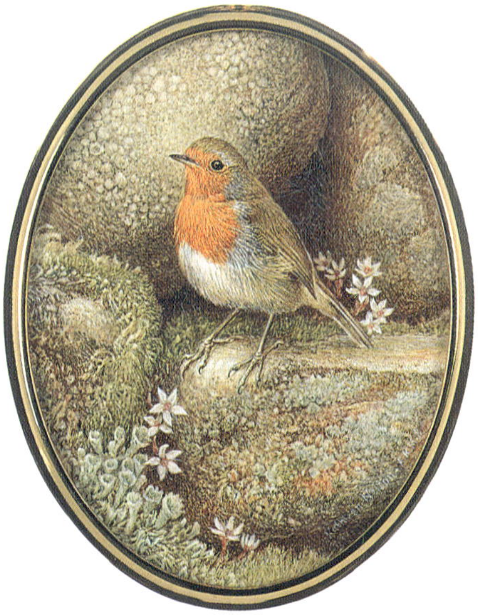

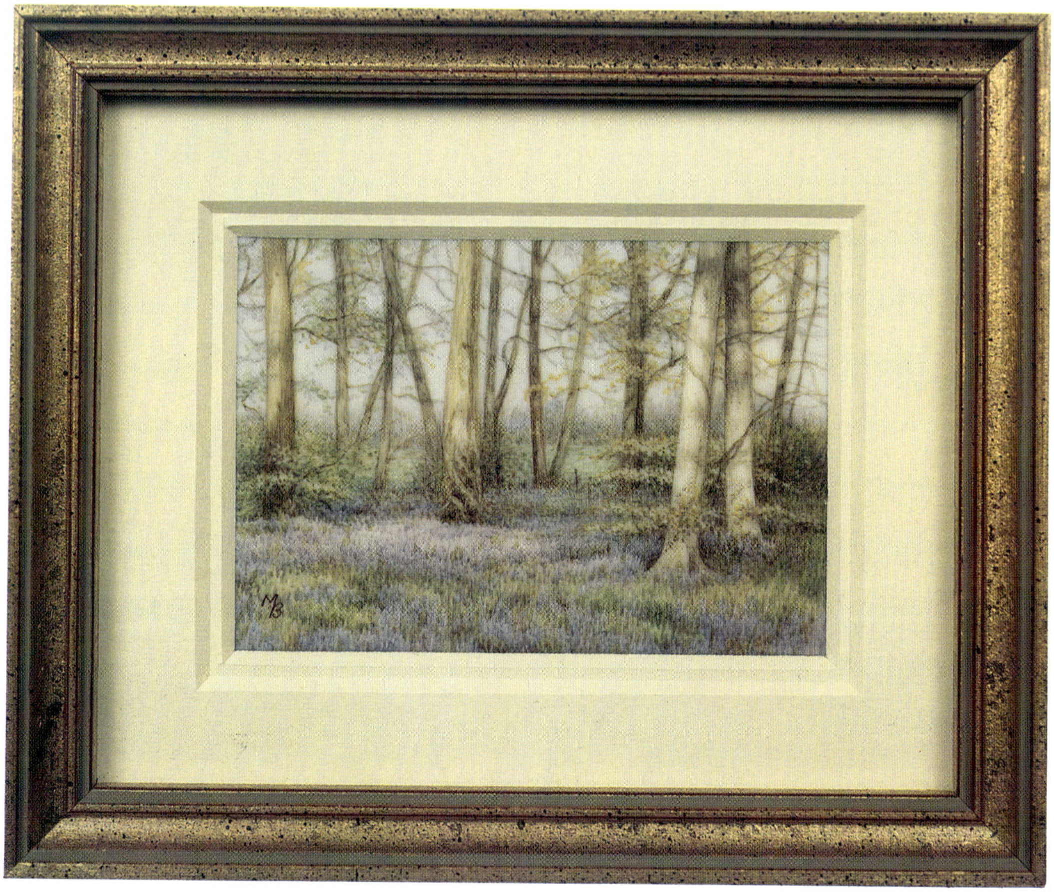

Margaret Anderson *ARMS HS MMAS SM*

Dana
(water-colour on Ivorine)

Mogs Among the Magnolias
(water-colour on Ivorine)
kindly lent by
Mrs. G.M. Wallwork

Lucy
(water-colour on Ivorine)

Margaret Anderson has been a professional artist for some eighteen years. Her work was accepted three times at The Royal Academy Summer Exhibition and she has also exhibited in Toronto, Canada and at the Bilan de l'Art Contemporain in Paris. She won the first prize at the Montana Miniature Art Society in the United States in May 1987.

An abiding love of animals led her to have a stand at Crufts for the first time sixteen years ago and since then she has exhibited there each year, selling to customers from all over the world. In 1984 she painted the Supreme Champion.

She lives now in the heart of the New Forest, fulfilling commissions for landscapes and miniature portraits of people, or of the animals they love.

Margi Cochran *ARMS MAA*

Arianne
(oil on Lumitex)

You and Me Against the World
(oil on Lumitex)
kindly lent by Miss E.Y. Wood

Friend of the Flowers
(oil on Lumitex)

Since 1975 Margi Cochran has gained considerable recognition as a miniaturist having been elected as an Associate Member of the Royal Miniature Society in 1987 and a Member of the Miniature Artists of America in 1989. She has had a long and successful career painting larger works beginning with portraiture, then embracing landscapes, still life, flowers, children and animals. Travel has enhanced her vision on all her subjects and the British Isles are her favourite source of material.

Born in Philadelphia, Pennsylvania, in 1925, she trained at the Philadelphia Museum School and then studied with renowned artists in New Jersey where she has lived for many years with her husband, Arthur Oschwald Jr.

In 1975 she entered the world of competition and won top awards in the first two national miniature shows where she exhibited. Since then she has been a consistent award winner and had many one-woman shows in galleries, participating actively in New Jersey, Georgia, Washington D.C., Florida and London annual exhibitions.

Her work is in private collections in the United States and abroad, including the permanent collection of the Miniature Art Society of Florida. She is listed in the 1994 Who's Who in Art in Britain.

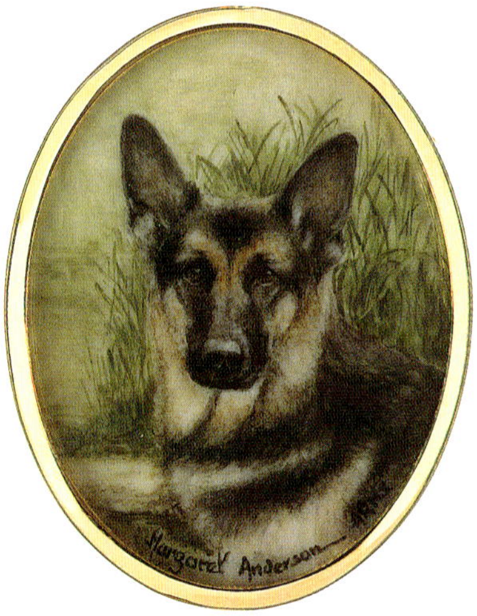
Margaret Anderson

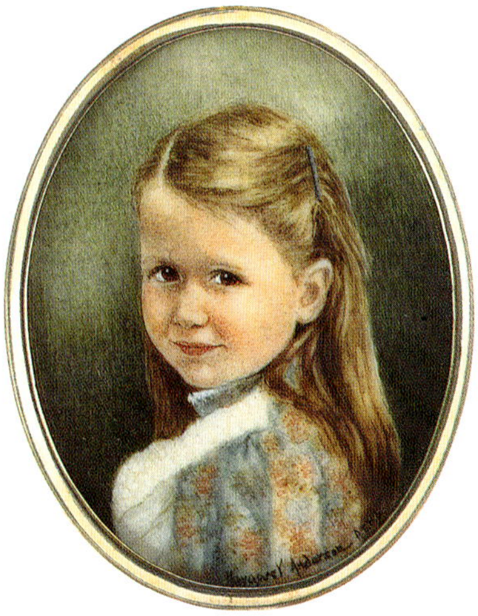

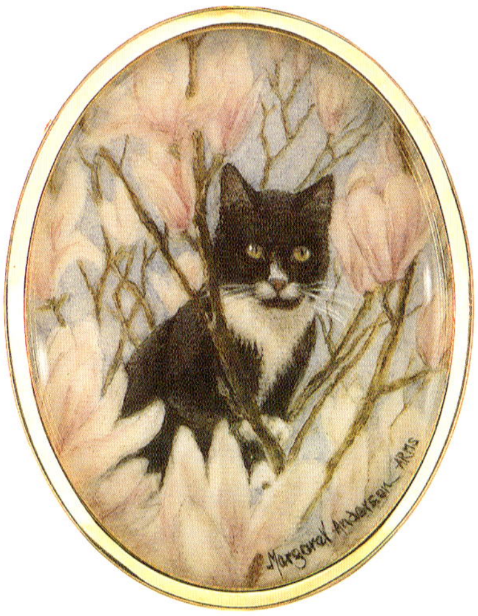

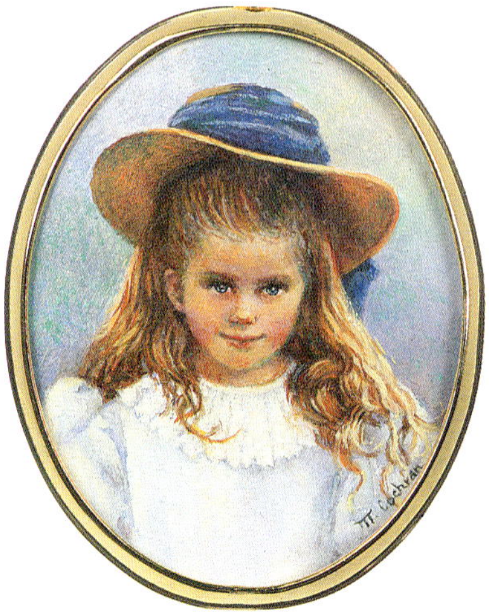

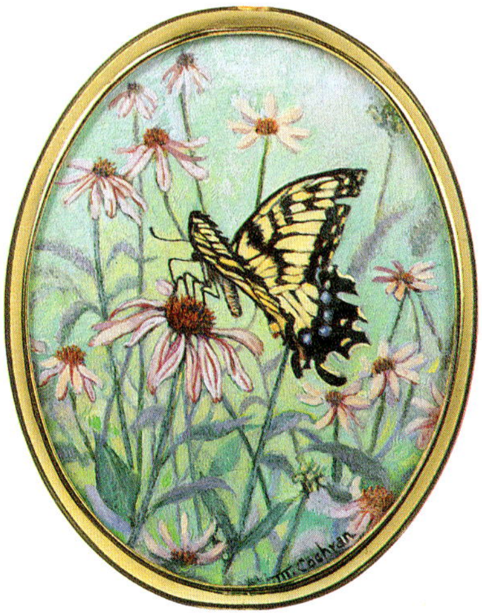

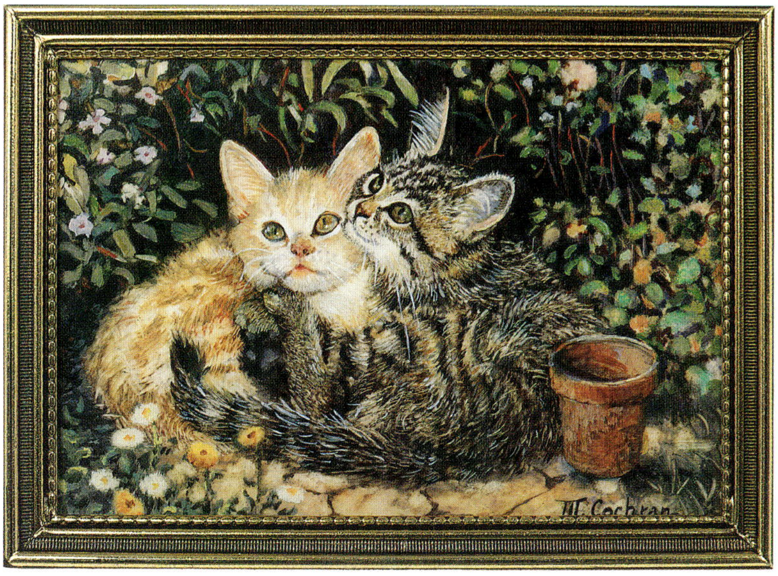
M. Cochran

Joan Patricia Carter *RMS SWA*

Tracy Waghorn
(water-colour on ivory)

Kim Carter
(water-colour on ivory)

Quinton Carter
(water-colour on ivory)

Joan Carter, born in Vancouver, Canada, daughter of Major J.F.B. Wilcox R.A., was educated at the Lord Selkirk School in Vancouver, then at the Colleges of Further Education at Ilford and Havering studying 'A' Level Art and Art History.

She is a writer, portrait painter, illuminator, illustrator and calligrapher working in water-colour, acrylic and silverpoint.

She became a Member of the Royal Miniature Society in 1986 and of the Society of Women Artists in 1985. In 1974 she won a Gold Medal at the Paris Salon, was a finalist in the Hunting Group Prize in 1980 and received an Honourable Mention for the Gold Memorial Bowl later on. She donated the miniature of the President, set on the pedestal of the Bowl. Joan has exhibited at the Paris Salon, the Royal Academy, the Miniature Art Society of Florida and had many one-woman shows.

She has published four general books, two art books, numerous Remembrance Books in Britain and abroad, art work for 'Herbs and Spices' for the Search Press and a book cover for Fowler Wright. She has given various talks, broadcasts and written articles. She signs her work J.P. Carter, with a harpoon and two fish swimming in opposite directions.

Christine Hart-Davies *BA (Hons.) RMS FSBA HSF*

Ricky
(water-colour on paper)

Blackberries
(water-colour on vellum)

Christine Hart-Davies was born in the Midlands. After reading Fine Art and Typography at University, she worked with a London design group designing and producing educational books. Eventually she settled in Dorset and began to combine her twin interests of painting and natural history in the form of botanical water-colours.

She has illustrated a large number of books and held many successful exhibitions in Britain and abroad. Her work is included in collections world-wide, notably in the Hunt Institute of Botanical Documentation in the United States. Her paintings of mosses and lichens have been awarded the Gold Medal of the Royal Horticultural Society four times and she holds another for her paintings of European orchids.

She is a committed member of several conservation organizations and has travelled extensively in Europe, Australia and the Americas to study and paint the native flora. In 1993 she joined an expedition to Sumatra to paint rain forest plants.

Christine is a Member of the Royal Society of Miniature Painters, a Founder Member and Honorary Secretary of the Society of Botanical Artists and a Founder Member of the Hilliard Society. Her miniatures, many painted on vellum, are of plants, plant habitats and gardens.

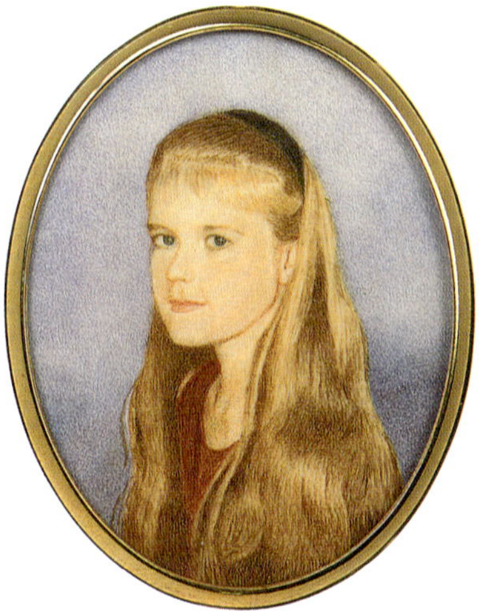

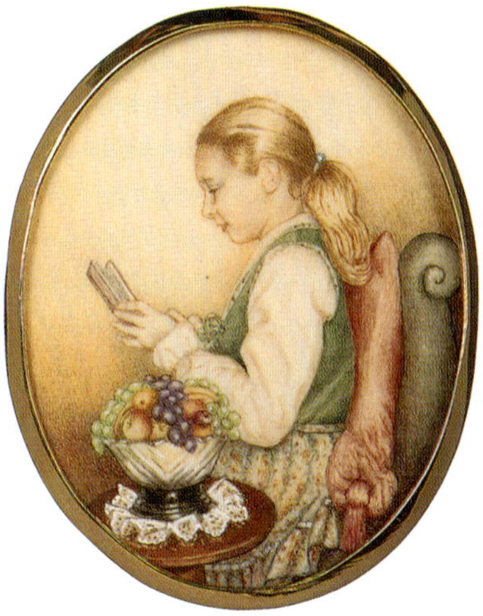

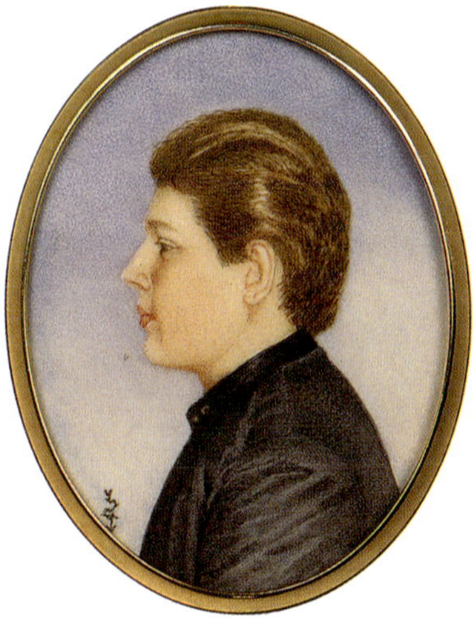

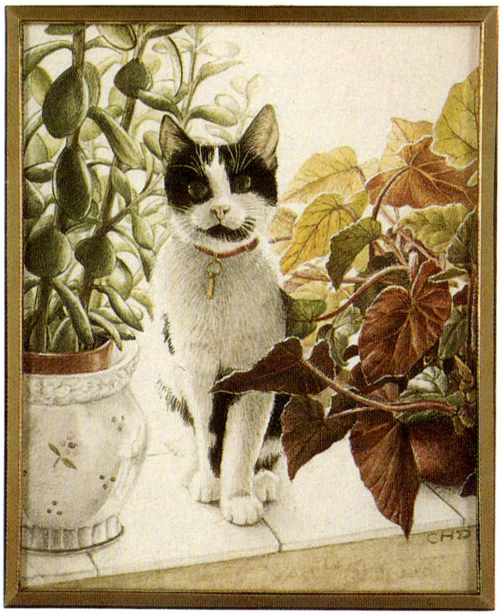
CHD

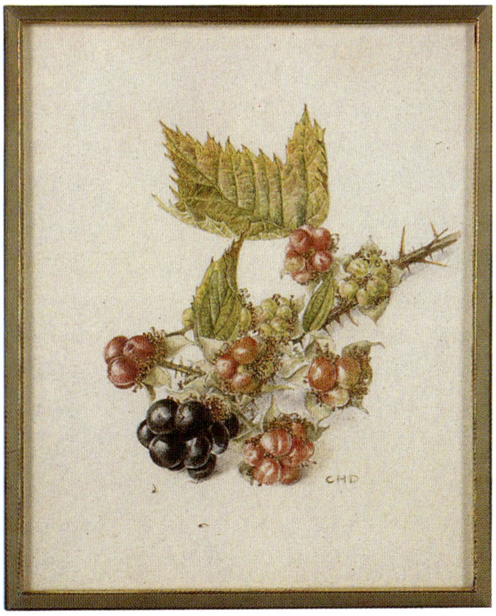
CHD

Professor Barbara Tate

PSWA RMS FSBA ASAF FRSA

Praises to Serapis
(oil on Ivorine)

To Wordsworth
(oil on Ivorine)

Born on June 2nd. 1927, she studied at Ealing Art School from 1940 to 1945. In 1951 she married James Tate ARMS FRSA and from 1956-1960 ran a jazz band agency with him and jazz clubs throughout England and Europe.

In 1968 she won the Paris Salon Silver Medal, the Gold in 1969 and in 1971 the Prix Marie Puisoye. She was elected an Associate of the Royal Society of Miniature Painters in 1971, a Member in 1972.

In 1972 she received a Special Mention Palme d'Or des Beaux-Arts, Monte Carlo and the Grand Prix de la Côte d'Azur. She lived in Chateau d'Oex in Switzerland and in 1980, on her husband's death, spent two years travelling between Switzerland and England, eventually deciding to live in England.

In 1984 Barbara was elected Vice President of the Society of Women Artists and President in 1985. In 1993, Honorary Professorship of The Thames Valley University was conferred upon her.

She has exhibited with all the Royal and other important Societies in London; at the Royal Academy of Arts, the Paris Salon and various exhibitions in France, Rome, Nice and Monte Carlo. She signs her works 'Barba' Tate and many have been reproduced.

Ida Teuton *BA ARMS HS*

The House Next Door
(water-colour)
kindly lent by Mrs. L.R. Bailey

Ida Teuton was born in Co. Down and educated at Methodist College and Queens University, Belfast, graduating in Social Sciences. A year later she undertook a post-graduate course at Edinburgh University.

In 1954, on returning to Northern Ireland, she worked firstly in a hospital and then in Community Psychiatric Services. In 1973 she became Assistant Director of Social Services on the newly formed Eastern Health and Social Services Board, retiring in 1983.

She always enjoyed drawing and painting, winning many major prizes in her student days. On retirement she became more and more interested in detailed painting. In 1985 she visited the Royal Miniature Society exhibition, was intrigued, tried it out and it 'got her'.

She has exhibited with the Royal Miniature Society, the Royal Ulster Academy, the Hilliard Society, the Ulster Society of Miniaturists and in galleries and exhibitions throughout the country. She paints scenery in most media, but prefers oil on Ivorine, and is interested especially in the texture and pattern of trees.

Vice President of the Ulster Society of Miniaturists (now dissolved), she is Vice President of Bangor Art Club and a member of the Arts Council (NI) Association.
Ida is married and has one daughter.

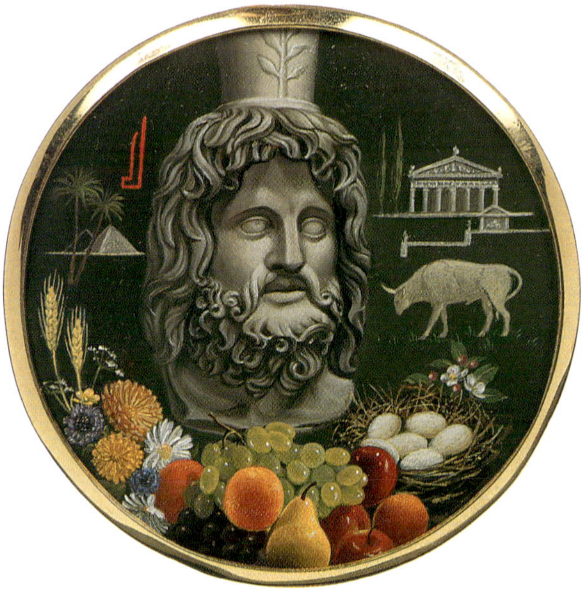

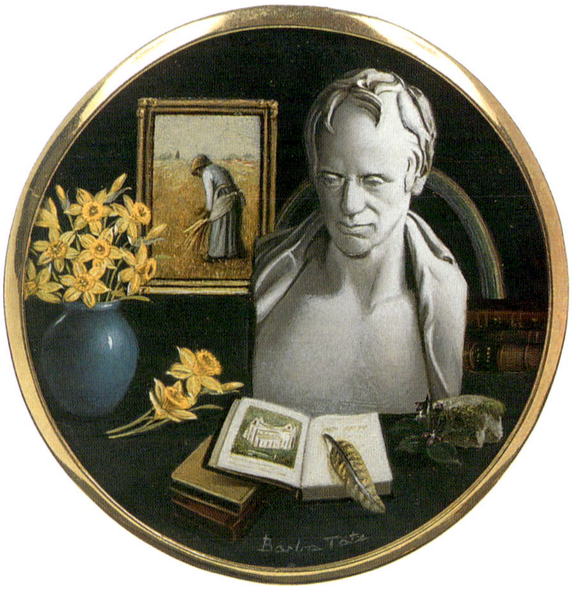

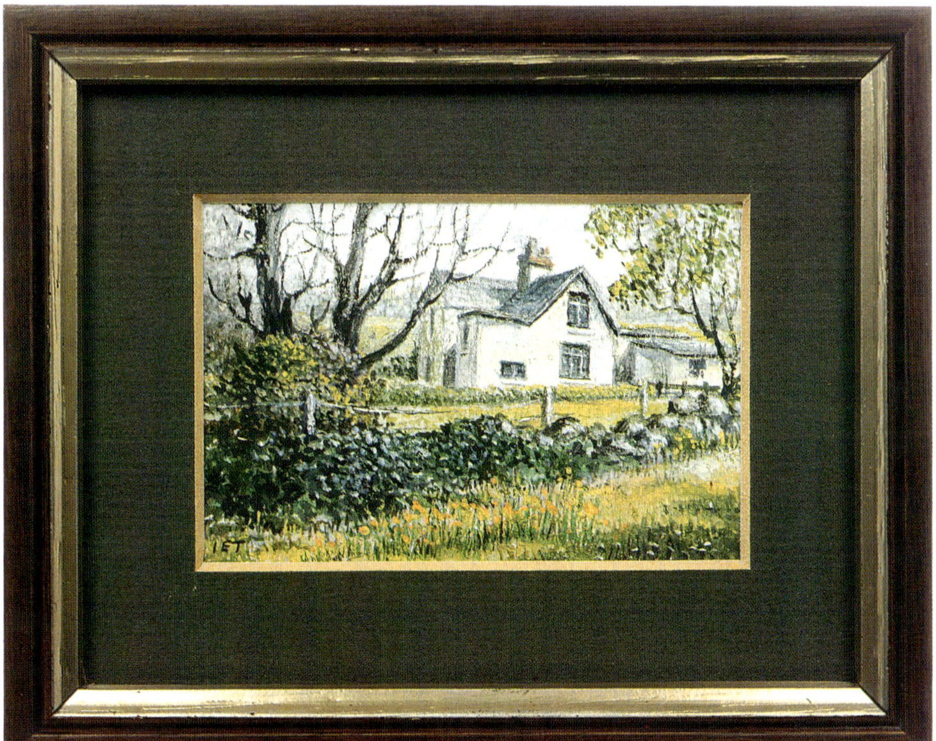

Joyce Rogerson *RMS SWA MASF HS*

Coal Tit
(water-colour on Ivorine)

In the Violet Wood
(water-colour on Ivorine)

Joyce, who has been painting and sketching wildlife and nature around her from an early age, began painting miniatures in 1983 of these same subjects. Her main interest was ornithology, which took her on visits to many bird sanctuaries, and she walks in the countryside carrying binoculars and sketch book.

She was elected a Member of the Royal Miniature Society in 1988, is a Member of the Hilliard Society, the Miniature Art Society of Florida and the Society of Women Artists. She exhibits in London at the Llewellyn Alexander Gallery and the Medici Gallery which has published one of her paintings as a greetings card.

She has had work accepted and hung by the Society of Wildlife Art of the Nations (SWAN) and was 'highly commended' for the Ulster Savings Perpetual Trophy in 1991 and 1992. In 1993 she won first prize in the 'Birds and Animals' category at the Miniature Art Society of Florida exhibition with third prize at the Georgia Miniature Art Society. In 1995 the Llewellyn Alexander Gallery awarded her a Commendation of Excellence.

Anne Mortimer *RMS SBA*

Woodland Primroses
(water-colour)

Anne Mortimer is one of this country's most imaginative illustrators. After studying Natural History at Dyfed College of Art she specialized in wildlife illustrations. Her designs show a freshness which has been successful in reproduction for cards, stationery, prints, plates and tableware world-wide.

After becoming a full member of the Royal Miniature Society her talent was recognised by being awarded a Gold Memorial Bowl Honourable Mention for an outstanding miniature in 1988. She is also a member of the Society of Botanical Artists and is acclaimed as certainly one of the finest contemporary painters of cats in the world to-day. She has illustrated two children's books on 'Tosca the Cat', which have been adapted for children's television, and in 1994 she was working on illustrations for an American children's classic, 'A Pussycat's Christmas'. Anne lives on Exmoor in the National Park, Somerset, where her surroundings provide inspiration and reference for her paintings.

She also runs a successful gallery in Dulverton, promoting interest in wildlife with paintings of animals and birds. Her main delight is in walking on the moor which inspires her work.

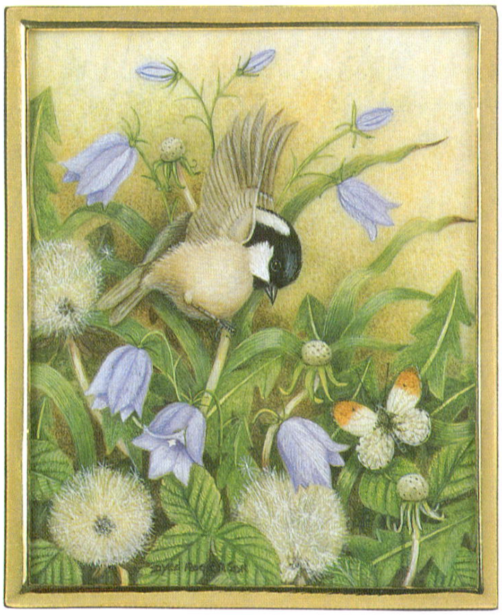

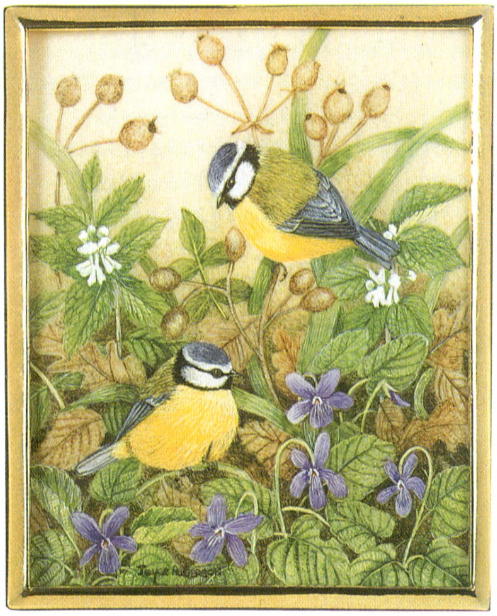

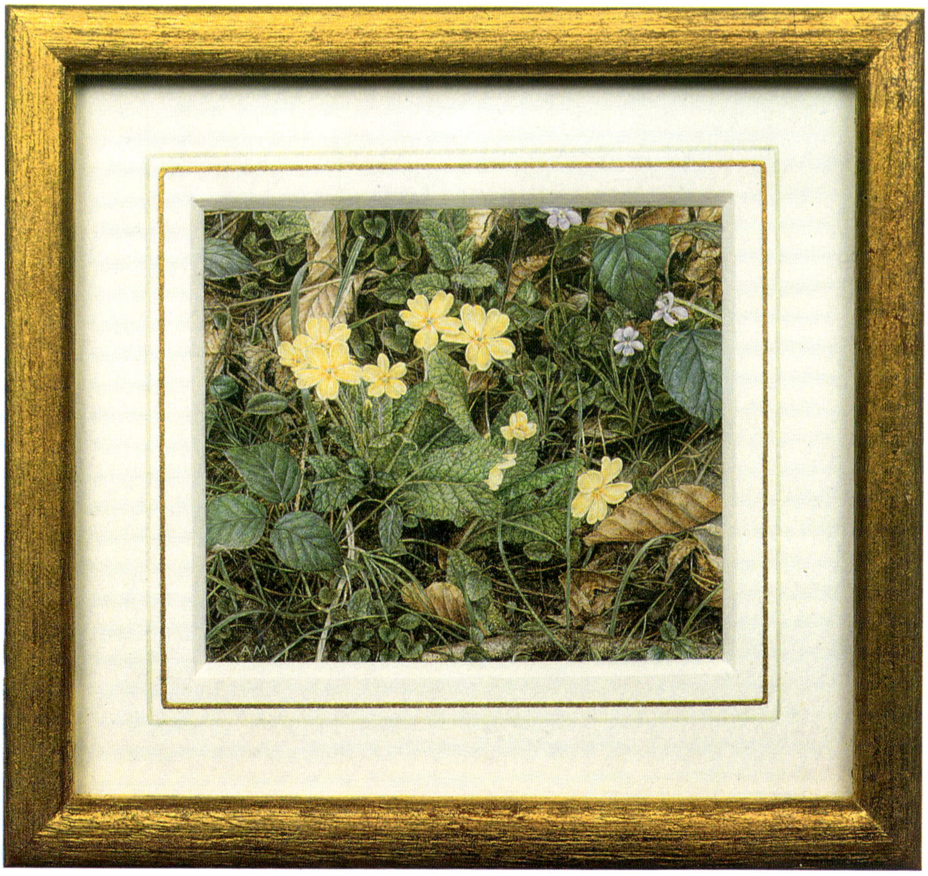

Michael W. Coe *ARMS HS*

Girl with Recorder
(water-colour on Ivorine)

Boy with Engine
(water-colour on Ivorine)

A self-taught water-colour artist, he became a full-time professional in 1975 and his finely detailed paintings of British birds have been shown with National Societies including the Royal Academy Summer Exhibition.

He progressed to painting portrait miniatures in 1990. Since then, his work has been exhibited at the Royal Miniature Society, the Hilliard Society and the Royal Academy Summer Exhibitions, as well as in America. He is a Member of the Hilliard Society and an Associate Member of the Royal Miniature Society where his work was first shown in 1991, receiving a Gold Memorial Bowl Honourable Mention. The following year he won a further Honourable Mention and the Best Non-members Award. In 1993 he received the Bell Award for Best Portrait at the Hilliard Society, second prize in Portraiture at the Georgia Miniature Art Society and the Mundy Sovereign Portrait Award at the Royal Miniature Society's exhibition.

Christopher Hope-King *ARMS SM (London) HS*

The Spanish Ambassador
(water-colour and gold leaf on Bristol board)

Destiny, Rubáiyát 49
(water-colour on Bristol board)

Christopher Hope-King was born in Yorkshire in 1951 and moved to Dorset at the age of five. He is self-taught in his art but was influenced by his grandfather, who was also an accomplished artist.

His fascination with painting miniatures began due to his interest in antiques and the pictures of the sixteenth and seventeenth centuries.

He has had many one-man exhibitions and has exhibited at the Mall Galleries, the Royal Academy Summer Exhibition and with the Royal Miniature Society.

He is a Member of the Hilliard Society, the Society of Miniaturists and an Associate Member of the Royal Society of Miniature Painters, Sculptors and Gravers where he was awarded a Gold Memorial Bowl Honourable Mention in 1993.

He works in the studio, at his cottage in Dorset, overlooking the beautiful countryside where the peace and quiet give him the gentle atmosphere needful to inspire the painting of his miniatures.

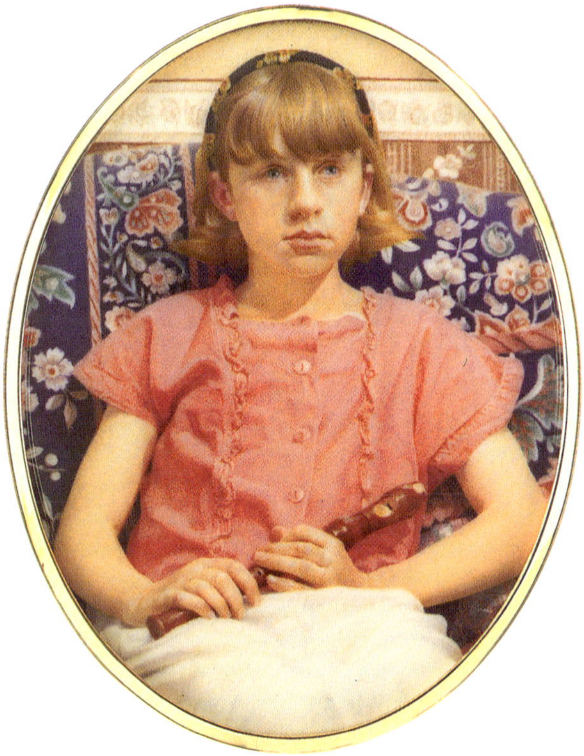

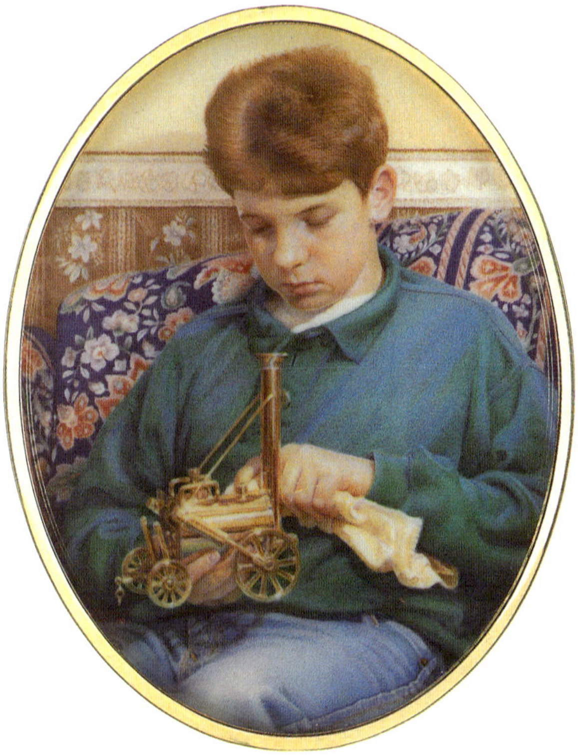

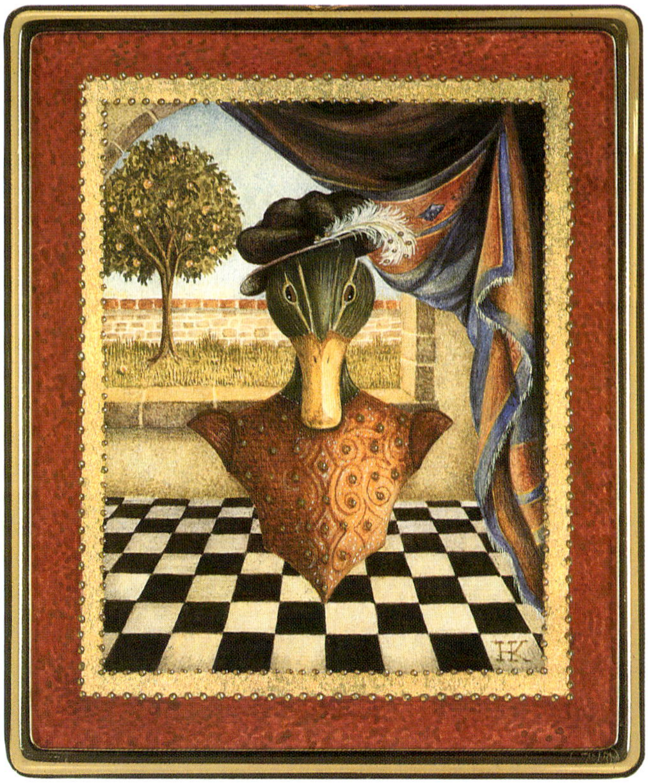

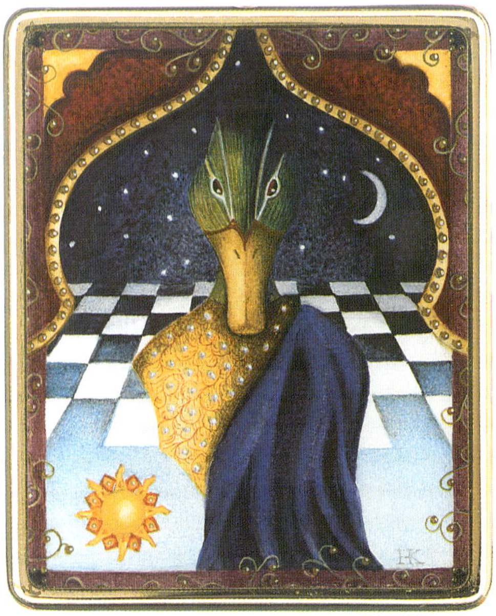

Heather O. Catchpole *RMS HSF MASSA*

Lucinda and Pollyanna
(water-colour on Ivorine)

Cocker Spaniel
(water-colour on Ivorine)

Deborah
(water-colour on Ivorine)

Canadian born, Heather Catchpole grew up in South Africa where she trained as a graphic artist. After travelling extensively she is now married and has a studio at her home in West Somerset.

Already a successful artist in pastels for portraits and pictures of dogs, she began painting and exhibiting miniatures in 1980, working in water-colour on Ivorine.

She is a Founder Member of the Hilliard Society of Miniaturists and also belongs to the South African Miniature Art Society. Her work has been exhibited widely in Britain and abroad.

She has friends all over the world and her work is to be found in private collections in many countries, as well as in several books on the art of miniature painting. Her enjoyment of the subject extends to giving illustrated talks on miniatures, silhouettes and their history.

'Some of the funniest people I know are dogs!'. With her sense of humour and her great love of dogs, a combination so often evident in her work, she was wonderfully equipped in 1994 to begin writing and illustrating her first book.

Elisa F. Cullyford *RMS MASF HS CPA*

Let There Be Peace on Earth
(water-colour and 23ct. gold leaf on gold paper)

Be it twelve art stamps as seen here in 'Let There Be Peace on Earth', or finely detailed paper-cuttings in black on white, the magical qualities of scissors and all things infinitely small held an early fascination for Elisa Cullyford.

Growing up in war torn Germany stirred her passion for books, art and nature. A scholarship in the United States opened her life to travel and spiritual freedom, followed by a career in languages, and she lives now in Phoenix, Arizona, with her two much-loved cats. Challenged by the medical diagnosis of 'less than a year to live', Elisa began to explore traditional paper-cutting in depth. Letting intuition guide her hand, she was able to cut ever finer and more intricate detail. Making miniatures became a healing activity, a window into the soul, discovering joy and transmuting pain into peace. With brushes, paint, scissors and paper, she created harmony, instinctively welcoming exhilarating ideas and spontaneity into her art.

Her miniatures have won a long list of awards, including Best of Show, Judge's Choice and Excellence in all Entries. She exhibits annually with Miniature Art Societies in the United States and in England.

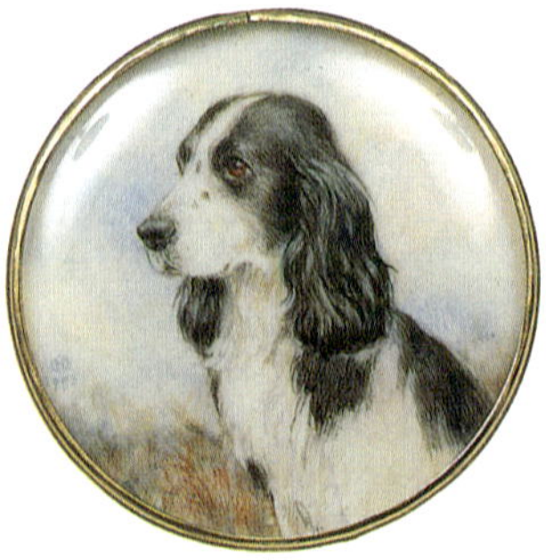

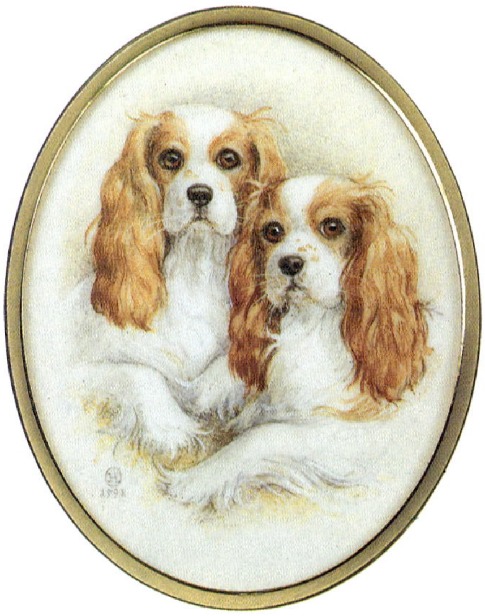

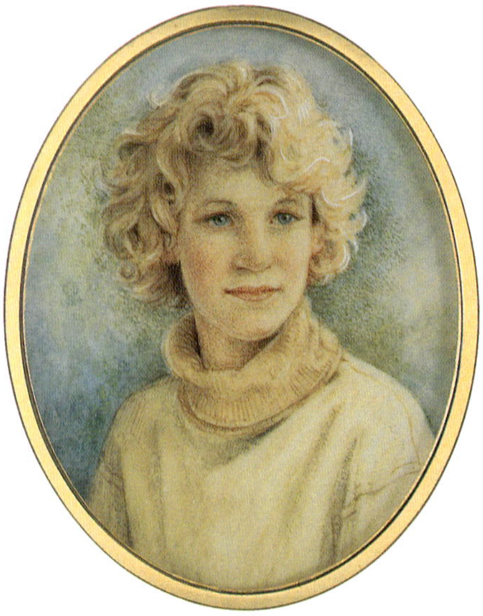

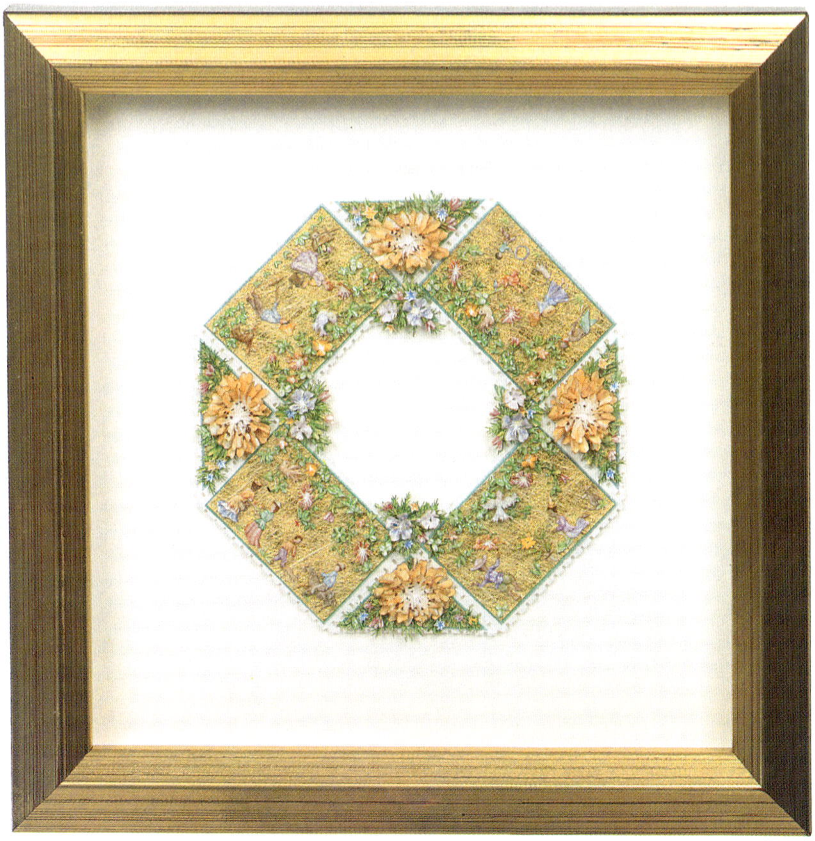

Jennie Edgar *NDD ARMS SWA*

Autumn Delights
(gouache on black paper)

Garden Fantasy
(gouache on card)

Jennie Edgar was born in Letchworth, Hertfordshire in 1940 and moved to East Anglia as a child. She developed her interest in art during long periods of illness and extended stays in hospital, following major surgery at Great Ormond Street Hospital in 1946 where she spent many hours painting, drawing and embroidering.

In 1963, as a scholar at Great Yarmouth College of Art, she gained a degree in Lithography and Printed Textiles. After leaving college she worked as a freelance designer in London before joining Ferguson Brothers, Carlisle, in their design studio.

She moved later to the Midlands, married and taught Art and Crafts in a secondary school. For fifteen years she lectured on painting and drawing to adult classes until forced to retire due to ill health. Jennie enjoys sketching and painting the local countryside. Her paintings are well-known for their characteristic dark backgrounds with detailed wildlife and botanical subjects, as are her miniatures.

She is a member of several art societies and has exhibited throughout the country. She has also had many one-woman exhibitions in the Midlands since the middle seventies and has work in a number of private collections in Europe and the United States.

Mary Dover *BA ARMS HS*

Autumn Tints
(water-colour on Lumitex)

The changing seasons are a constant source of inspiration for Mary's landscape and botanical paintings. She uses her own photographs or paints from life. A horse-chestnut tree in her garden first inspired her to record in water-colour the tree's cycle from bud to chestnut.

After training at Cardiff College of Art, she undertook freelance work for cartographical and engineering drawing offices. This detailed task laid the foundation for miniature painting many years later.

She is married with two grown-up children. When they left home she studied with the Open University for six years during which time her painting activities were minimal. Since graduating in 1990 she has concentrated on miniature painting.

She won an award for the best botanical painting of wild flowers at the Cardiff Horticultural Society Show and, in 1991 and 1993, the cup for the best miniature in the South Wales Art Society exhibition.

She exhibits with the Hilliard Society, winning the Best Novice Award in 1992, and her work is shown in London exhibitions and galleries. She was elected an Associate Member of the Royal Miniature Society, after exhibiting there for three years, and in 1994 won the Fairman Award First Prize.

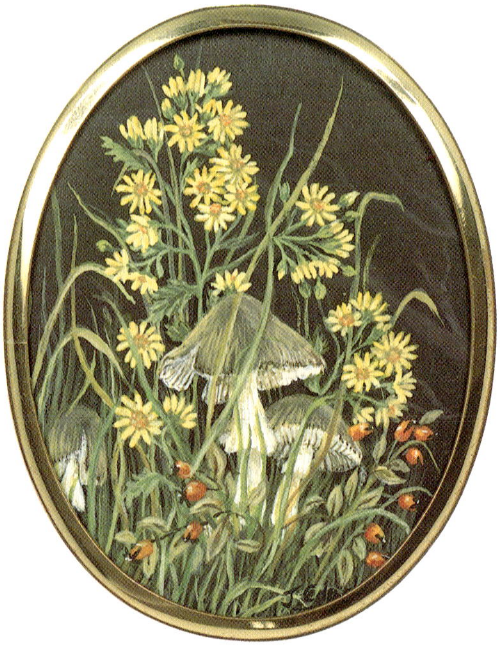

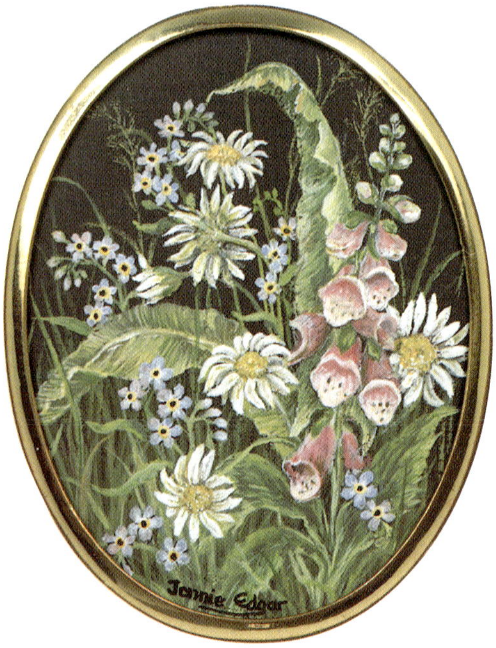
Jennie Edgar

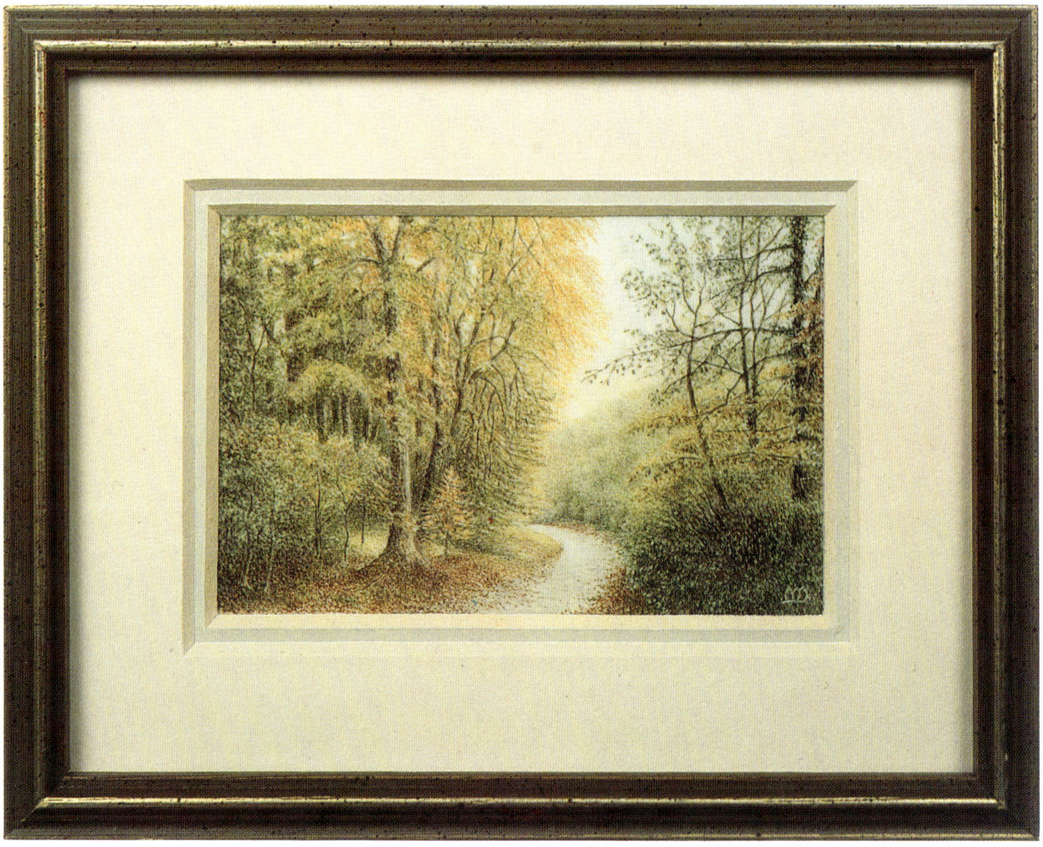

Elaine H. Fellows *BA (Hons.) RMS SWA HS*

Primo Violino
(water-colour on vellum)
kindly lent by
Mrs. Anita Emmerich, RMS

The Old Hunting Horn
(water-colour on vellum)

Encouraged by an art dealer she began miniature painting in 1986, exhibiting five works with the Royal Miniature Society. Next year she became a Member of the Hilliard Society and in 1988 began painting professionally. After a two-man exhibition in Hereford she was invited to Membership of the Society of Women Artists and to exhibit in several London galleries.

In 1989 she became an Associate Member of the Royal Miniature Society and was awarded a Gold Memorial Bowl Honourable Mention. The next year she received the Bell Award for Portraiture from the Hilliard Society and in 1991 a second Gold Bowl Honourable Mention, as well as the Madam MacCarthy Memorial Award for Portraiture in Ulster. In 1992 she won the Mundy Sovereign Portrait Award.

Her other interest is in early music. The musical instruments, used then, appear often in her miniatures and she plays the music herself on a variety of the authentic instruments. Her painting is influenced by Pieter Claesz and Jan Vermeer.

In 1992 she was elected a Member of the Royal Miniature Society and her fine work has been featured in the Antique Dealers and Collectors guide.

Joan Willies *RMS MPSG Hon.MASF HS GMAS FIGMA*

Miss Hayley Mills
(oil and alkyd on Ivorine)
kindly lent by Miss Mills

Still Life
(oil and alkyd on Ivorine)

Joan Willies lives in Florida but was born in Bristol, England, and from her earliest memory has always painted and drawn. Her parents made sacrifices to give her tuition in art and music.

She is a singer, but art predominates and she paints mainly miniatures. During the war her childhood paintings were printed as greetings cards sold to benefit the Free French led by Général de Gaulle. Her first sale was at four years old when her nursery school Principal purchased a painting for one penny! Drawing paper was scarce in wartime. The family butcher put extra sheets of white paper around the sausages telling her Mother 'For your little girl to draw on'.

In 1976 she was elected a Member of the Royal Miniature Society. Her Memberships include the Hilliard Society and the Miniature Societies of Florida, Georgia and Washington where she has won a number of awards. She paints a wide range of subjects, selling internationally: owners of her paintings include Royalty, with business and entertainment personalities.

She appears on television, has written articles for American publications, two books on the history and technique of the Miniature and is writing a further detailed treatise on Miniature Painting to be published in 1995.

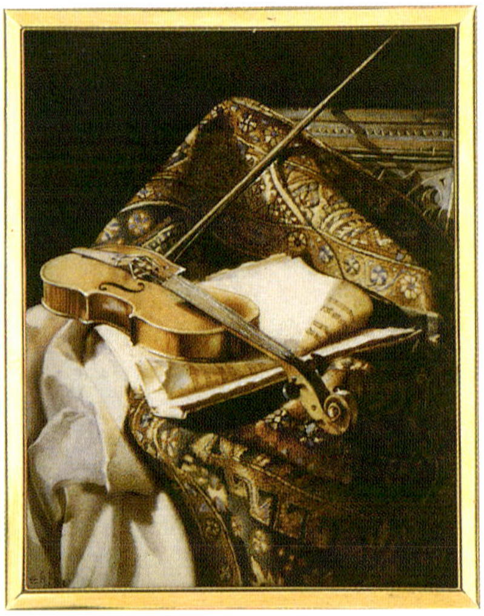

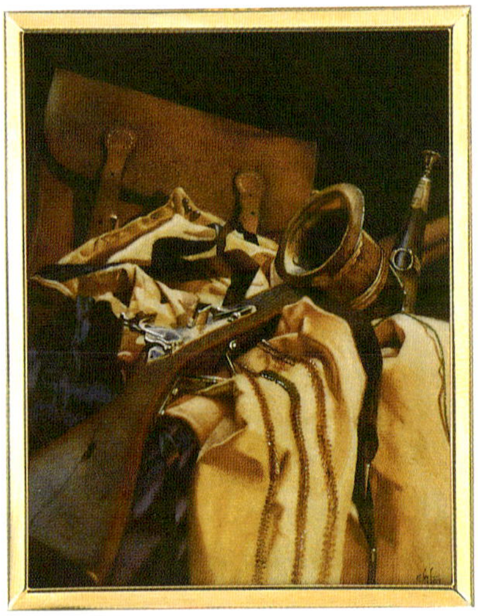

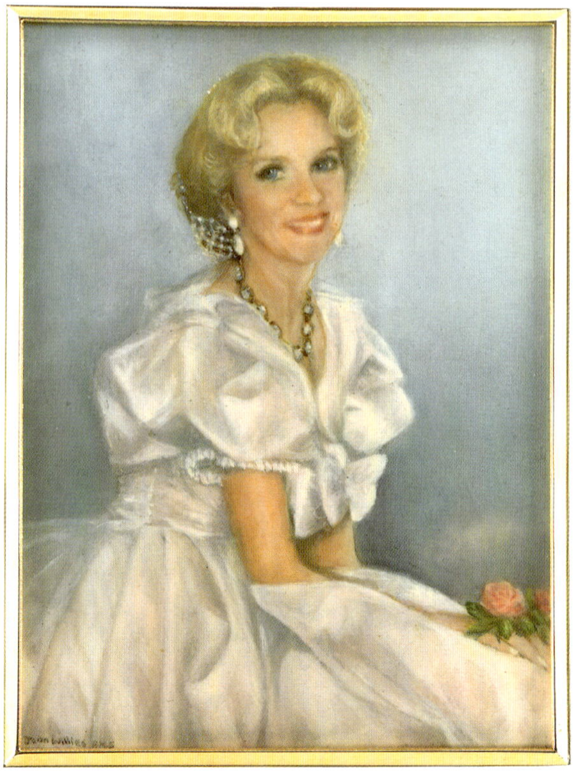
Joan Willies RMS

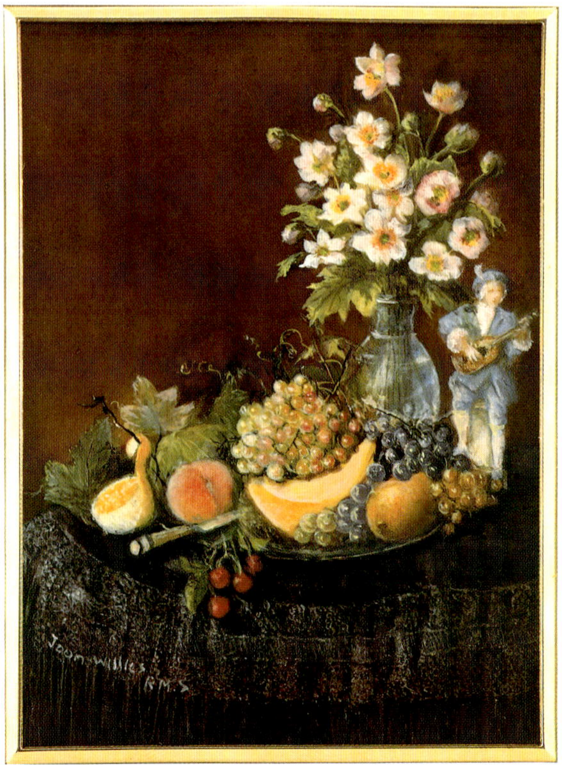
Joan Willies RMS

Barbara Penketh Simpson *ARMS HS*

Amy Hughes
(oil on Ivorine)

Annika
(oil on Ivorine)

Born in Crewe, Cheshire and brought up in North Wales, Barbara now lives outside London, with her husband and family, where she works part-time as a qualified nurse with sick, new-born and premature babies. She has had no formal art training but has always been creative and feels that she must have inherited her talents from her mother, who was an enthusiastic amateur water-colourist, and her father who is a natural draughtsman.

She has been painting seriously since the early seventies, finds portraiture fascinating and works on larger pictures in oils as well as miniatures. She considers herself extremely fortunate to have been tutored and encouraged by the world-renowned sculptor and painter, Barry Shiraishi.

Barbara first exhibited with the Royal Miniature Society in 1988 and was elected an Associate Member in 1989, winning the Mundy Sovereign Portrait Award in the same year. She has also had paintings exhibited in the Mall Galleries with the Society of Women Artists and has work in private collections in Germany and Canada.

She is a Member of her local Art Society and enjoys creative embroidery, sculpture, interior design and is a keen gardener.

Tom Dale *DA RMS HSF*

Mendip Snow
(water-colour on Arches paper)

Tom Dale is a Scottish miniaturist who lives and works in Somerset.

A Member of the Royal Society of Miniature Painters, Sculptors and Gravers and a Founder Member of the Hilliard Society, he studied at the Glasgow School of Art where he specialized in mural painting, stained glass and sgraffito. He also studied wood engraving and etching. Over the years he developed a pre-occupation with the discipline of miniature work and now the main of his output is in the genre of miniature painting covering a variety of subjects.

His speciality is water-colour landscapes of the British countryside where his paintings draw one's attention to the extraordinary beauty of the commonplace. On close observation you are drawn into a world of crisp information which can be hauntingly evocative. John Dalton, writing in the Guardian Arts Review, said 'Within an inch he can make the water lap gently at low tide or fix the atmosphere of a misty morning over fields.'

He exhibits with miniature societies and galleries in London, the West Country and overseas, his paintings being in private collections in over forty countries. His name is in 'Who's Who in Art' and 'The International Dictionary of Exhibiting Artists'.

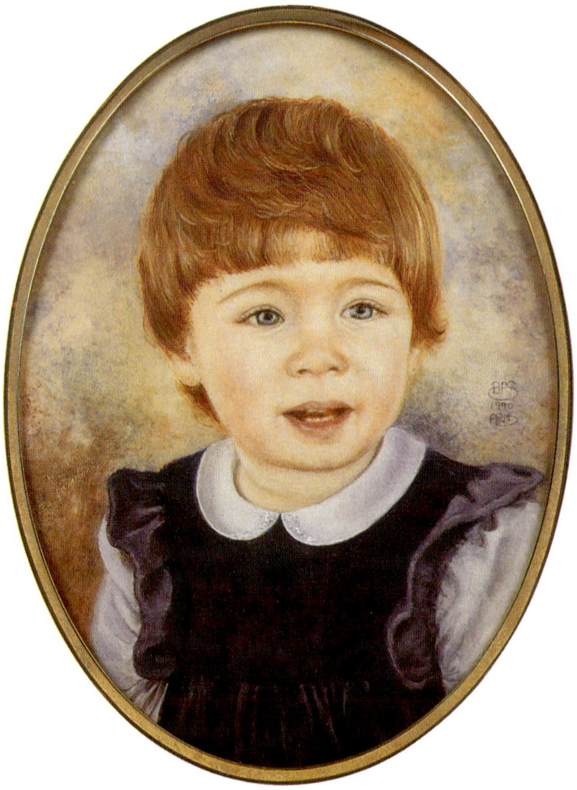

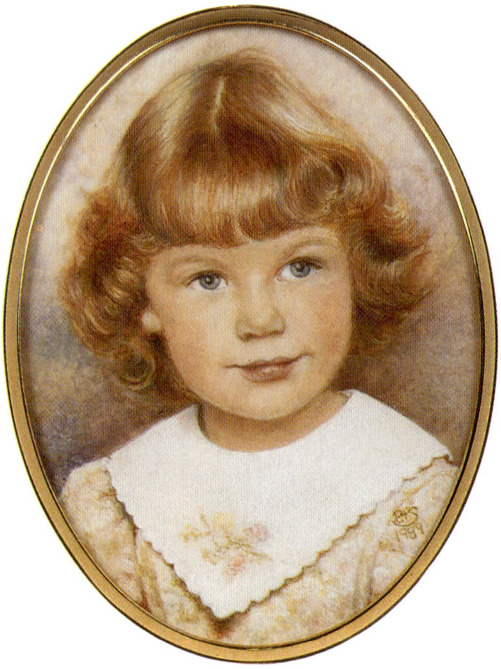

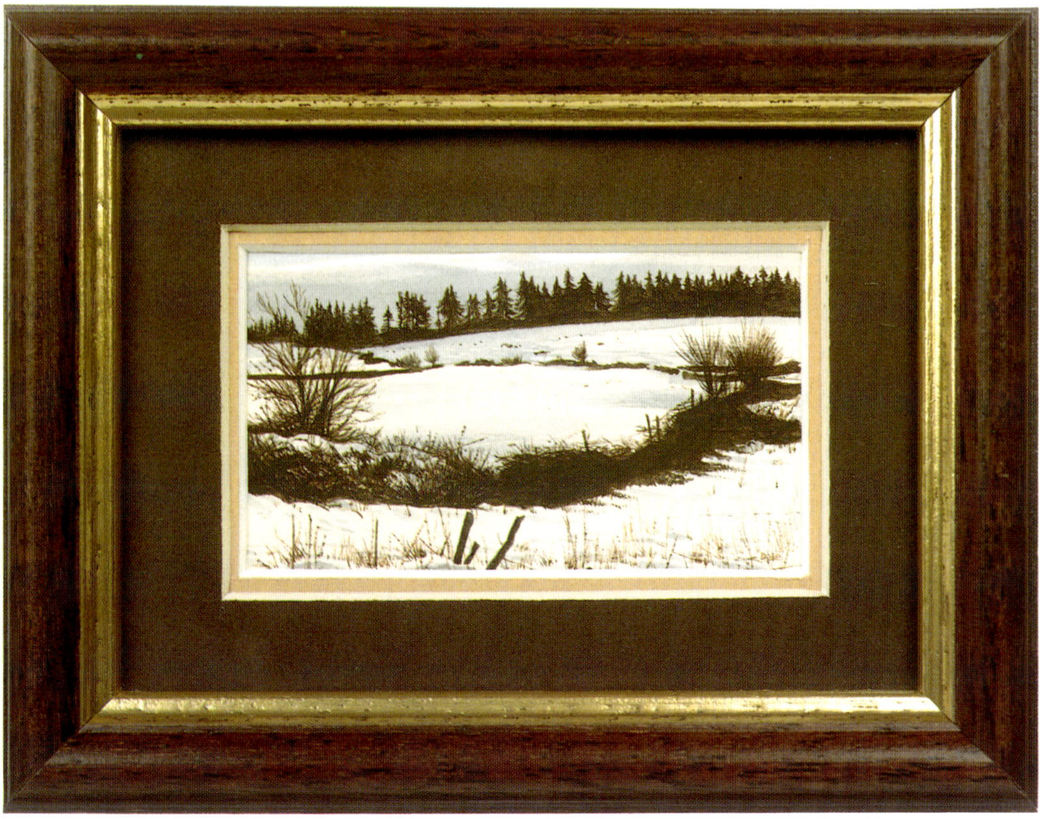

Julie Hockin *ARMS HS*

A Cornish Otter
(water-colour on Ivorine)
from the Diploma Collection

Bird of Darkness,
Bird of Light
(water-colour on vellum)

Autumn Inspiration
(water-colour on Ivorine)

Julie developed a fascination with miniatures at school. A first painting in a seashell of Charlestown harbour led to painting miniatures for a living in 1978 and reproducing her work in print in 1980.

She became aware of the natural beauty surrounding her and its fragility. She determined to capture it and encourage others, through her work, to develop their own awareness.

After election as a Member of the Hilliard Society she combined day-to-day sales and distribution of her printed work with painting original miniatures, mainly commissions. She gave talks on the origins of miniature painting and demonstrations of the techniques.

An illness in 1987 restricted her painting but by 1990 she was working with renewed perception. Her improved design won a Gold Memorial Bowl Honourable Mention from the Royal Miniature Society of which she is an Associate.

In 1991 she joined with a colleague and set up a company marketing her printed work in order to leave her time for concentrating on new designs. Commissions include designs for London Zoo's endangered species project, a Wildlife calendar, Christmas cards for two charities and stationery for the Royal Society for Nature Conservation.

She has held two personal exhibitions at Marwell Zoological Park and the National Trust's Cotehele House.

Joyce Wyatt *VPSWA RMS ASAF Hon.UA*

Elizabeth
(pencil and wash on Ivorine)

Harry
(oil on Ivorine)

Joyce Wyatt was trained at Hornsey College of Art with private tuition from Francis Hodge R.P. The famous Annigoni was a great friend to her and her family for over twenty-five years, giving her much guidance and advice. She is a Member of the Royal Miniature Society, Vice President of the Society of Women Artists, an Honorary Member of the United Artists and an Associate of the Société des Artistes Français.

Her one-man shows include 1966 and 1970 at the Mall Galleries, Paris and Biarritz in 1971 and Edinburgh (Festivalex) in 1980. She has exhibited with most Royal and other important Societies, including the Royal Academy of Arts, and at the Paris Salon where she was awarded the Prix Roland and an Honourable Mention in 1964, the Silver Medal in 1965 and the Gold Medal with Hors Concours in 1969.

In 1977 she painted a fresco in Italy, dedicated by the Bishop of Pistoia, and she has a large painting of the Nativity in St. Andrew's Church, Totteridge, dedicated in 1976.

Much of her work is in private collections in Great Britain and other countries, including portraits commissioned by their Royal Highnesses the Prince and Princess Michael of Kent.

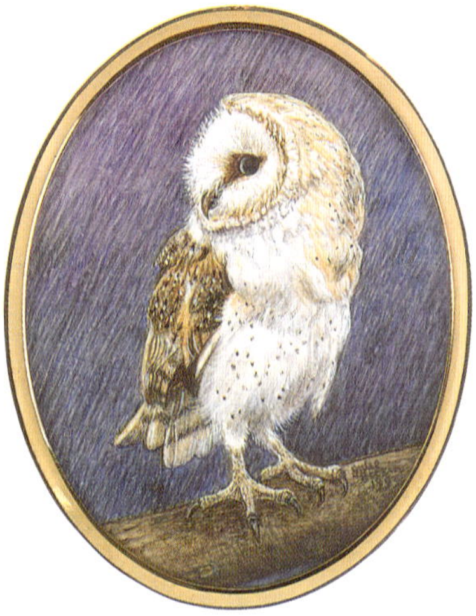

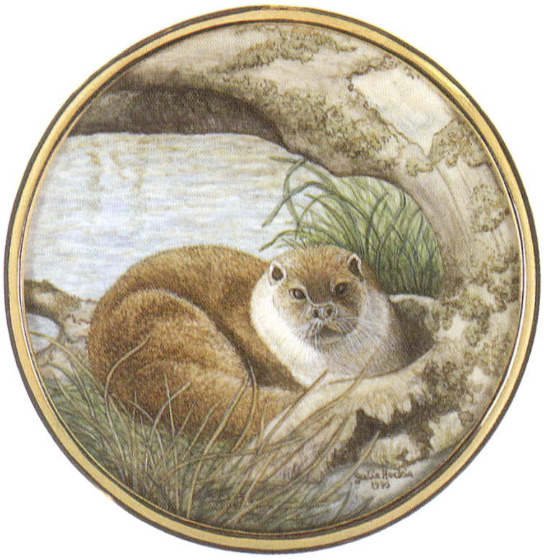

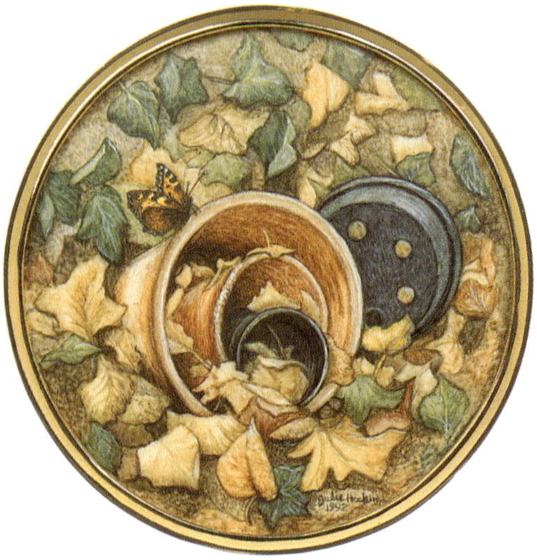

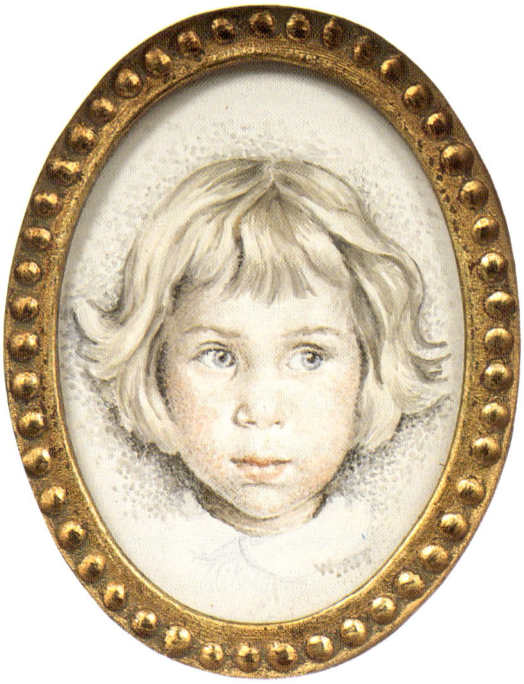
WYATT

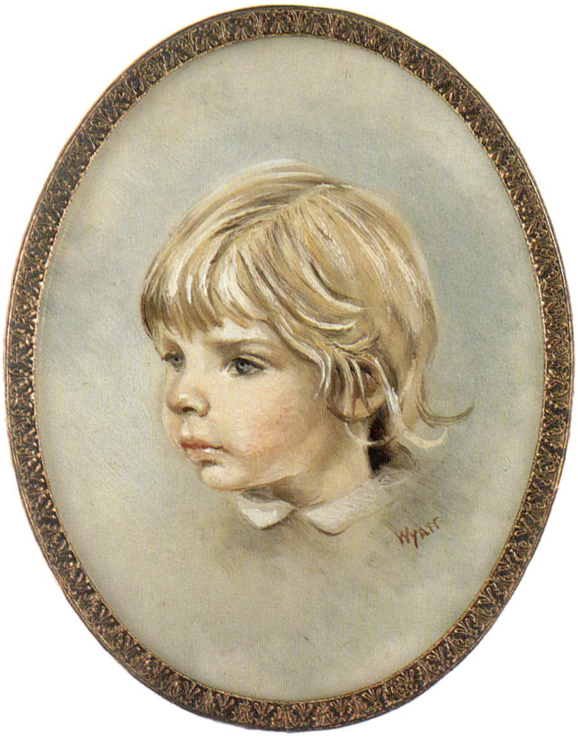
WYATT

Margaret Adams *RMS HS*

Lucy Gaze
(water-colour on Ivorine)

A Man in a Pink Turban
(water-colour on Ivorine)

Margaret Adams was born in Haslemere and spent her childhood in the scenic area of Hindhead. She painted from an early age and, on leaving school, went to the Farnham School of Art and trained in photography and miniature painting at the Bloomsbury Trade School. She then became a retoucher at Shaw Wildman's Studio.

She was one of Somerset's first land girls and stayed on the land until 1945. When the war ended she worked as a welfare officer in Italy, Austria and Malaya. In 1951 she married Bill Adams in Penang where they lived until 1960. They had six children. Margaret compiled the Penang Guide Book, illustrated with her photographs, and made fifty paintings of Malayan flowers which were identified at Kew Gardens Herbarium. From 1979 she studied in Jeff Pickering's studio for five years.

After her husband died she returned to miniatures, using water-colour on Ivorine, and first exhibited with the Hilliard Society in 1989 when she won the Suzanne Lucas Novice Award. In 1990 she became an Associate of the Royal Miniature Society and in 1991 received a Gold Memorial Bowl Honourable Mention. In 1992 she was elected a Member.

Robert Hughes *RMS SM (London) HS*

Sherbourne Church
(oil on board)
kindly lent by Jill Pickenpaugh PGMAS

Robert was born in London in 1934 but now lives in Wiltshire surrounded by the beautiful countryside which inspires his landscape paintings.

He started painting professionally in 1982 without formal training. His first exhibitions in Marlborough gained him a reputation in the art world and he exhibits now in London, York, Salisbury and Wells.

In 1986 he was elected an Associate of the Royal Miniature Society and a Member in 1989: also he has been a Member of the Hilliard Society of Miniaturists since 1986.

He works at home in his studio, adjoining a gallery, and supplies galleries in other parts of the country, occasionally undertaking commissions.

Like many artists, he listens to music while painting which helps him to create his fine miniatures. He achieves the detail in his paintings without a magnifying glass, but uses up to twelve different brushes. He works mostly in oils, varying his media with gouache and water-colour, and his palette is based on eight earth colours with black and white. Once he has painted the main scene he often adds figures and animals.

His paintings are in private collections in Great Britain, the United States, France, Japan, Australia and New Zealand.

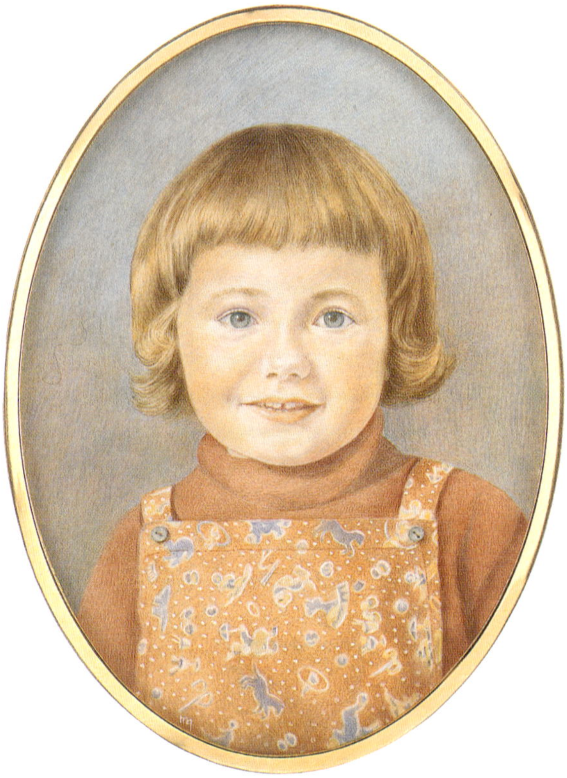

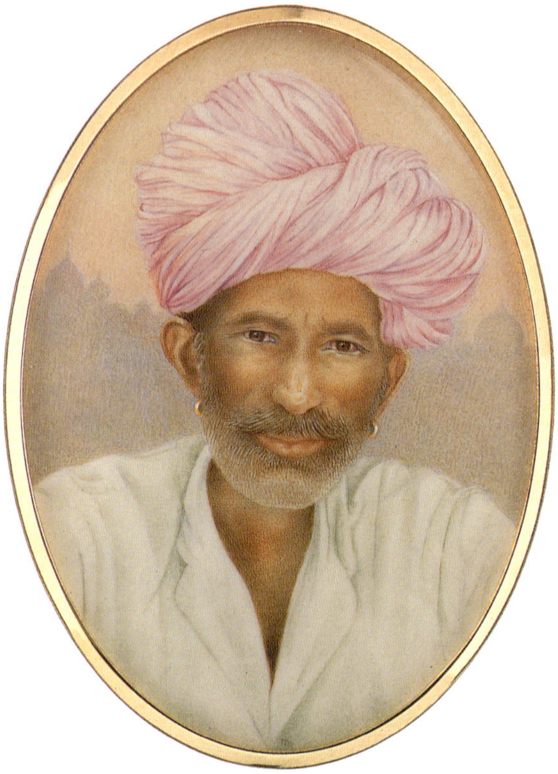

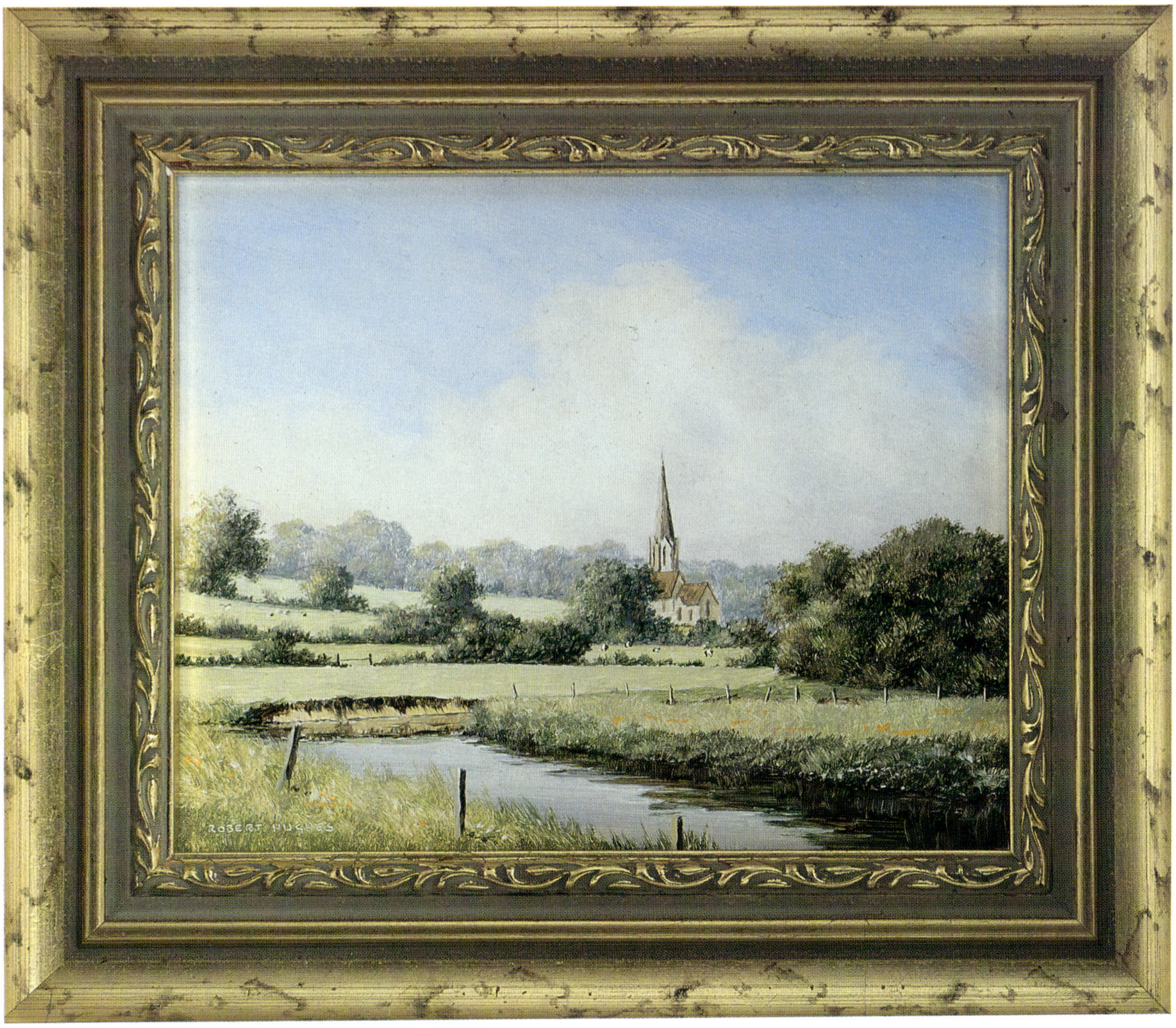
ROBERT HUGHES

Barbara Allen Watkinson *RMS AE*

Young Girl
(rhodochrosite and enamel)

Lucrezia Borgia
(gold and silver, enamel and precious stones)

Siamese Dancer
(gold, silver and enamel)

Engaged for over two years and left some money by a godmother, she married and they chose a honeymoon instead of a new road to their newly-repaired farmhouse. They travelled to South Africa, Australia, toured the United States from San Francisco; took ship to Japan, China and along the Yang-tzi Kiang gorge; went on to Bali, Japan and at last sailed home through the Mediterranean. They collected many lovely things, all stolen in one burglary after another.

Discouraged by dreadful weather they sold the farm, moving to Harrogate, but visited their cedar-wood house on a Scottish loch where she had time for painting and submitted work to the Royal Miniature Society.

Inspired by a beautiful enamel picture of homing sheep at sunset and being presented by her husband with a laboratory and kiln, she borrowed an instruction book, bought gradually other equipment for working stone and metals, then launched into her exquisite work on figurines combining precious and semi-precious stones, gold, silver and enamel. She created them in all shapes and sizes, from imagination or history. Many collectors have longed to possess these beautiful pieces but Barbara loves each one too much to contemplate depleting the family.

Guy R.H. Shaw *BA (Hons.) ARMS*

Introspection
(boxwood)

Wild Seed
(permafreeze mammoth tusk)

Red Dragon
(staghorn)

Baku Kurai
(staghorn)

Born in 1951, Guy gained a B.A. Fine Art (Hons.) at Newport College of Art in 1974.

Introduced to Netsuke in 1978 he recognized his future career. The years would have been bleak without his wife's encouragement and support from two collectors, Miss B. Nind and Dr. Neil Lawson-Baker. Then in 1986 he met Michael Birch, the first professional Netsuke artist in the West, who helped him to find a United States market.

He has shown in over twenty exhibitions and one-man shows at the British Museum, the Los Angeles County Museum of Art, in London, New York, Miami, San Francisco, Chicago, Vienna, Tokyo, Paris and Barbados. His work is found in major collections world-wide.

His sculpture, largely allegorical, explores human relationships through the rhythms of natural forms, stepping sometimes into Japanese mythology to embody a good idea. He enjoys the challenge of difficult materials and these include emerald, coprolite (fossilized dinosaur dung), woods, burrwoods, antler, mammoth ivory, corals, amber, shells and horn.

A Vice President of the Western Netsuke Carvers Association, he has lectured in England, the United States and Austria and, independent of agents, is unlimited in exhibiting around the world. Present major exhibitions include London in 1994 and New York in 1995.

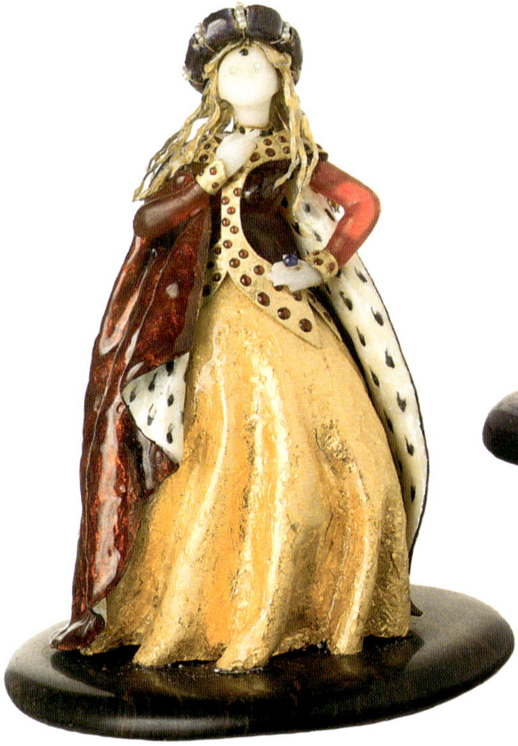
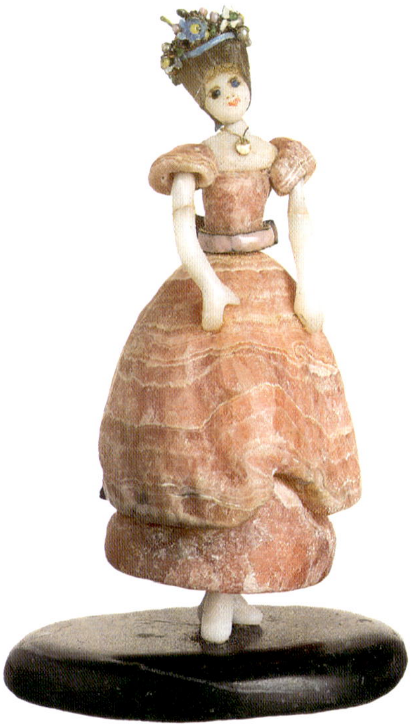
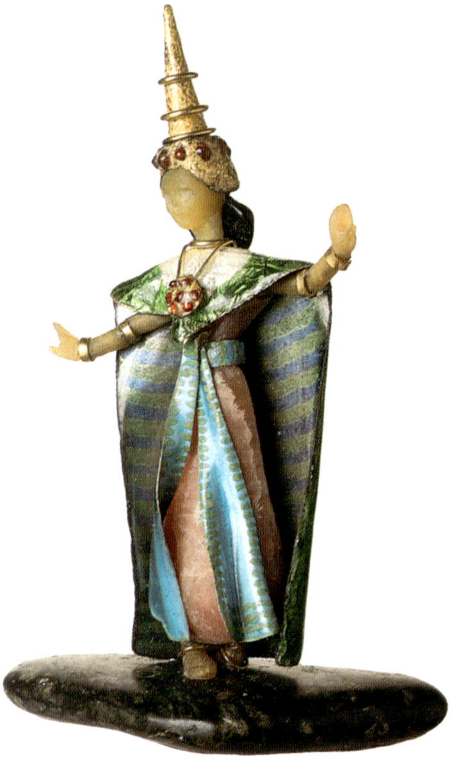
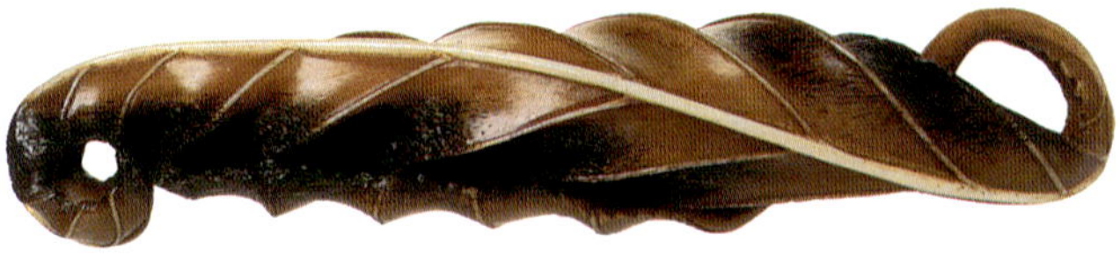
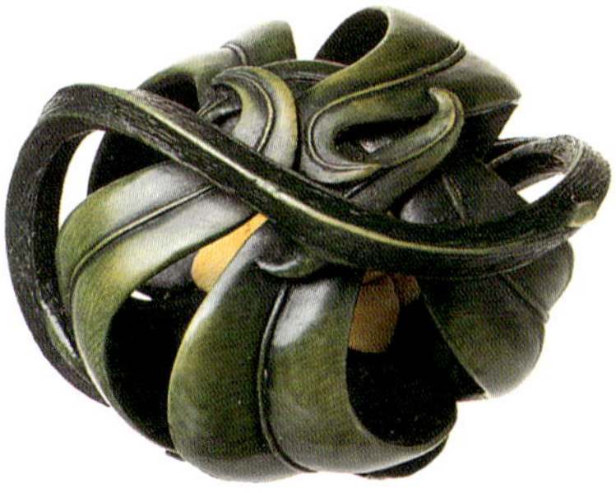
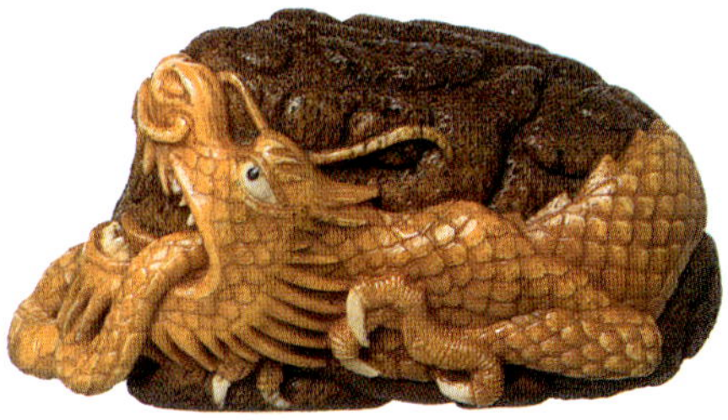
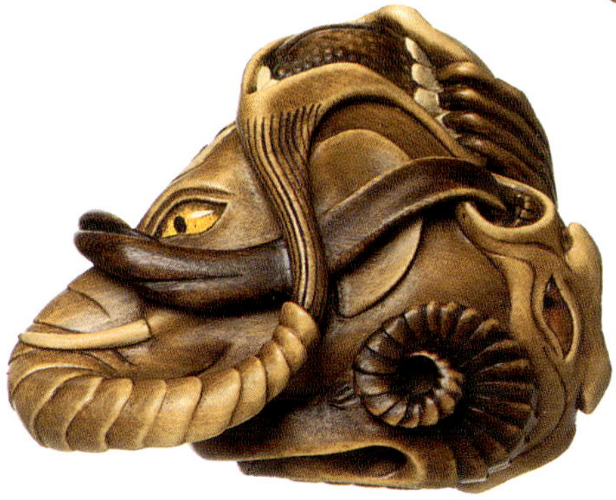

Barry Toshio Shiraishi RMS

Sleeping Mermaids
(cold-cast bronze)
kindly lent by the President

Born on May 5th 1938 in South-east London, he has a Japanese father and an English mother.

He attended the Woolwich Polytechnic Art School and studied under Heber Mathews. His early professional work was in silk-screen printing, sign writing and interior design.

He is employed, currently, as an Adult Education teacher which spans the instruction of art, sculpture and the assistance of students with learning difficulties. His free time interests include boating, camping, flying kites, gardening and cooking.

Barry is renowned as a freelance painter and sculptor, fulfilling private and Company commissions. At present he is heavily involved in many commissions for the Franklin Mint Company and the pieces are exhibited and sold in all major countries. These works are, in the main, miniature ornamental gardens, figures in period costume, eggs and, most recently, pop groups in bell jars.

The inspiration for the subjects of his own work is primarily creative fantasy around the female form, as in the Sleeping Mermaids. These works are acquired mainly by collectors in Europe.

He uses all the media for paintings and ceramics with cold-cast bronze for sculptures.

Linda Soar DSR(R) ARMS

Dragon
(cold-cast bronze)

Born in the London Borough of Greenwich in 1955 she was educated locally, achieving the qualifications to train as a Radiographer and, in 1975, gained her Diploma (DSR(R)). She married in 1976 and, in 1982, her son was born.

Artistic ability runs through all her maternal family, showing strongly in her Uncle who was an extremely successful architect. Although she enjoyed art at school she neglected it until after her son's birth when she joined local classes and met the tutor, Barry Shirashi, another RMS member. There she discovered that her talent lay in sculpture.

The technical work can be hard to accommodate in a non-studio setting, without specialist equipment and materials. The problem of size means that working on a small scale can help to overcome some difficulties, though presenting others, and with Barry's training and encouragement she was drawn towards miniature work. Since then she has worked with him on a commercial basis and had commissions of her own.

She began to show in 1985, notable exhibitions being those of the Royal Miniature Society and the Society of Women Artists. In 1989 she won the Bidder and Borne – Royal Miniature Society Award for Sculpture and in 1990 was elected an Associate Member.

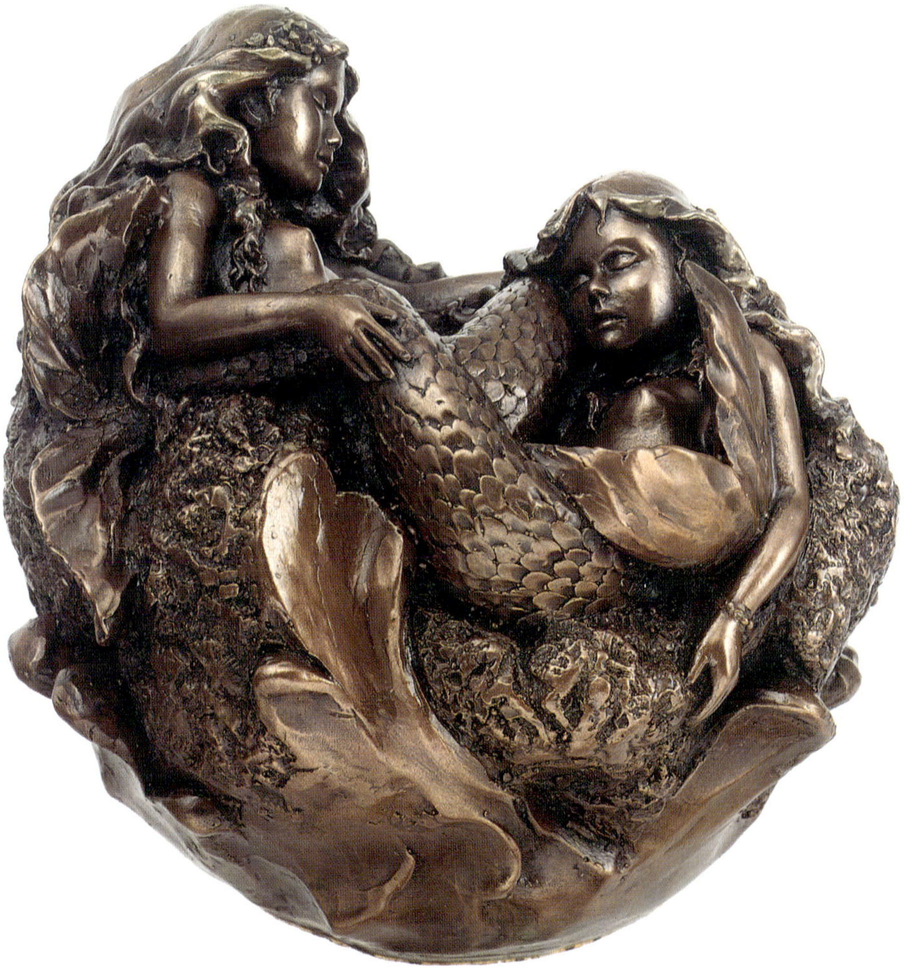

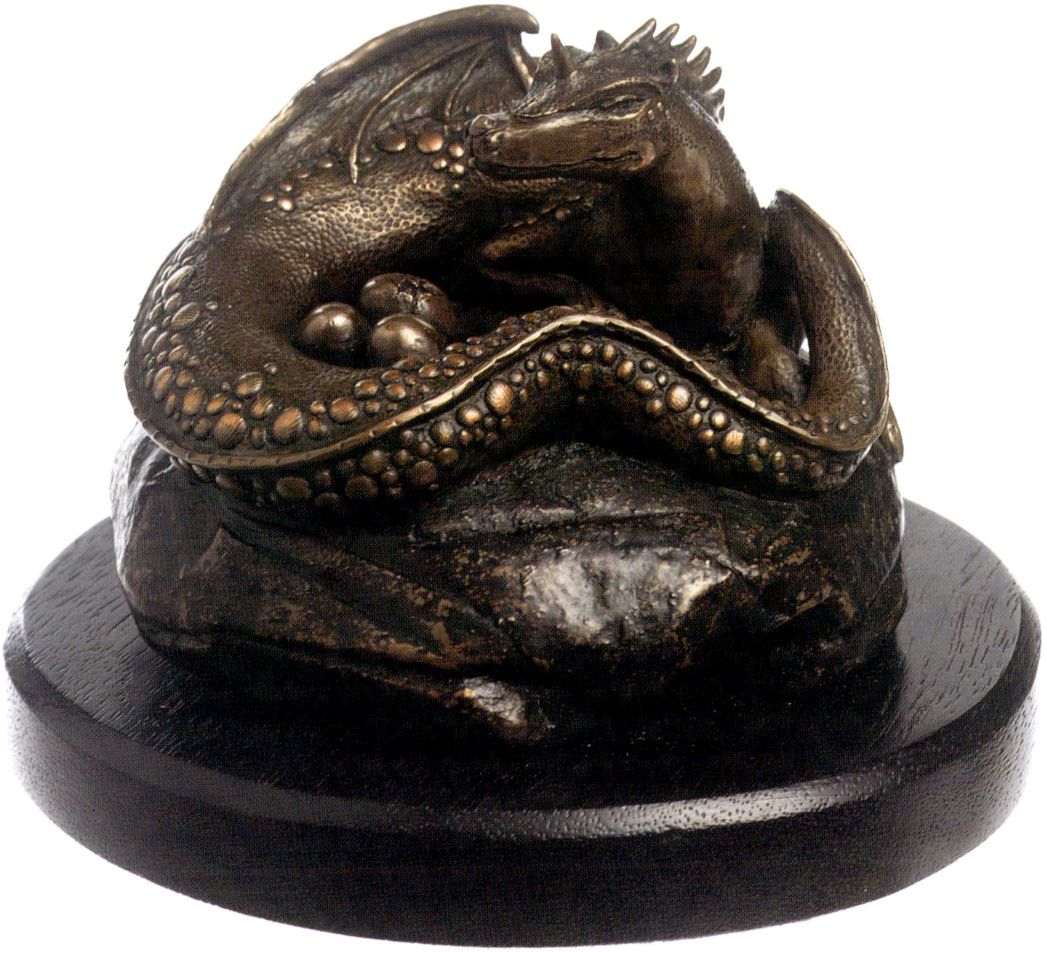

John Sabel RMS

A French Lady | **Lady of the French Court** | **Lily Langtry**

Marie Antoinette | **An English Lady** | **Example of Reverse Piercing**

(the vitreous enamel portraits are set in gold with silver and precious stones.)

He is descended from the Sabelinsky family of jewellers who worked almost exclusively for Russian nobility, then fled Russia to arrive in England in the late 1800's.

Born in London in 1922 he was educated at Hillhead and became a jeweller in 1938, learning enamelling and jewellery from his grandfather. He worked in Paris with the celebrated designer Leo Weith, returning to London at the outbreak of war to serve as a pilot in the R.A.F. When Paris was liberated he was posted to Le Bourget, linked up again with Leo Weith and practised his art when flying duties permitted.

Demobilised, John returned to work in Paris and London specializing in the making of individually commissioned fine jewels. As a miniaturist he created portraits worked in vitreous enamel, a medium lending itself to jewellery applications.

His creative work, love of music, poetry and the arts contrasted with his passion for sport, especially rugby, worrying his parents lest injury should cut short his career. Fortunately 'the Devil looked after his own'.

Winner of a Gold Memorial Bowl Honourable Mention he made history as the first artist invited to Royal Miniature Society Membership at his initial exhibition.

Commander Geoff Hunt RN RMS HS

HMS Victory Breaking Through the Line at Trafalgar
(acrylic on papier maché box)
kindly lent by David Haynes Esq.

Geoff Hunt joined the Royal Naval College, Dartmouth, in 1949 and spent nearly forty years in the Royal Navy, serving both as seaman officer and fighter pilot. He had always sketched and painted and as a midshipman relished the obligation to illustrate his journal. Thereafter he kept many ship 'line' books (a humorous, illustrated record) and developed a flare for caricature.

He always painted at sea, using oils and concentrating on marine and aviation subjects. Towards the end of his naval career he took up miniature painting after decorating an antique snuff box for his wife's collection.

He now spends most of his time painting, predominantly miniatures of eighteenth and nineteenth century sea battles, clipper ships and yachts. The challenge is not only to portray in miniature details of sails and rigging or the state of sea and sky; equally important, and more demanding, is the need to achieve a sense of action, movement and atmosphere which in life involves all the senses, but in art is limited to sight.

His work is widely collected, both at home and abroad. Other subjects include birds, animals, architecture and portraits, but he remains fascinated fundamentally by the sea which he knows so well.

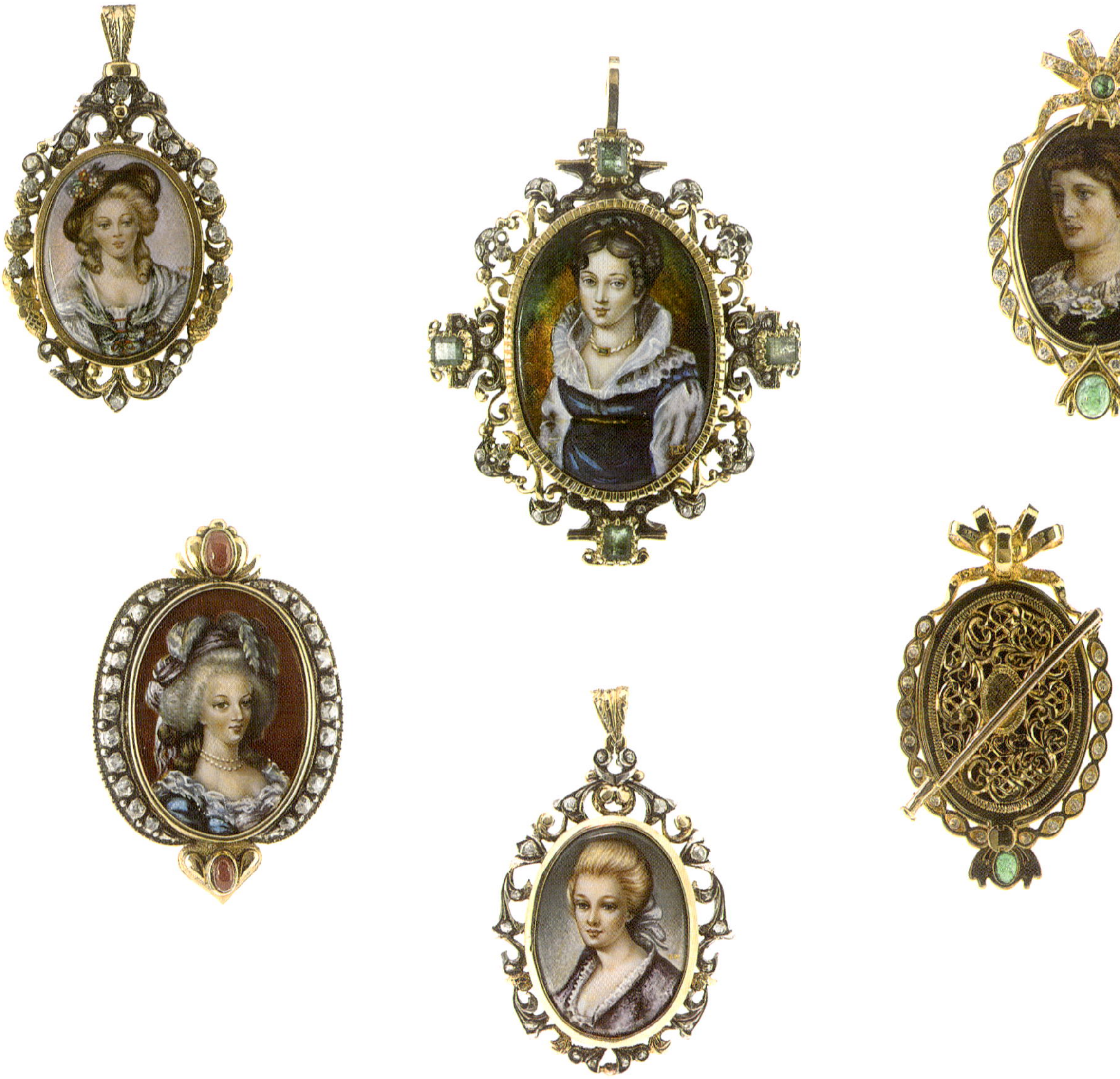

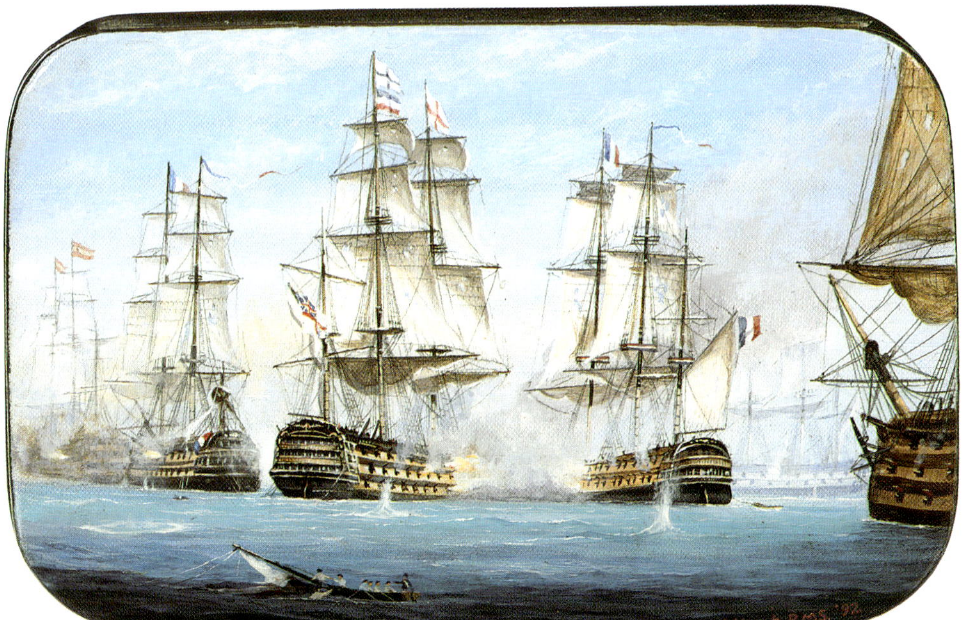
G.W.G.Hunt R.M.S. '92

Jenny Kennish *RMS SWA FSBA*

Early Spring
(porcelain)

Jenny studied Botany, Zoology and Art, became a qualified teacher in 1965 and taught until the birth of her two children. Family life interrupted study although she continued water-colour painting.

She decided to work in clay after watching a demonstration of porcelain sculpture. First she used stoneware, then discovered porcelain with which she explored the realistic portrayal of plants.

Deciding on original sculptures, she enjoyed the freedom of design and delicacy of modelling this method allowed for each sculpture, of an actual scene, as a finely detailed portrayal of flowers and animals.

A sculpture takes up to a month's work, but specimens have to be studied first. Each leaf and petal is made separately and assembled while the clay is wet Animals have accurate anatomical detail. The sculpture is left until dry, then fired slowly, the temperature rising over twelve to fifteen hours. When cold it is painted and re-fired, sometimes four or five times, until nature's colours are reproduced as accurately as possible. Although she uses the same subjects occasionally, the design is never repeated. Each sculpture is unique.

She exhibits widely and as a Member with the Royal Miniature Society and the Society of Botanical Artists.

Kay Thetford Kendall *RMS SWA*

Cheetah Brooch
(silver)

Dragon Pendant
(silver)

Born and educated in Manchester, she trained as a physiotherapist and, on qualifying, went almost immediately into private practice which led to other openings in health and beauty treatments. At this time the arts and painting were her hobbies and she studied extramurally at Art College. She has been creating sculptures for over twenty years and, realizing that this field of art was her metier, she left medicine and became a sculptor full-time.

From the first, child portraiture took much of her time, but her marriage to Wilmer Kendall led to smaller works: figurative pieces and semi-abstracts in bronze, which she and her husband cast and finished themselves. Lately she has been concentrating on miniatures in silver and sculptural jewellery.

She has exhibited widely in London, Paris, Venice, Switzerland and the United States. Her awards include the First Sculpture Prize at the Grolla d'Oro in 1981, in 1986 a Gold Memorial Bowl Honourable Mention and the Bidder and Borne Sculpture Award. In 1982 she executed two orders for the New Towns Commission in Hertfordshire.

She was elected a Member of the Society of Women Artists in 1980, an Associate of the Royal Miniature Society in 1984 and a Member in 1988.

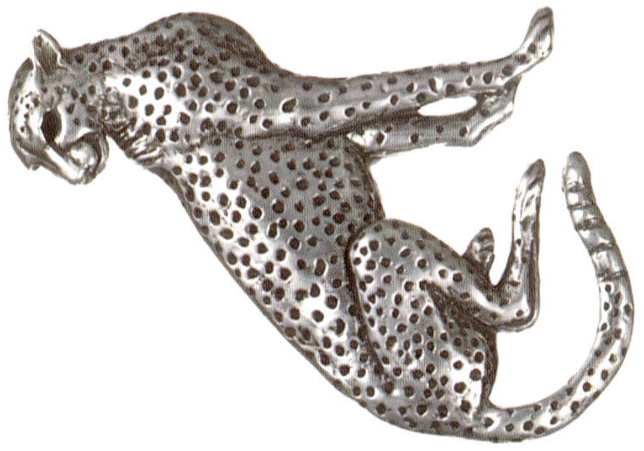

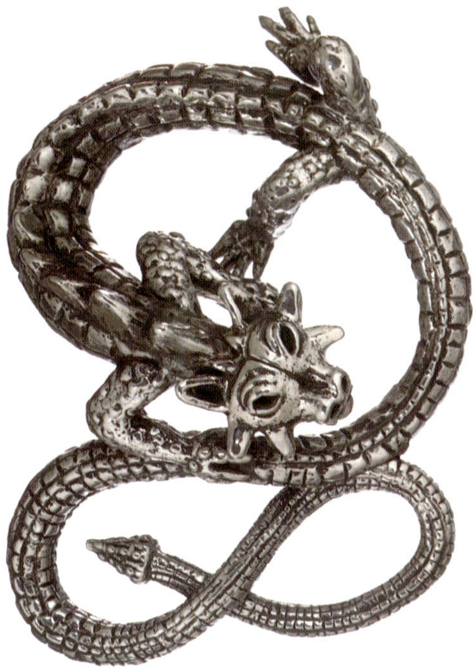

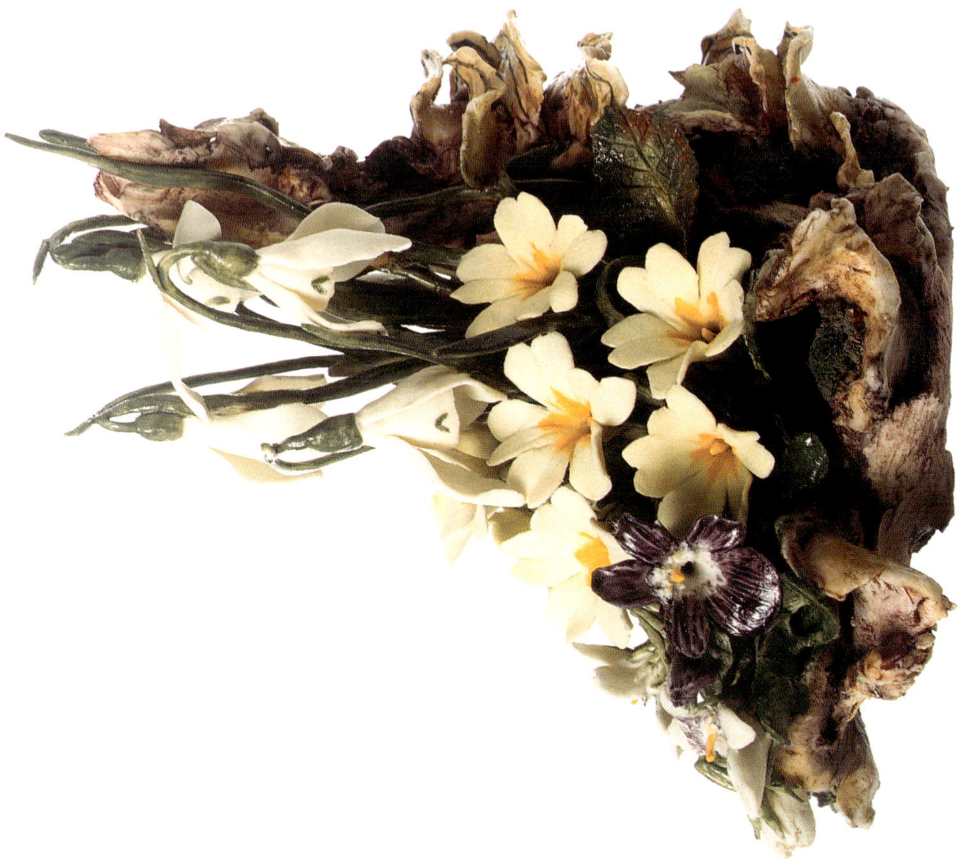

Wing Commander (retired) Derek Le Roy Bird RMS

Kashmir King Chess Piece
(ivory)

Kashmir Bishop Chess Piece
(ivory)

Kashmir Rook Chess Piece
(ivory)

Derek le Roy Bird had a long and interesting career in the RAF as a pilot and in administration. He was a senior test pilot, a chartered engineer and was awarded the Queen's Commendation for Valuable Service in the Air. A member of various expeditions for the RAF to the Himalayas, East Africa and New Zealand, he led the RAF Ellesmere Island Expedition to the Arctic Circle in 1967, becoming a Fellow of the Royal Geographical Society in 1968. He retired from the Service in 1978.

At seven years old he made original models. On retiring he reverted to this interest, attending the London College of Furniture from which he graduated with First Class Honours in 1979.

He has exhibited for fifteen years with the RMS, became an Associate Member in 1985 and a Member in 1988. He won a Gold Memorial Bowl Honourable Mention in 1987, a High Commendation in 1989, also the Bidder and Borne – Royal Miniature Society Sculpture Award in 1994.

He works in ivory, exotic hardwoods, tortoiseshell, mother-of-pearl, amber, jade and buhl, carving chessmen, boxes and animals, and restores antique chess sets, objets d'art, model aircraft and ships.

Pamela de Ville RMS

Adriana
(bronze)

Her passion for sculpture was aroused, and her life enriched, by working with that fine artist, the late T.B. Huxley-Jones, FRBS, RBSA, ARCA. She left art college during the war to do four years' army service and could practise again only when marriage and schooling allowed. Under Huxley-Jones' leadership her eyes were re-opened dramatically.

It was a great satisfaction when her work reached the standard to be exhibited competitively with the Society of Portrait Sculptors, the Manchester Academy of Fine Art and to be held in private collections in Australia, Canada, the United States, Germany and Saudi Arabia as well as in Britain.

She casts all the smaller work in real bronze and achieves this by having attended a foundry course, to the consternation of her husband when she set up a furnace to produce molten metal. It was thrilling to use the ancient lost wax method and, unusually for a sculptor, to handle every stage herself. Knocking off the mould to reveal the finished product is the final excitement.

She felt her efforts were truly rewarded in 1978 when she received an invitation from the Queen who wished to see an example of the work.

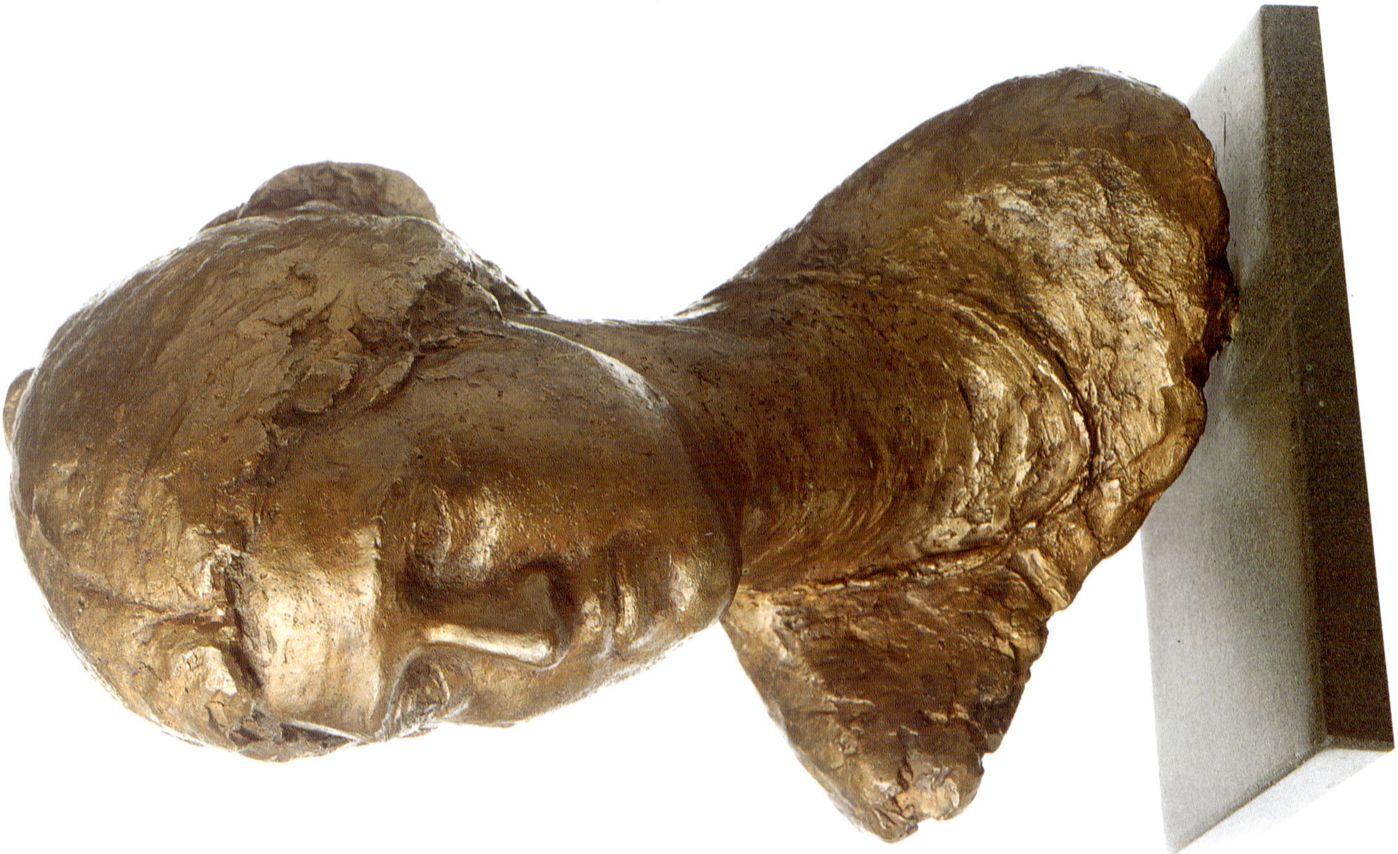

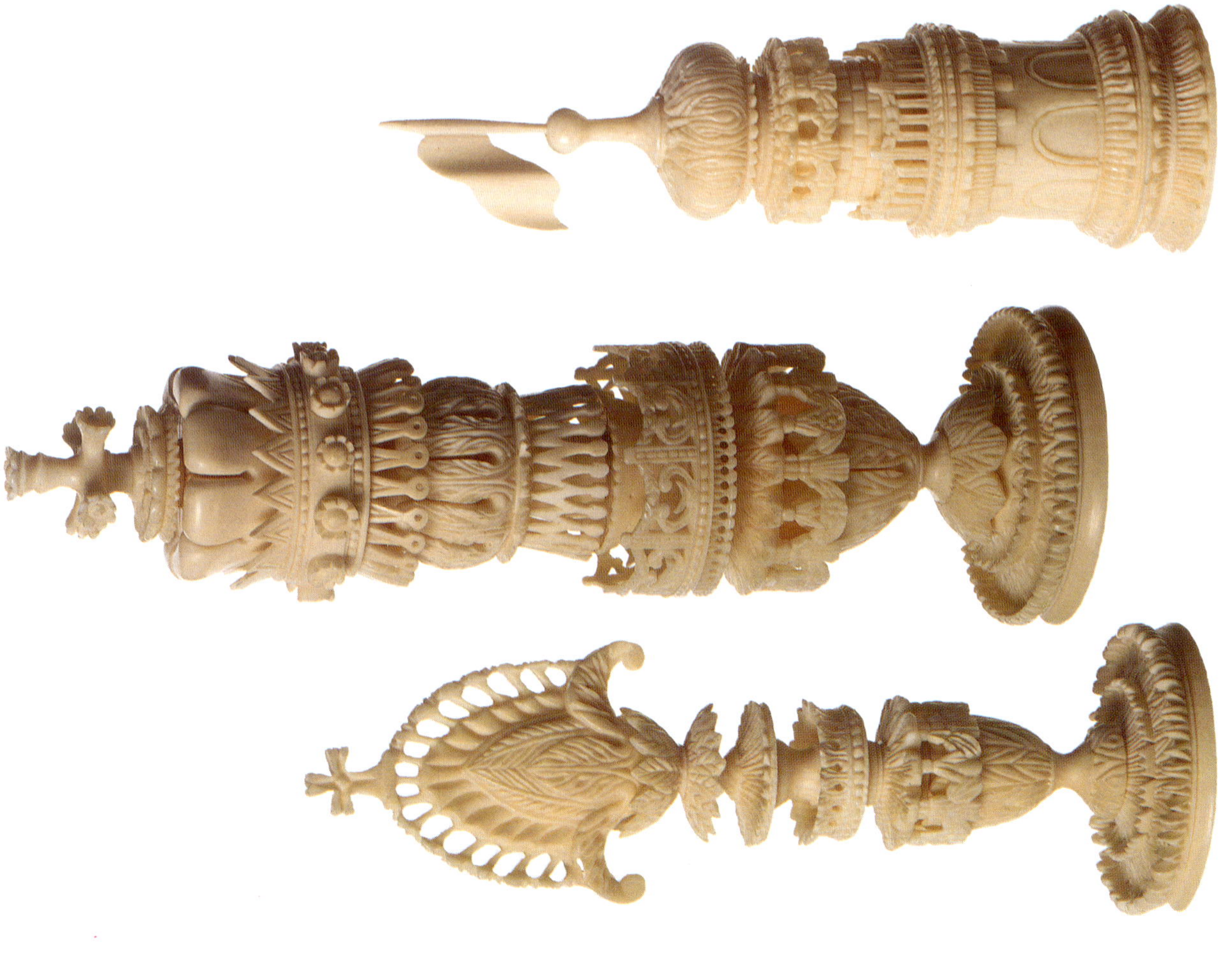

James F. Cumberland-Brown *ARMS HS*

The Endeavour
(scrimshaw)

Born in 1934 James Cumberland-Brown's early artistic abilities were the only ones which could guarantee consistent appearances at the annual school prize-giving. This promising start came to an abrupt end when he left school and emigrated to the Australian out-back in 1951.

It was not until 1975, living in the whaling port of Albany, Western Australia, that he became fascinated by the ancient art of scrimshaw, practised by sailors in the old days, and took up pencil and engraving tools once again. From early experimental dabbling, living in complete artistic isolation, he developed an intricate and individual style which soon saw his work in exhibitions and selling at Sotheby's.

Almost twenty years later he is a full-time and passionate scrimshaw artist with works featured in private and public collections world-wide. He exhibits annually with the Royal Miniature Society, where he was awarded a Gold Memorial Bowl Honourable Mention, and the Hilliard Society. In 1991 a work of his was shown at the International Festival of Miniatures in Montelimar, France.

Australian galleries in Sydney and Canberra feature his pieces which are also in the National Maritime Museum and the Murdock University Art Collection.

Nada Marija Pedley *RMS*

Orphan's Plea
(chocolate black clay)

She was born in Gorenjska near Bled in Slovenia where she grew up and did her schooling. From an early age art was her best subject and in 1967 she graduated in Commercial Art in Ljubljana, afterwards working as an arranger. In 1968 she came to England to learn English, married here and had three children.

Meanwhile she began studying pottery and ceramics at the Horsham Art School and soon afterwards exhibited paintings and ceramic work at local exhibitions in West Sussex.

For the past nine years she has exhibited her work at the Royal Miniature Society, becoming in 1991 an Associate and in 1994 a Member of the Society. In 1990 she had won the Bidder and Borne Award for the finest sculpture exhibited that year.

In 1989 she was introduced to the firm of Royal Doulton which gives her regular commissions for prototype figures.

Her crinoline lady 'Mary' was chosen as the Figure of the Year for 1992 and in 1993 the lovely 'Orphan's Plea' was awarded a Gold Memorial Bowl Honourable Mention, with a Second Mention in 1994.

Her greatest wish is to achieve excellence in her chosen art form, from which she derives the highest personal and artistic pleasure.

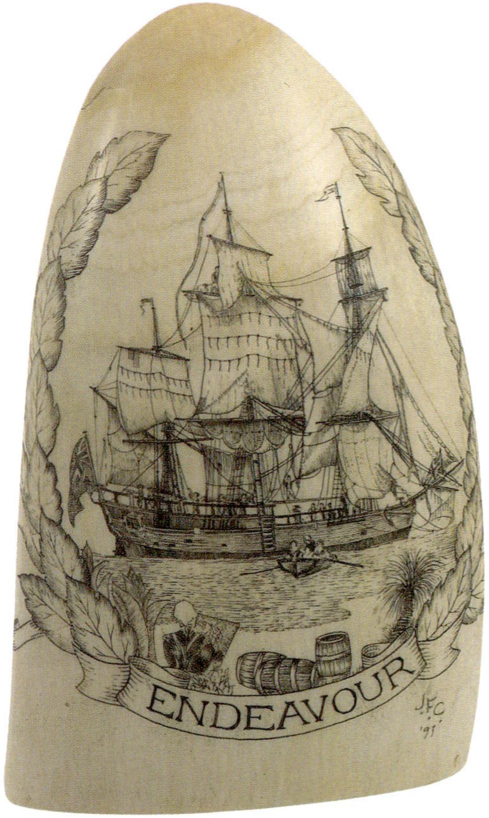
ENDEAVOUR

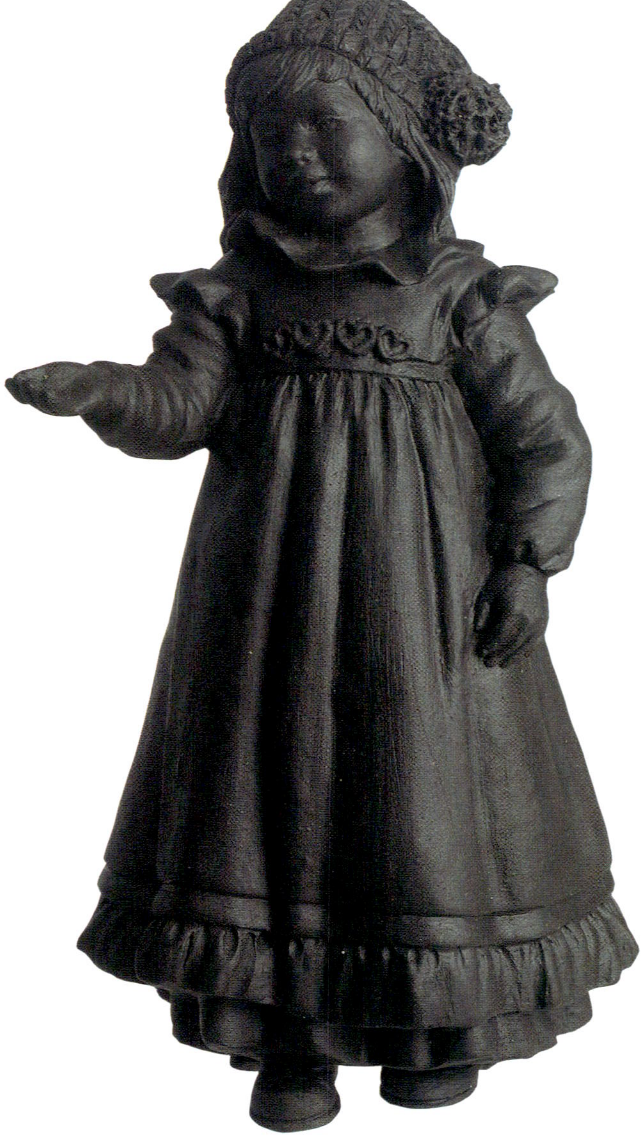

Judith Syverson RMS

Story Time
(acrylic on Ivorine)

A resident of the beautiful Flathead Valley of north-western Montana, Judith does most of her work on location. Her paintings of western wildlife, landscapes and wild flowers reflect the way things look to-day flavoured with the pioneer spirit of yesterday. The fascinating true stories of homestead scenes enrich the history of these uniquely western landscapes. Another important area of Judith's work is that of her Victorian paintings. Authentic gowns are used to recreate the grace and beauty of the era.

Exhibiting with many miniature art societies in the United States, she was placed first and second at the Montana Miniature Art Society's Third International Show and first in Landscape at the Miniature Art Society of Florida's Seventh International Competition.

Judith's paintings may be found in both private and corporate collections throughout the United States, Canada and Europe.

Muriel Constance Smith RMS

Keith Ford
(water-colour on old ivory)
kindly lent by Mrs. D.S. Ford

Lady May Abel Smith
(water-colour on ivory)
kindly lent by Lady May

Muriel was born in Nottinghamshire, where she was educated, and spent her life in Nottingham. She was an artist of the highest quality, with a talent bordering on genius, which began to be manifest at the age of six when she won her first prize.

She studied at Nottingham College of Art. When her talent made her Aunt offer a London training her parents refused to allow it.

She remained at the College for fourteen years where she intensified the study of every aspect of her art, perfecting her skills. She was taught also by Alyn Williams, the Founder President of the Royal Miniature Society, of which she was proud to become a Member in 1954.

The delicacy of her work was unsurpassed. She exhibited five times at the Royal Academy of Arts, the Royal Miniature Society, galleries in the United States, a one-woman show at the Walker Galleries in Bond Street and at the Paris Salon where she was awarded both a Mention d'Honneur and a Silver Medal. She travelled extensively painting eminent families, including Royalty, her work adding up to over seven hundred portraits during a career spanning more than sixty years. Her special gift was an insight into her sitter's character, visible in the expression of the eyes. She refused several proposals of marriage, preferring her independence and devotion to her work.

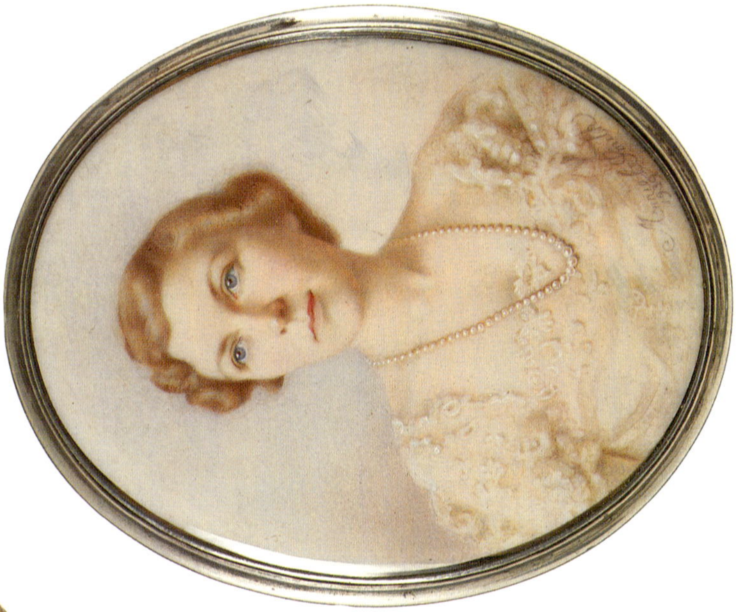

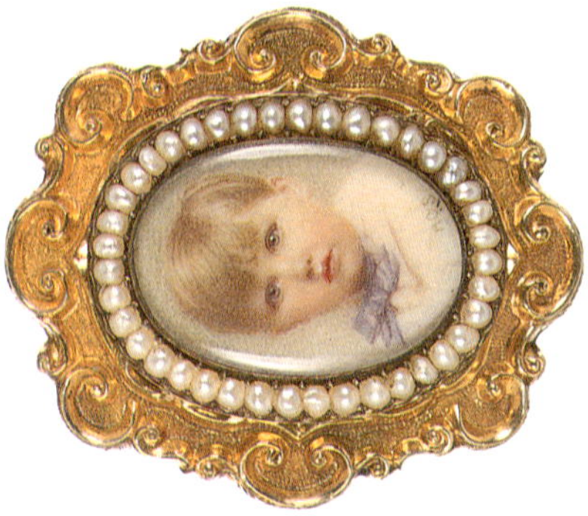

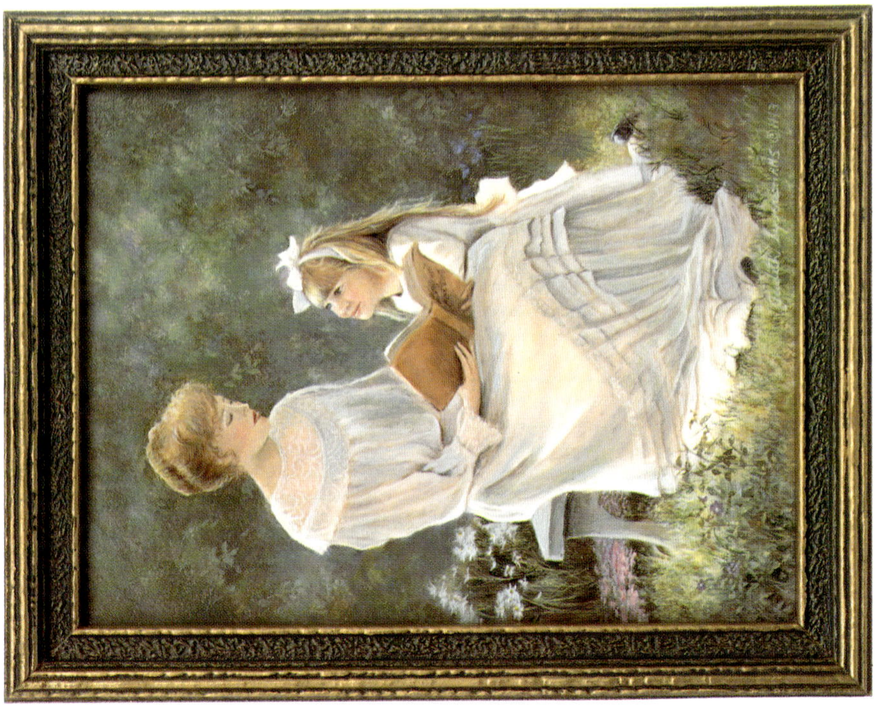

Mary McLean *RMS HS*

Harvest Moon
(water-colour on vellum)
from the Diploma Collection

Mary McLean lives in Dorset surrounded by the birds and wildlife she loves to paint. She first exhibited her work at the Old School House Gallery, Woolland, Dorset in 1990. The same year her miniatures were accepted by the Hilliard Society and the Royal Society of Miniature Painters, Sculptors and Gravers.

In 1991 she had her first successful one-man exhibition of fifty miniatures at Woolland and was elected an Associate Member of the Royal Society of Miniature Painters, Sculptors and Gravers, becoming a Member in 1994. Although painting a variety of subjects in water-colour on Ivorine and vellum, Mary is particularly well known for her pictures of birds, poultry and waterfowl. Five reproductions of her work were used to illustrate the front cover of 'Fancy Fowl', a specialist breeders' magazine.

She exhibits at provincial galleries in Woolland and Sturminster Newton, as well as in London with the Royal Miniature Society and the Llewellyn Alexander Gallery. She is a regular exhibitor at the Royal Academy Summer Exhibition and her work has been shown in galleries and exhibitions in Europe, the United States and as far away as Japan.

Stuart Perkins

NDD (Hons.) ATD RMS MPSG MASF HS GMAS MAA

Still Life in Bowl, Mango and Lace
(water-colour on card)

Still Life - Cup and Saucer with Fruit
(water-colour on card)

Stuart Perkins studied Fine Art at the Leicester College of Art gaining First Class Honours in Sculpture. His early training in figurative clay modelling is evident in the strength of form achieved in the design of his miniatures.

He has lectured on pottery and sculpture in English Art Schools and from 1978 to 1985 earned a living as a craftsman potter. He has exhibited with the Royal West of England Academy, the Royal Water Colour Society and the Royal Society of Miniature Painters, Sculptors and Gravers of which he became a Member in 1991.

Following a lecture tour, invited by the Florida Clay Workers Guild, he became interested in miniatures and since 1986 has exhibited regularly in the United States with the four major East Coast Societies. He has won thirty-one awards in international shows during eight years including fifteen firsts. This was rewarded in 1990 by Signature Membership of the Miniature Artists of America. He became the first European to hold membership both of this and the Royal Miniature Society.

Stuart works in water-colour on card and with oil on vellum. He paints mainly landscapes, often of the Forest of Dean and the Wye Valley, with forays into still life.

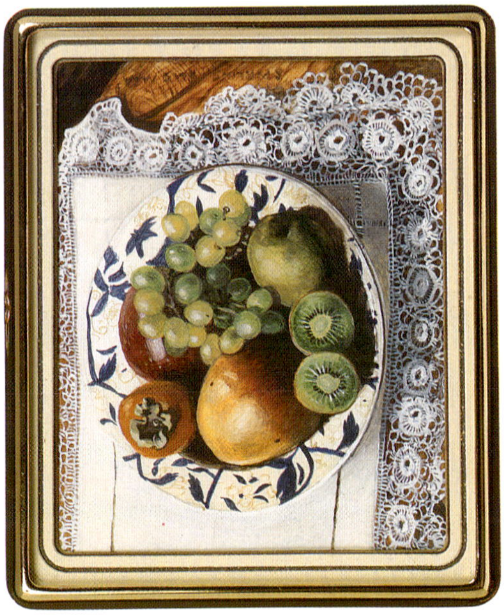

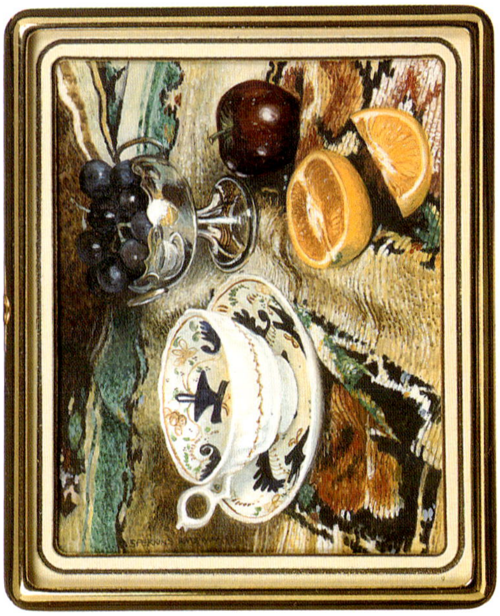

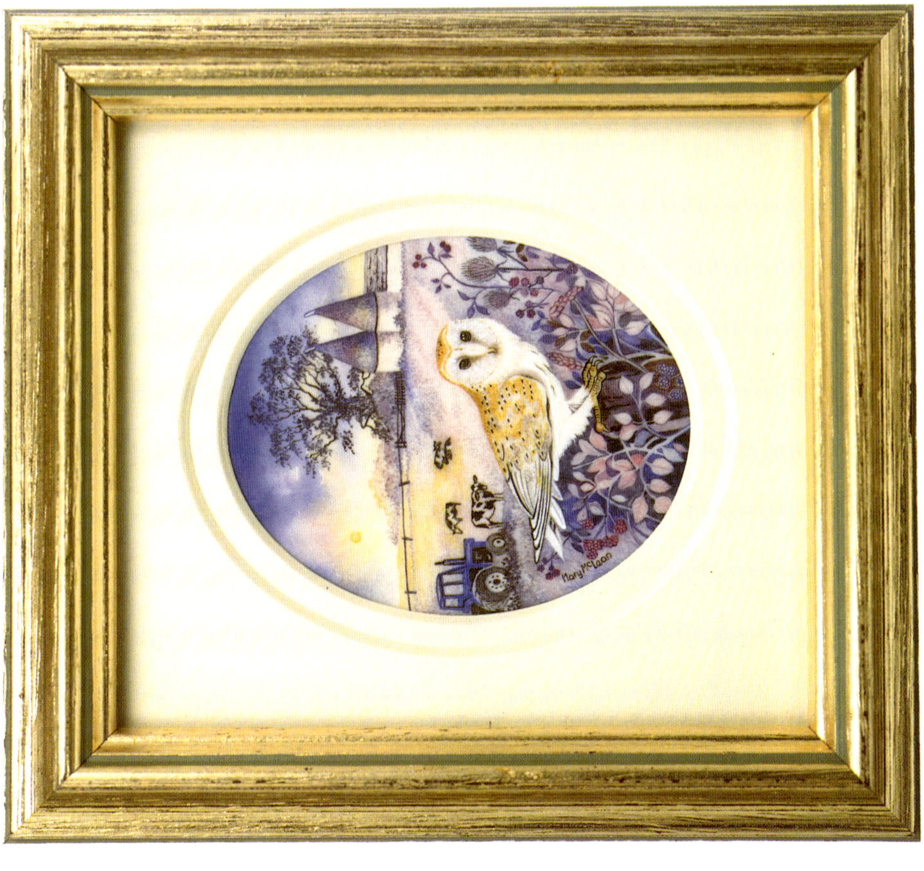

Doreen Medhurst *RMS SWA SBA*

The Weald of Kent
(acrylic on Ivorine)

St. Mary Bourne, Hampshire
(acrylic on Ivorine)

Married and living in Kent, she was self-taught and, interested in painting from the age of five, entered many newspaper competitions, gaining prizes of ten shillings or one pound. Evacuated during the war to Cornwall and Wiltshire, she started sketching the different landscapes. During the 1950's she travelled the length and breadth of England as a portrait photographer.

She returned to the Press in 1971, entering 'The People' Housewives Painting Competition, where she had animal portraits exhibited at the Festival Hall for three consecutive years.

She began landscape miniature painting and exhibited with the Royal Miniature Society when it was at the Mall Galleries. Her medium is acrylic with which she paints on Ivorine.

She is a Member of the Royal Miniature Society, the Society of Botanical Artists and the Society of Women Artists, finding her subject matter on the coast and in the rural and village life of Britain.

She has had several one-woman exhibitions in Kent and Sussex and designed greetings cards for Lings in 1993. Her work is shown at the Llewellyn Alexander Gallery, the Alfriston Gallery the Elan Art Centre in Sevenoaks and her paintings are in private collections in America, Australia and Japan.

John L.M. Weeks *FNCM ARMS*

Magdalen Tower, Oxford
(water-colour on Ivorine)

He was born in Chelmsford, Essex where later he held his first musical position as church organist, before moving to Bracknell. He trained as a musician, with appointments as organist and choirmaster, and teaches privately the piano, flute and the theory of music.

Both music and art have always been of great importance to him. He wanted to draw and paint when he was very young. While studying music at Colchester he was given instruction in art by Mr. John Buhler and during his musical career was able to give time to painting as well. He developed a style which strives for realism. As well as larger works in oil and water-colour he paints miniatures on vellum or Ivorine, using traditional techniques. Most music lessons fall in the evenings leaving him daylight hours for painting.

In 1987 he was elected an Associate Member of the Royal Miniature Society with which he exhibits each year. Subjects vary, but are often landscapes and architectural scenes, also portraits. He has had several one-man exhibitions and also shows his work at a gallery near Wokingham in Berkshire.

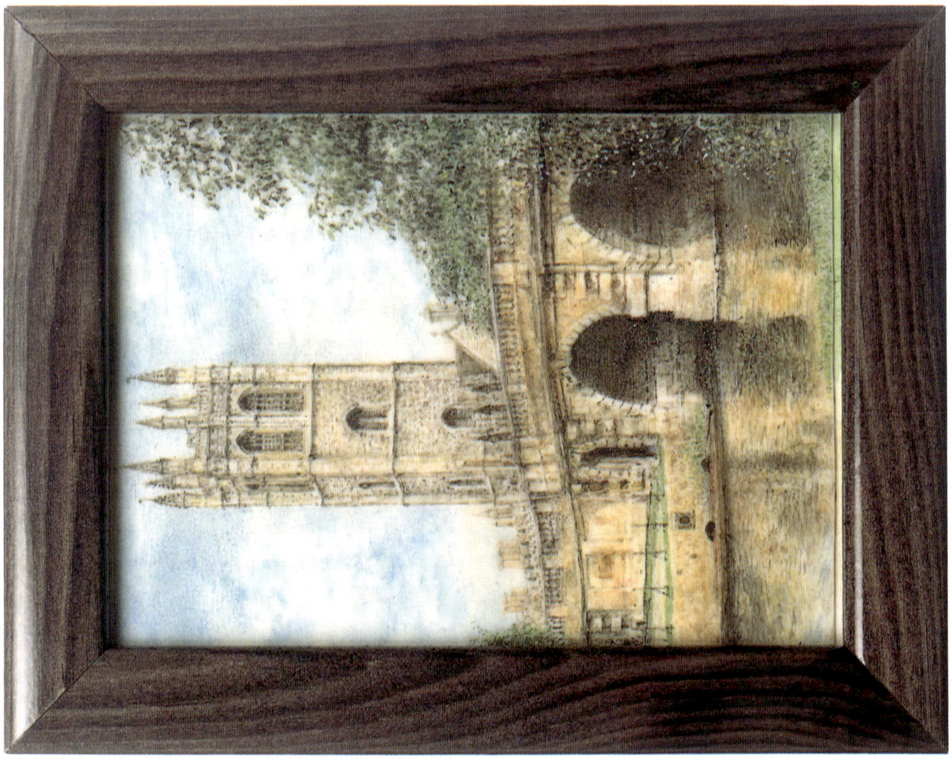

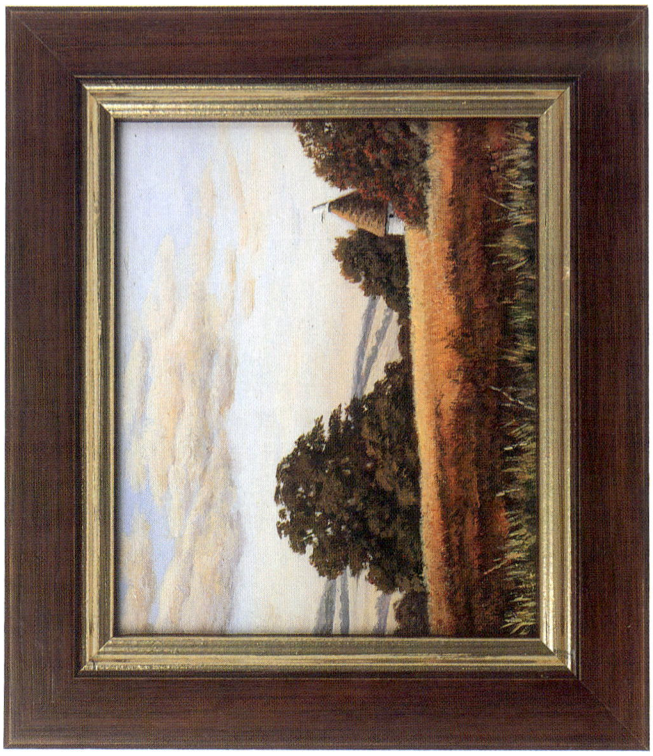

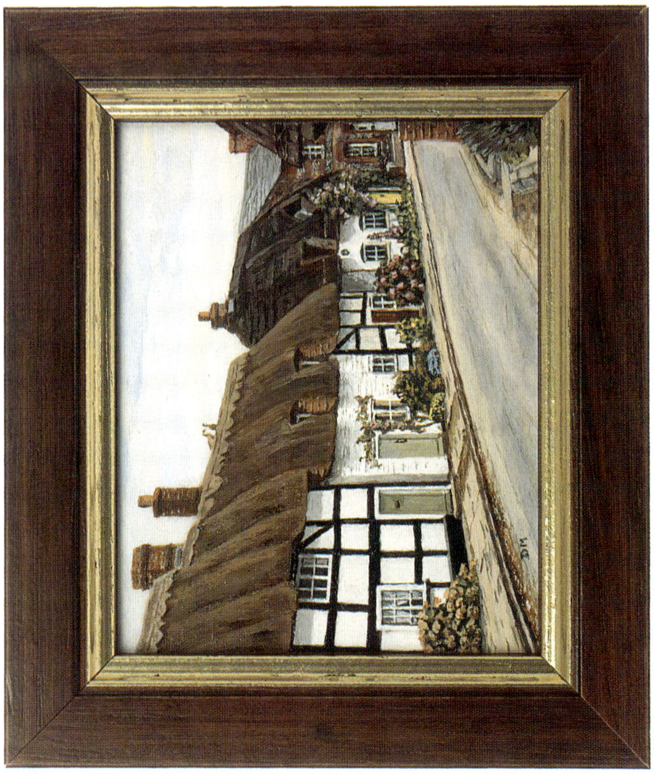

Dianne Branscombe *ARMS SWA HS*

Miss Lisa Branscombe
(water-colour on Ivorine)

Autumn Fruits
(water-colour on Ivorine)

Born in Norwich in 1949, Dianne Branscombe lives with her husband and two children in the Broadland village of Surlingham. Since early childhood she has always been interested in painting and studied art at the University of London Goldsmiths' College. During her subsequent teaching career in Norfolk she pursued her love of painting and held her first solo exhibition in 1983. Every year since she has staged successful annual exhibitions in Norwich and also exhibited extensively in East Anglian and London galleries.

Dianne paints portraits, landscapes and still life in oils and water-colours. Her use of a palette of pure pigments gives her paintings transparency and luminosity. The country feel to Dianne's pictures reflects her way of life, her deep interest in growing fruit and vegetables, making bread, cakes and preserves and many of these appear in her work.

She has exhibited with the Royal Miniature Society every year since 1986 and in 1993 became an Associate Member. She is a Member of the Hilliard Society of Miniaturists, exhibiting with them since 1988, and in 1994 became a Member of the Society of Women Artists. She has shown work at the Summer Exhibition of the Royal Academy of Arts.

Vera Ibbett *RMS FSSI*

The Bridle-path
(gouache on Ivorine)

Morning Gallop
(gouache on Ivorine)

Vera Ibbett studied figure and portrait painting under Innes Fripp RA and brush lettering under William Sharpington at the City and Guilds School of Art, London. Her interest in hedgerow and meadow flowers was encouraged and developed by John Nash RA. She holds the Royal Horticultural Society's Silver Grenfell Medal for Botanical Illustration and the London College of Printing Diploma for Graphic Reproduction.

In 1971 she was elected a Fellow of the Society of Scribes and Illuminators for one book, Flowers in Heraldry, which made her the subject of the 1974 Thames Television series 'The Craftsman'. Two years later, that book was published by the Alcuin Society, Vancouver, British Columbia, Canada. She taught calligraphy at the Reigate School of Art in the eighties and inscribed and illuminated the Battle of Britain Roll of Honour for Biggin Hill.

She was elected an Associate Member of the Royal Society of Miniature Painters, Sculptors and Gravers and exhibited at the Royal Academy Summer Exhibition, later qualifying for full Membership of the Society in 1990. Her work today concentrates mostly on fine animal portraits, often in a landscape setting. She designed the lettering for the latest Royal Miniature Society Catalogue cover.

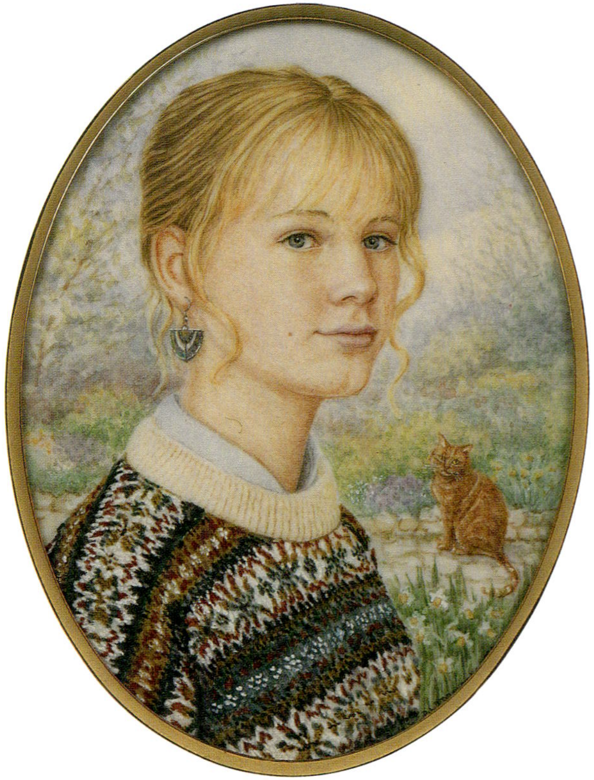
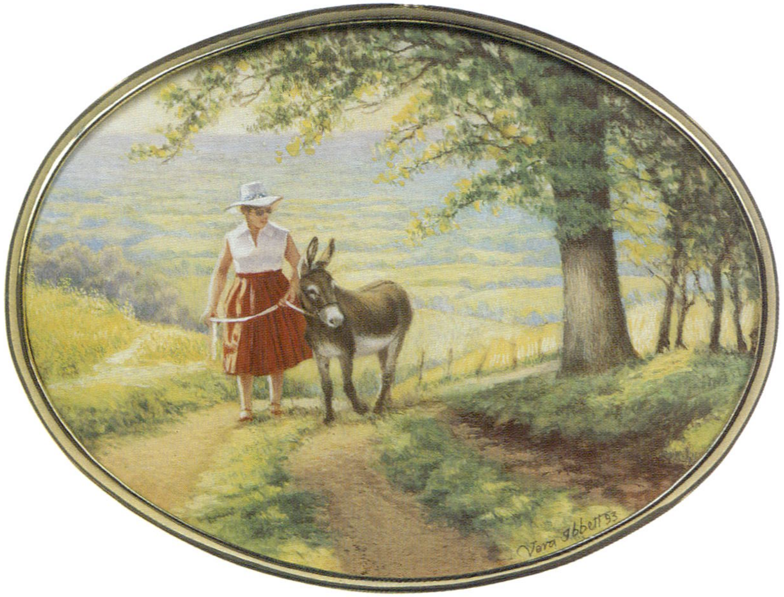
Vera Abbott93
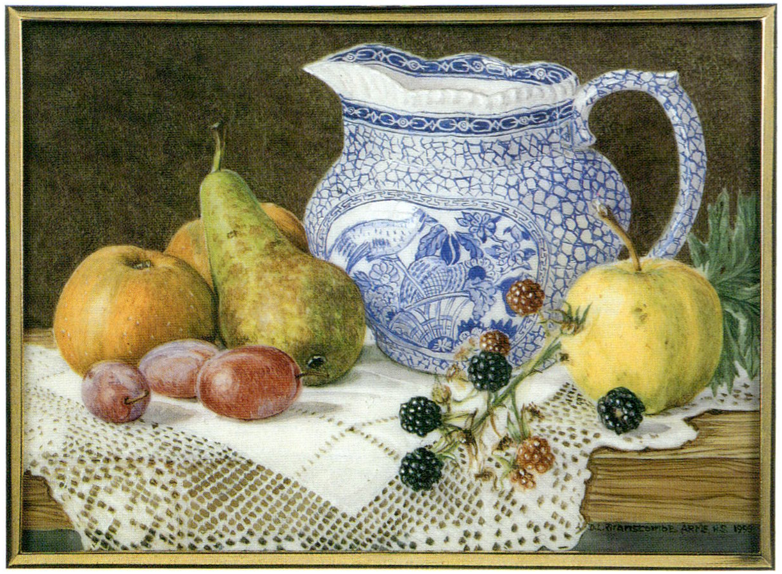
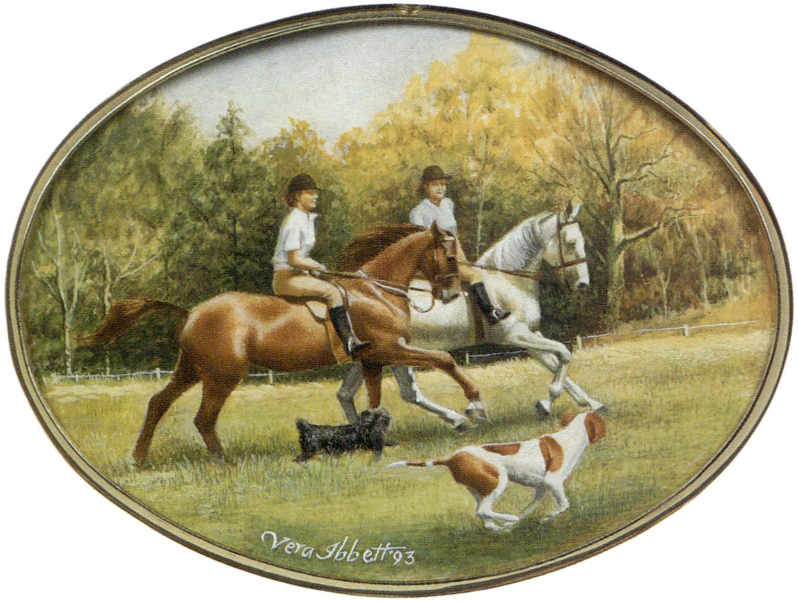
Vera Abbott93

Sheila Harwood Parry *RMS FRSA HS*

Portrait of the Artist
(gouache on vellum)

She was born in Salford, Lancashire and won a scholarship to Salford College of Art where she studied for two years. She became a professional textile designer, continuing her studies at evening classes, and was awarded an Exhibition Tenable by the College Governors.

She lived in Australia for ten years and worked there as a freelance for five studios. Returning to Britain she resumed her art career.

After exhibiting with the Royal Miniature Society she became an Associate in 1972, a Member in 1976 and showed at the Royal Academy and the Paris Salon where she was awarded the Honourable Mention Diploma.

She was elected a Fellow of the Royal Society of Arts in 1971 and had many works published by Royles and other publishers.

Elected an Artist Member of the Fine Arts Trade Guild and then to the Executive Council, she served seven years as Warden and Master's Warden.

Sheila has exhibited internationally in London, Florida, Washington and Australia winning eight awards in Florida, Montana and Washington.

She paints mostly with gouache on vellum or card and signs her work S.H.P. Her paintings are in private collections in Italy, France, Australia, America and Great Britain, also in the Municipal Gallery of Fine Art, Southport.

Enid Clarke *ARMS*

The Sewing Basket
(oil on Ivorine)
from the Diploma Collection

Tea and Scones
(oil on Ivorine)

Enid Clarke is a Norfolk-born artist who, after twenty years exhibiting her flower paintings widely throughout East Anglia, began to be fascinated by miniatures.

In 1983 she met Sheila Sewell RMS from whom she received tuition in the specialized art of miniature painting.

Her work was accepted and hung in the Royal Miniature Society's annual exhibitions and she was elected an Associate Member of that Society in 1989; also she was awarded a Gold Memorial Bowl Honourable Mention in 1990.

Since 1987 her work has been hung regularly in the Royal Academy Summer Exhibitions.

In 1989 she won the Rose Bowl Award for the best miniature in the exhibition from the Society of Miniaturists in Yorkshire and was Highly Commended in the East Anglian Open Arts Exhibition held in King's Lynn in 1992.

Her work is shown regularly in London and she has presented, this year, one of her best pieces to the Royal Miniature Society's Diploma Collection.

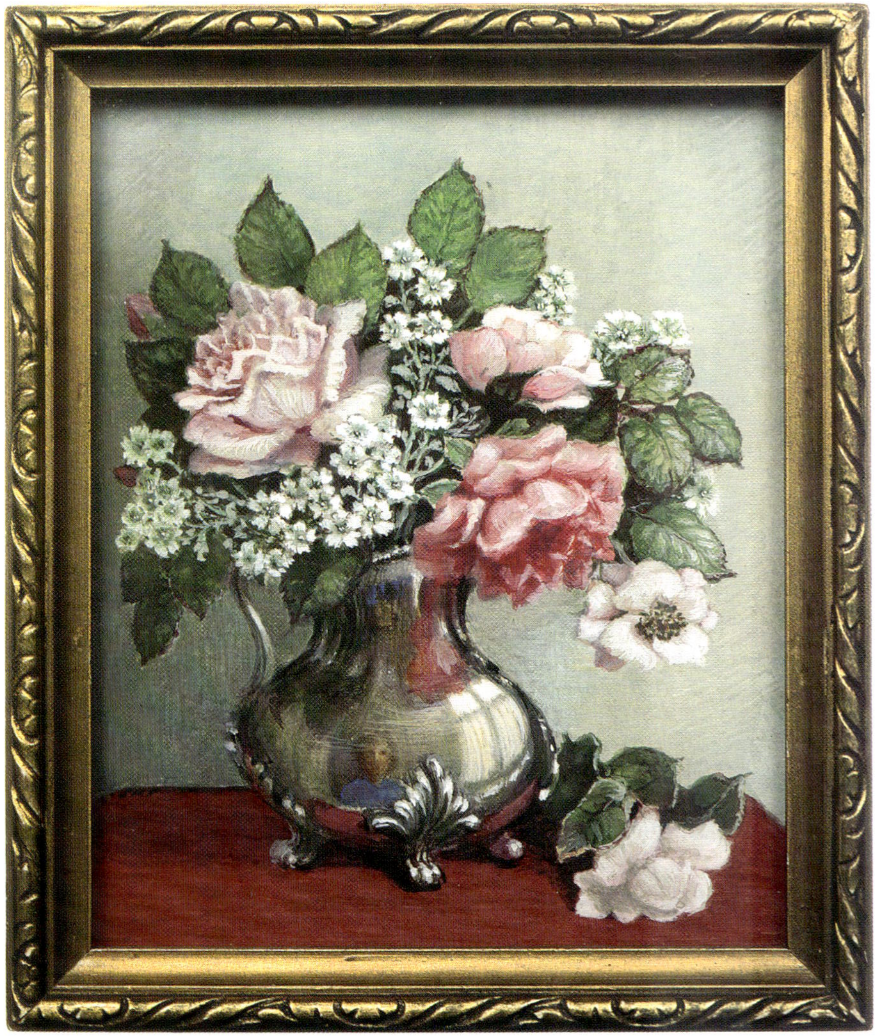

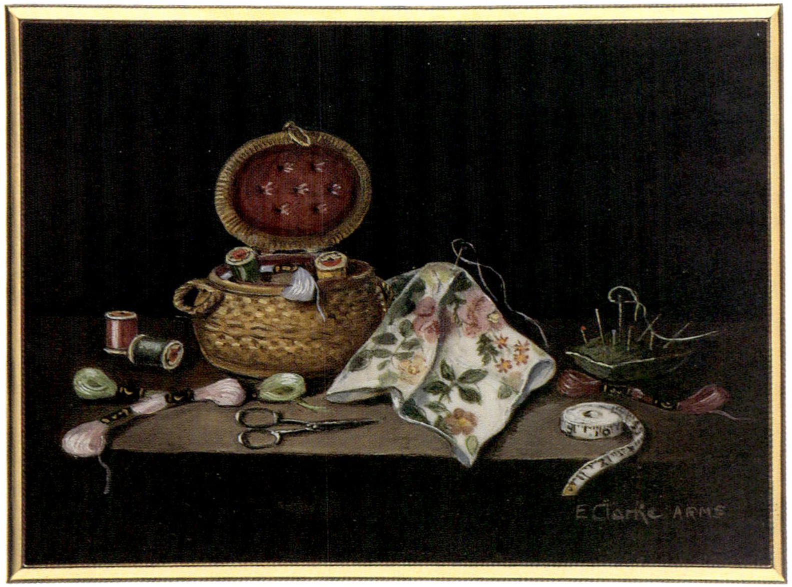
E.Clarke ARMS

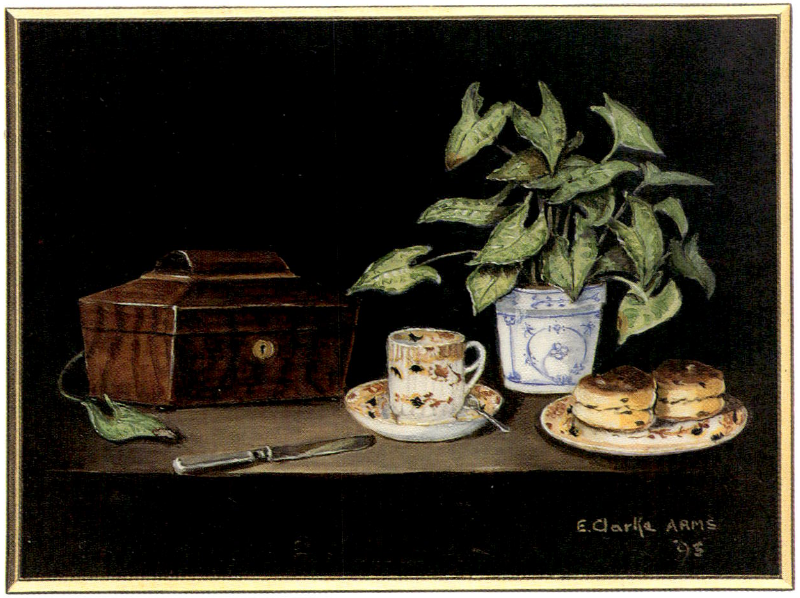
E.Clarke ARMS
'95

Pat Heatley

Mod. BA (Hons. in Science) RMS USWA HS

Gouramis
(gouache on Ivorine)

The Music Room
(gouache on Ivorine)

Her best subject at school was art but her father advised a University degree as providing a secure financial future. She decided on Natural Sciences as some drawing would be required. Obtaining an Honours Degree from Trinity College, Dublin, she followed a science-orientated career through research, lecturing and teaching. On retirement in 1983 she taught herself water-colour painting, mainly flowers and still life, in all possible detail. Seeing these works at the Royal Ulster Academy Phyllis Arnold urged her to paint miniatures. She became a Founder Member of the Ulster Society of Miniaturists in 1986 and was awarded the Ulster Bank Perpetual Trophy in 1987 and 1991, the Madam MacCarthy Mór Memorial Bowl in 1989 and the Northern Bank Perpetual Trophy in 1992. She has exhibited with the Hilliard Society since 1987 and the Royal Miniature Society since 1989.

She was elected an Associate of the Royal Miniature Society in 1990 and a Member in 1993 when she won a Gold Memorial Bowl Honourable Mention and a First Prize Fairman Award. In 1994 a second Honourable Mention followed.

She paints in water-colour and oils, using gold and silver leaf. Her subjects include musical instruments, flowers, birds and fish.

Elizabeth R. Meek *ARMS HS*

Greek Lady
(oil on Ivorine)
kindly lent by Muriel Hutton

From the age of eleven Elizabeth wanted to be an artist and when she was twelve her first work was exhibited with the Royal Drawing Society in London. Unable to attend Art College, she trained as a nurse at Westminster Children's Hospital. Throughout her nursing career she painted and drew, often using her colleagues as subjects. Before leaving nursing she did two large paintings for the Children which hang at the Westminster and Chelsea Hospitals.

In 1978 she turned to art. She is self-taught and enjoys painting people from all over the world, using oil on Ivorine and the finest of brushes for the exquisite detail.

She exhibits annually with the Royal Miniature Society and the Hilliard Society. She has shown work in London at the Mall Galleries, in Yorkshire and Paris, at the British Painters and the Society of Women Artists Exhibitions and the Barbican Centre.

At the Hilliard Society Elizabeth has won the Bell Best Portrait Award and the Suzanne Lucas Award for Best In Exhibition. At the Royal Miniature Society she has been runner-up for the Gold Memorial Bowl twice and received one other Honourable Mention. She has sold work in France, Italy, Australia and Great Britain.

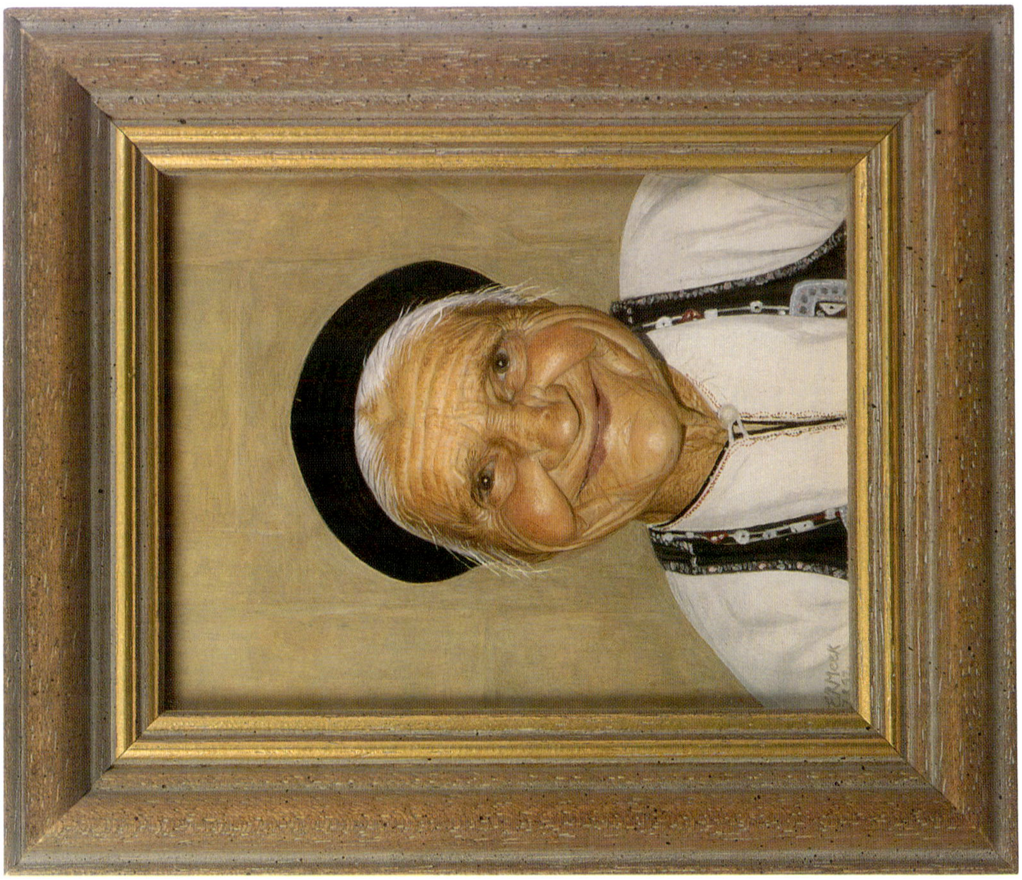

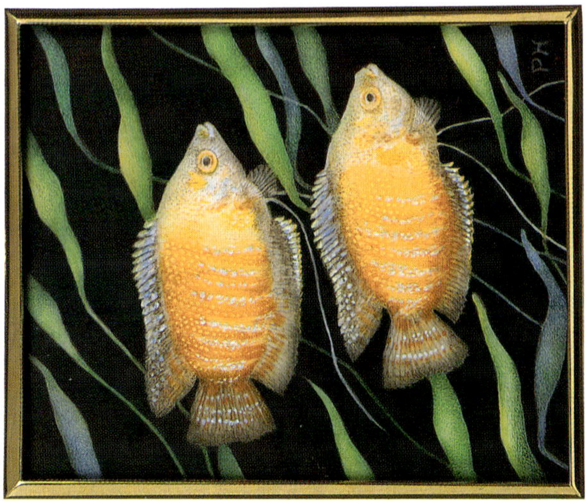

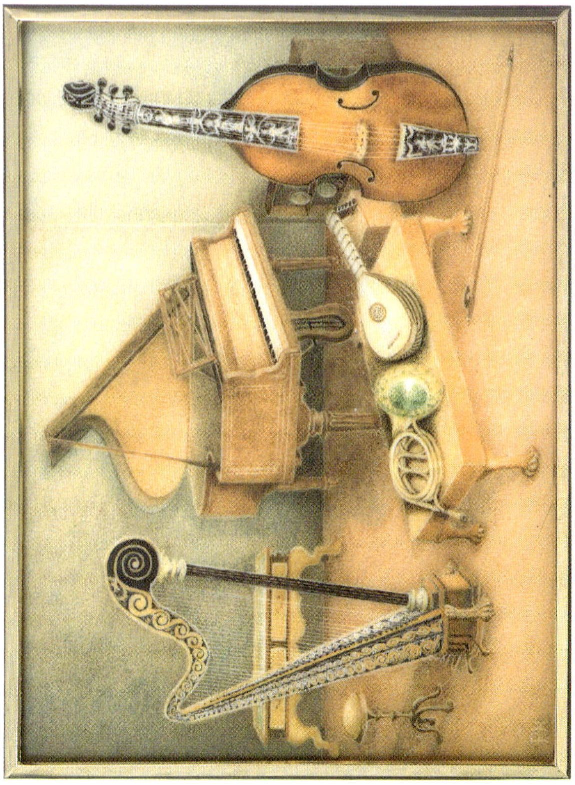

Vivien Jane Mullett *ARMS HS*

High Snab, Newlands Valley, Cumbria
(water-colour on Arches paper)

She was born in 1952 in Oxford and studied Fine Art at Reading University, concentrating on three-dimensional work. She became aware of natural law, sacred geometry, human nature and purpose and worked on the mathematical structure of Islamic patterns. She respects the planet we live on, hoping to convey its beauty to the viewer.

Vivien organized The Workshop for amateurs and youth clubs with a community screen-printing shop and dark-room, the first available to the public.

Miniature landscapes intrigue her, for within a tiny framework lies an immense view to step into with its space and distance. Her landscapes are extraordinarily fine in execution and have a delicate aura which is rare and of great appeal. Her first miniatures were painted as presents until she was persuaded to send to the Royal Miniature Society. She has shown there since 1984, winning a Gold Memorial Bowl Honourable Mention in 1987 and 1992 when she was elected an Associate. She has had work in the Royal Academy Summer Exhibitions, the Hilliard Montelimar Exhibition in France and a three-woman show in London. At the Miniature Art Society of Florida she was awarded first prize in water-colour of animals and birds.

John Dean *RMS SM FRSA*

Yokohamas
(oil on ivory)

Autumn
(oil on ivory)

He is a self-taught artist painting both large river land-scapes and miniatures in oil.

He was born in Grassington, North Yorkshire on March 25th, 1930. The son of Newland Walton Dean, Master Butcher, he was educated at the Grassington Church of England School, thereafter training as a Master Butcher.

He worked in farming and the building trade, was experienced in dry-stone walling and was the Search Leader of the Upper Wharfedale Fell and Cave Rescue Team from 1952 to 1959. A Founder Member and then President of the Upper Wharfedale Museum Society, he took up art on leaving the Royal Army Service Corps. He exhibited with the Royal Miniature Society, the United Artists, the Society of Miniaturists, the Yorkshire Artists, the International Art Fair at Olympia, the Salon des Nations in Paris and many others, originating ivory piano key miniatures.

His work has been purchased by Shell Oil International, A.E. Auto Parts, Lord Harewood, the Earl of Burlington and many others and is collected in most countries of the world. It has also been reproduced in England and Guernsey as prints and cards.

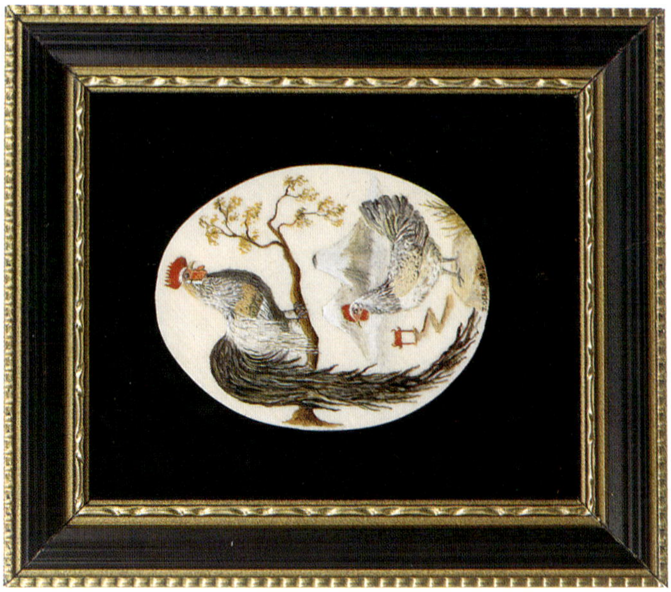
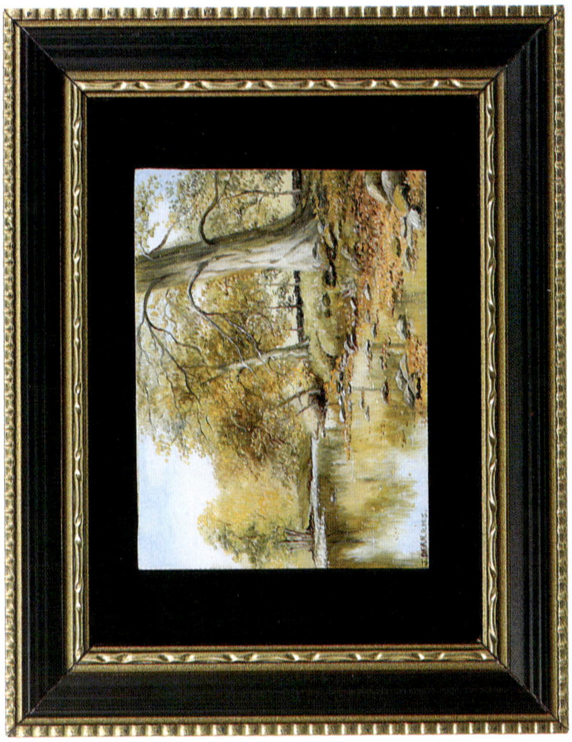
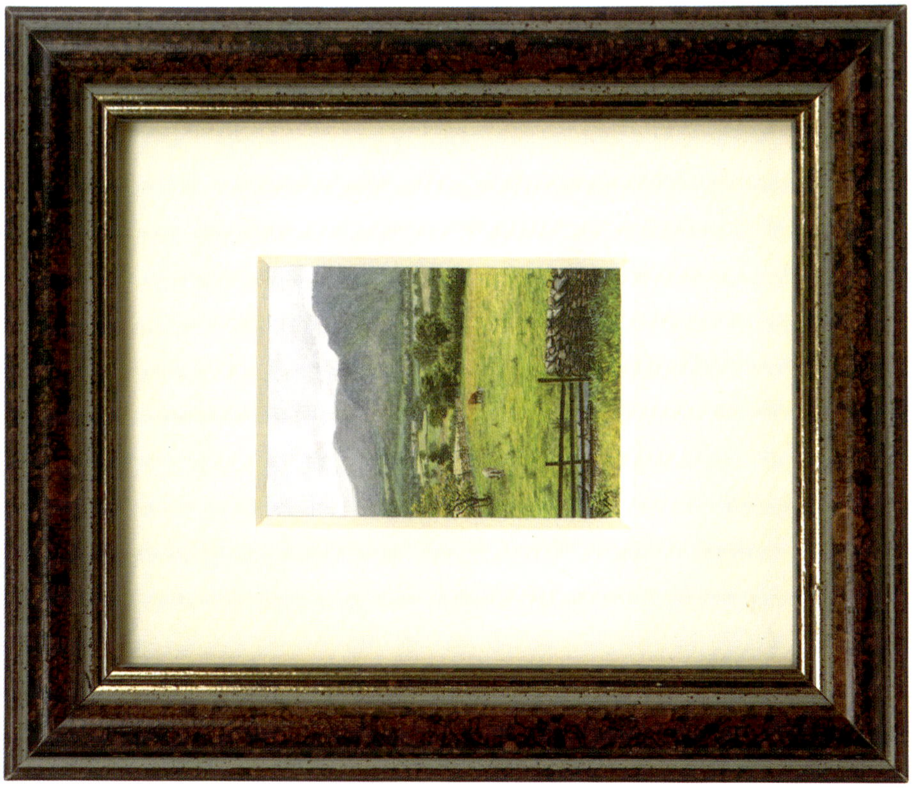

Florence Young *RMS SWA ASAF HS*

London Antique Stand
(water-colour on vellum)

The Nore Lightship
(water-colour on vellum)

She is a Member of the Royal Miniature Society, the Society of Women Artists and the Société des Artistes Français. She gained a Mention Honorable, the Prix Marie Louise Jules Richard, for the year's best miniature, and a Silver Medal. She won a Diplôme d'Honneur at the Galleries Vallombreuse, Biarritz.

She has exhibited with the United Society, the Royal Water Colour Society's Flower Exhibition, The Royal Institute Galleries' Summer and Winter Salons, the Pastel Society and with other Royal Miniature Society Members at the Royal Institute of Painters in Water Colours. She has had work in the Royal Academy of Arts Summer Exhibition.

She lectures and demonstrates to various groups, including voluntary therapy for people with mental troubles. She tutors landscape painting at Holiday Fellowship centres and also miniature work at Fittleworth, West Sussex.

Commissioned work includes portraits of Princess Diana, the late Very Reverend Dean of Christchurch College, Oxford and the one-time Mayor of Hillingdon Borough. Commercial commissions have been for the Post House Hotel Heathrow, Diaform, Swedish Tools Ltd. and Williamson's Watercress Growers of Wiltshire; Hillingdon Borough Leisure Services and Barclays Bank, Uxbridge have acquired her work. She covers a wide range of subjects.

Maureen J. Norton *RMS*

The "Ethel Ada" of Shotley
(oil on Ivorine)

Pause for Reflection
(oil on Ivorine)

Maureen Norton started painting in early childhood but was not able, unfortunately, to take up offered academic and art scholarships. She spent many years in the Civil Service but continued painting, constantly sketching country and marine subjects. Consequently she is largely self-taught and in the 1960's began showing oil paintings of East Anglia in shared and one-man exhibitions. Also she exhibited as an Associate Member in the United Artists exhibitions at the Mall Galleries.

Subsequently she turned to miniature painting and, after exhibiting successfully in the Bankside and Mall Galleries, was elected a full Member of the Royal Society of Miniature Painters, Sculptors and Gravers in 1990.

A shared family love of marshes, estuaries and sailing enables her to be afloat and still sketching (though slightly damp!), constantly gathering material for marine subjects for both miniature and larger paintings. Attention to accuracy is the hallmark of her work as boat owners can be extremely particular about the smallest detail.

Commissions include country estates in Norfolk and East Anglian scenes for Germany, Mexico, France and the United States of America.

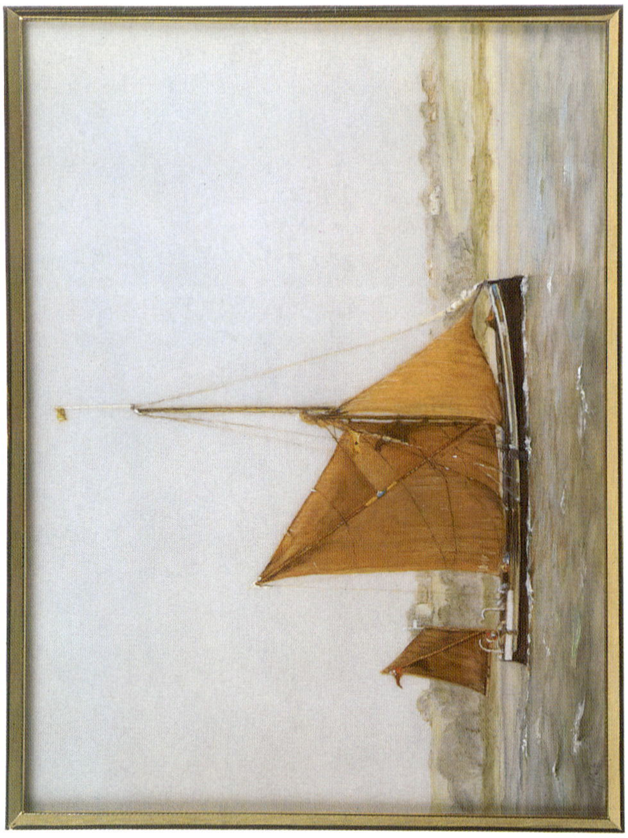

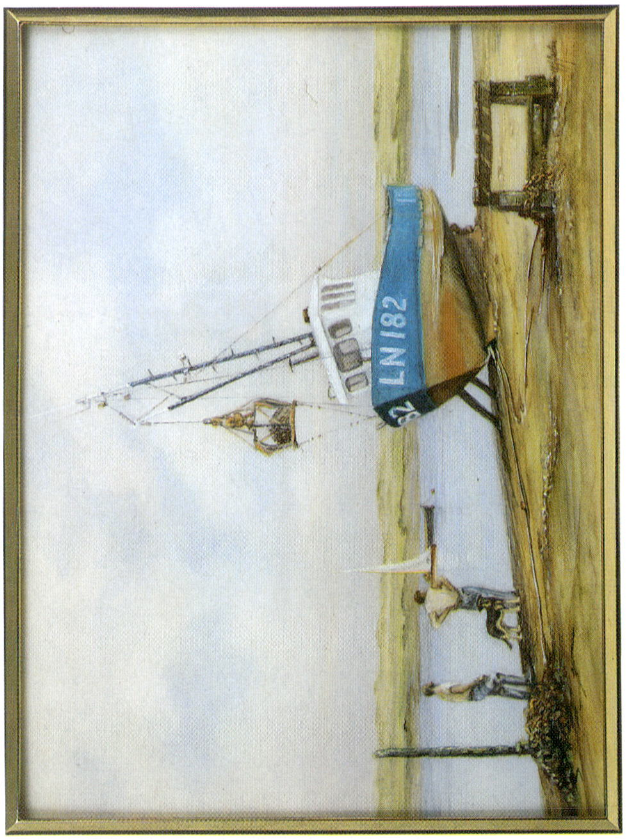
LN182

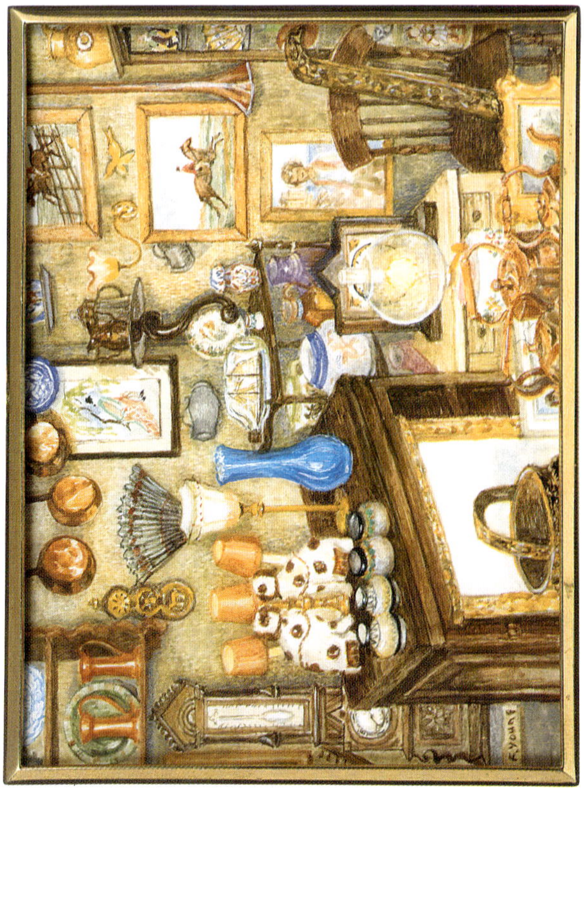

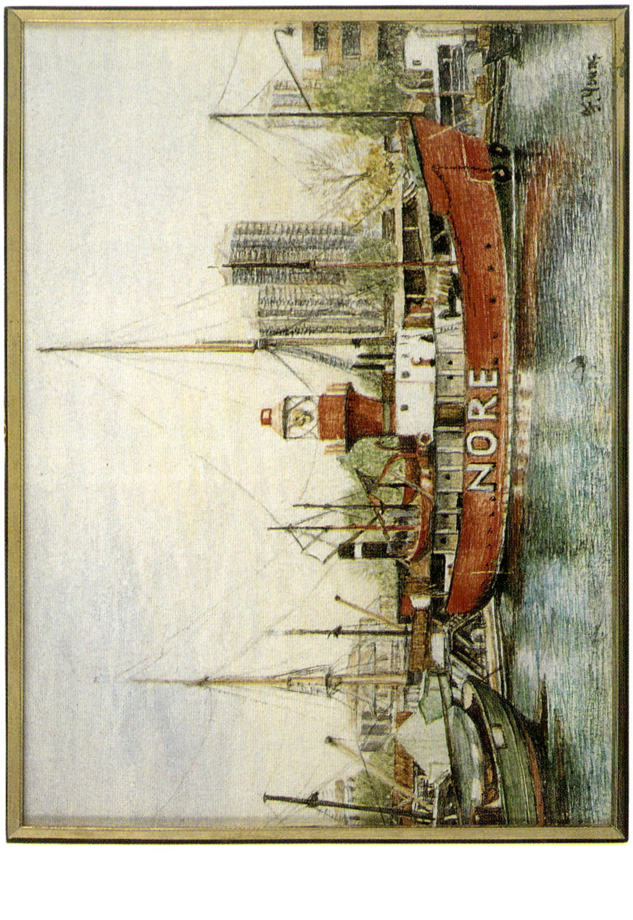
NORE

Carrie Muskett *ARMS*

Welsh Sunset
(gouache, pen and ink)

She was born in 1952, has been painting for over twenty years and has had one-man and shared exhibitions in London, Ely and Stamford.

She started painting miniatures in 1991 following a commission for a book jacket from the publishers Michael Joseph.

In 1992 five of her paintings were accepted by the Royal Society of Miniature Painters, Sculptors and Gravers for their Exhibition.

She exhibited at the Royal Academy Summer Exhibition in 1993, was elected to Associate Membership of the Royal Miniature Society at their 1993 exhibition and was awarded a Gold Memorial Bowl Honourable Mention.

Her work, interesting in its combination of gouache with pen and ink, is unique in its intensely decorative quality and richness of colour, with the forms in her pictures complementing each other in a symphony of shapes and shades. Her detail is remarkable and she sustains her gift for design in a harmonious border, painted with the same minute care, the whole carefully framed to emphasize the colours of her work.

Kate Dornberger Taylor

BA RMS MPSG MASF HS GMAS

Creaming Surf
(water-colour on paper)

Forest Floor
(water-colour on paper)
kindly lent by the President

Born in Pittsburgh, United States in 1926 she received a Bachelor of Arts Degree from Chatham College, Pittsburgh in 1948. Later she studied with Murray Hantman and others in New York and on Monhegan Island, Maine. She exhibited in various group and one-man shows until in 1967 she married Kenneth Taylor, an English antique dealer, became a British citizen and moved to Somerset. Her work is in water-colour, oil and acrylics, for large pictures as well as miniatures, and she has paintings in private collections in the United Kingdom, the United States, Canada, Europe and Australia. She is a Member of the Royal Miniature Society, the Hilliard Society, and also of the American Miniature Art Societies of Florida, Georgia, Montana, New Jersey and Washington D.C. where she has won a total of eleven awards with a first for Abstract in Washington.

She paints largely from memory and imagination, the pictures being derived or abstracted, rather than copied, from nature. They are not necessarily to be understood mentally or realistically, but should be felt and reacted to emotionally, as the mind and heart react to music, so that one may enter into them and let the imagination wander there.

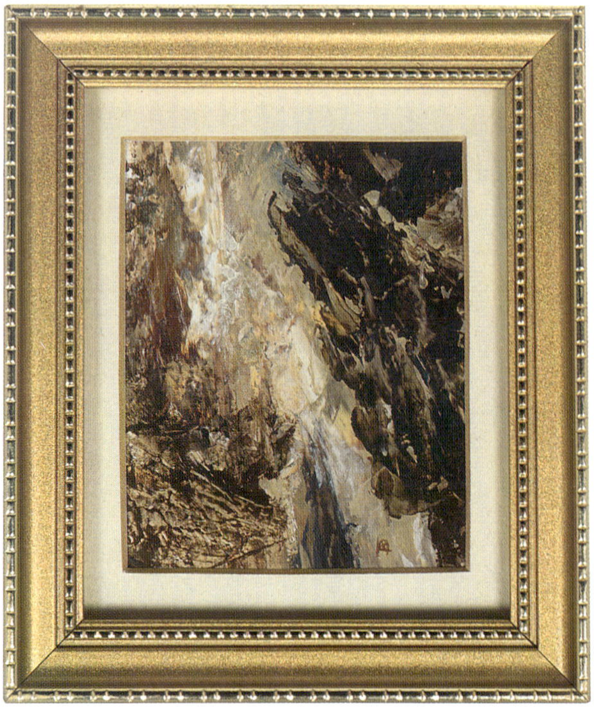

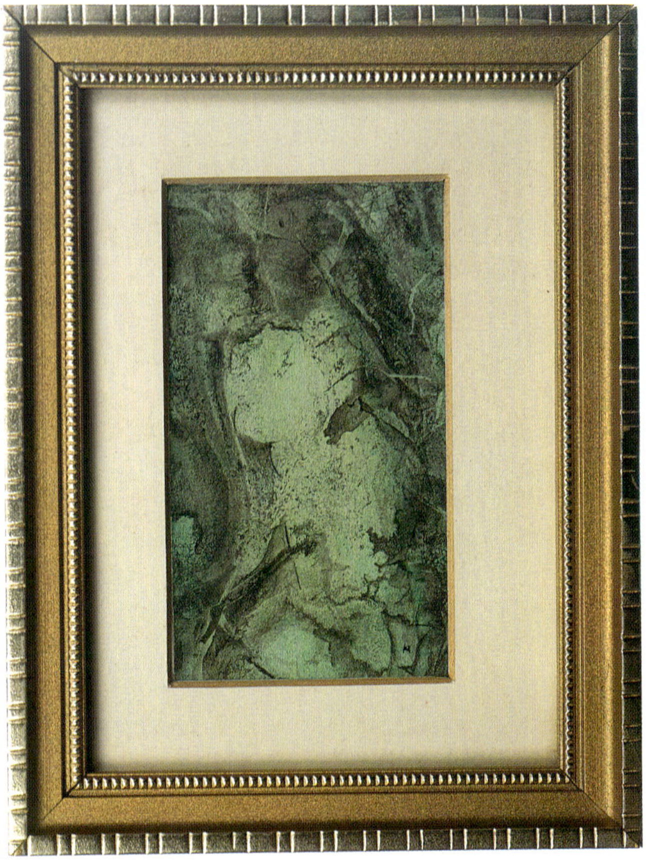

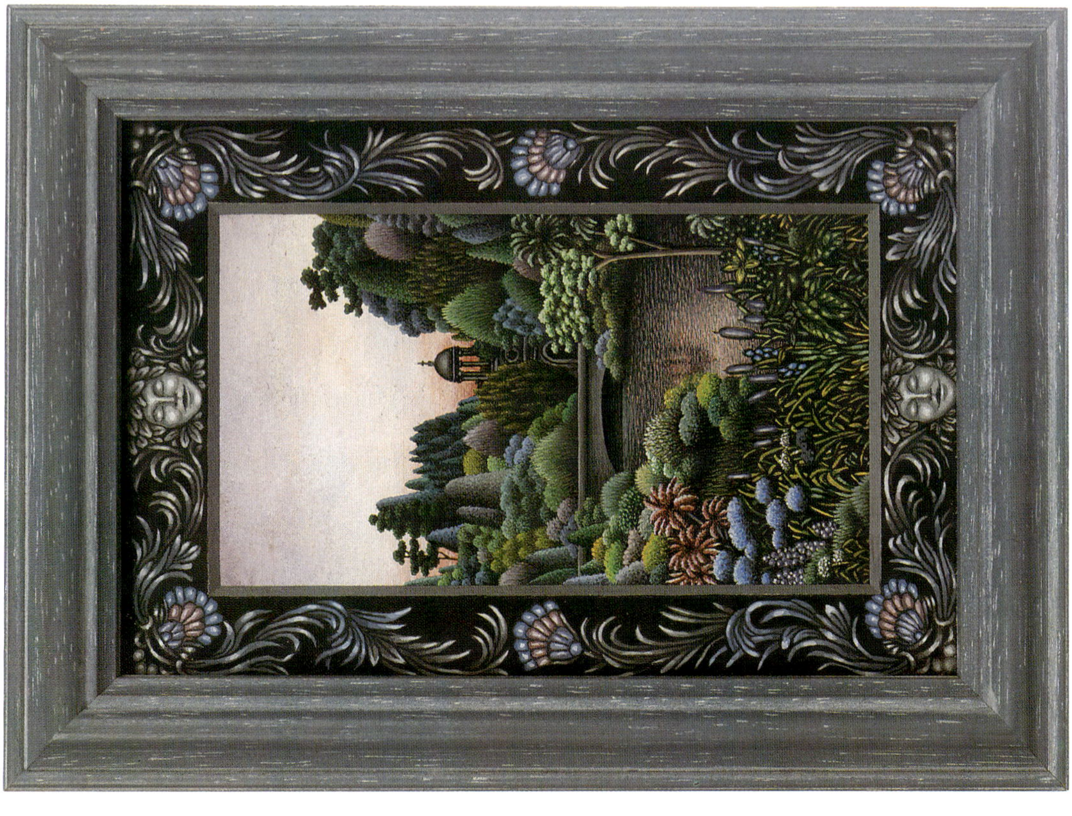

George Simpson RMS

Adlestrop
(gouache and gold leaf on paper)

Born a true Londoner within the sound of Bow Bells, he has lived in London all his life. He learned calligraphy at Orange Hill School, Edgware at the tender age of eleven.

His education was interrupted by service in the Royal Air Force, therefore he is largely self-taught. He is still researching his subject passionately and is a freelance calligrapher, designer, teacher and lecturer.

A full Member of The Royal Society of Miniature Painters, he has exhibited with the Society for many years, as well as having one-man shows in various parts of London. He carries out commissions regularly for private individuals and for a number of national and international organizations. His work is represented in many personal collections world-wide. He has been teaching calligraphy in Adult Education Centres and Residential Colleges for more than twenty years.

His published work 'Writers and Hampstead', a literary anthology written entirely in various calligraphic alphabets, was commissioned by Hampstead Arts Council in 1987. His other interests are Victorian literature, music, the theatre and particularly opera.

Christopher Guise ARMS

The East Indiaman Alfred
1291 tons, built at Blackwall in 1845 for Green's Blackwall Line
(oil on Ivorine)

The East Indiaman Monarch
1440 tons, built in 1844 for Green's Blackwall Line
(oil on Ivorine)

Born in 1928 in India he was educated at Charterhouse and Brasenose College, Oxford. After National Service he worked in India for some years. Married, with two children, he has lived at Hurstpierpoint in Sussex since 1957 where he was on the staff of Hurstpierpoint College from then until 1988.

He has had a life-long interest in ships and sailing since early years spent in southern Cornwall. He took up marine painting in his early forties and began miniature painting some ten years later. His preferred medium is oil painted on wooden panels or Ivorine.

His large work and miniatures have been exhibited in sailing centres in Britain and the United States, principally in New England. He shows in London, Washington, New York and San Francisco.

He has exhibited with The Royal Miniature Society since 1983 and was elected an Associate Member in 1988.

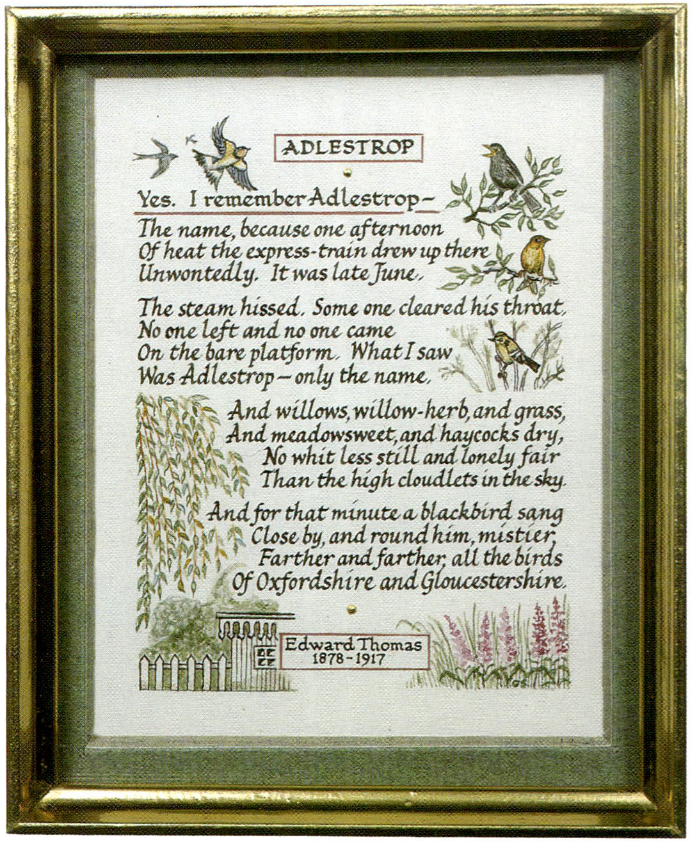
ADLESTROP
Yes. I remember Adlestrop–
The name, because one afternoon
Of heat the express-train drew up there
Unwontedly. It was late June.
The steam hissed. Some one cleared his throat.
No one left and no one came
On the bare platform. What I saw
Was Adlestrop – only the name.
And willows, willow-herb, and grass,
And meadowsweet, and haycocks dry,
No whit less still and lonely fair
Than the high cloudlets in the sky.
And for that minute a blackbird sang
Close by, and round him, mistier,
Farther and farther, all the birds
Of Oxfordshire and Gloucestershire.
Edward Thomas
1878 – 1917

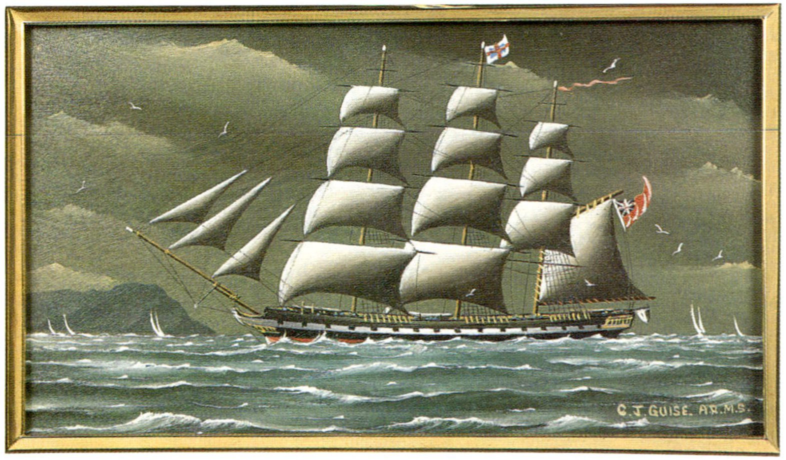
C.J. GUISE. A.R.M.S.

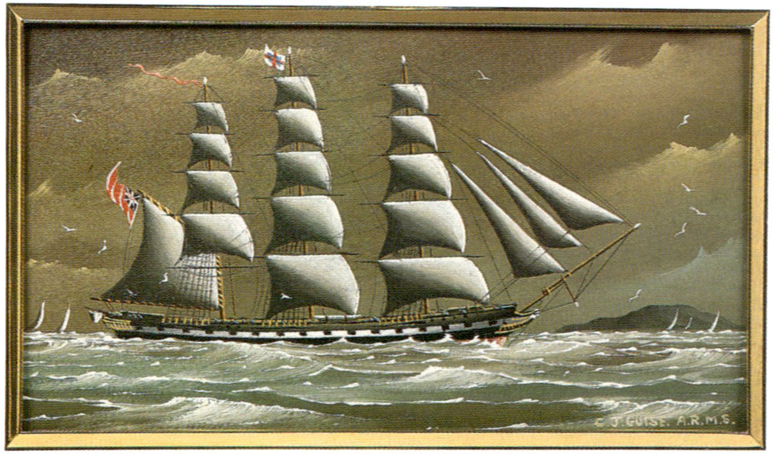
C.J. GUISE. A.R.M.S.

Rosalind Pierson *RMS MASF HSF*

Winter Light
(water-colour on Bristol board)

The River Tavy
(water-colour on Bristol board)

Rosalind studied at the Ruskin School of Drawing, Oxford, although painting miniatures before then. When she left she had no clear idea what to do following her training. She first exhibited at the Royal Academy in 1974 and held a successful exhibition in her home town, Tavistock, which encouraged her to work for another exhibition each year.

She exhibited with the Royal Miniature Society in 1975, becoming an Associate in 1977 and a Member in 1979, then decided to send to the Paris Salon. Elected an Associate Member of the Société des Artistes Français, she was awarded a silver medal in 1978 and a gold in 1981. She has exhibited in Canada, America, Monaco and Ulster, winning in 1994 the Excellence in all Entries Award at the Florida annual exhibition.

In Britain her work was in demand all over the country as she held exhibitions in different areas. In 1978 her first exhibition in Wells, Somerset, led to her becoming the Co-founder of the Hilliard Society of Miniaturists.

Though painting many beautiful country scenes she likes to specialize in Dartmoor landscapes, not an easy subject in miniature. She loves to walk on the moors with her three miniature poodles.

Geoffrey Norman Evans *ARMS HS*

The Woodcarver
(water-colour on vellum)
kindly lent by J.L. Morton Esq.

Born and educated in Cheltenham, Gloucestershire, Geoffrey Evans won a scholarship to Cheltenham College of Art. His studies interrupted by World War II, he was employed as a draughtsman by the Folland Aircraft Company, followed by three and a half years' military service at home and abroad. On leaving the Army he joined the Gloucestershire Constabulary.

He served for twenty-five years as a Police Officer, then spent ten years with the Legal Department of Avon County Council, during which painting was restricted to leisure time.

Retiring in 1988 on health grounds, he was able to devote much more time to his first love, Art, and took several courses experimenting with different media.

In 1992 he became interested in miniatures and joined the Hilliard Society, concentrating almost exclusively on this form of art. In 1993 he became an exhibiting Member, with six miniatures accepted for the May exhibition, and began exhibiting in London galleries.

He submitted five miniatures for the 1993 exhibition of the Royal Society of Miniature Painters, Sculptors and Gravers which were accepted, one being awarded a Gold Memorial Bowl Honourable Mention, and he was invited to be an Associate Member of the Society.

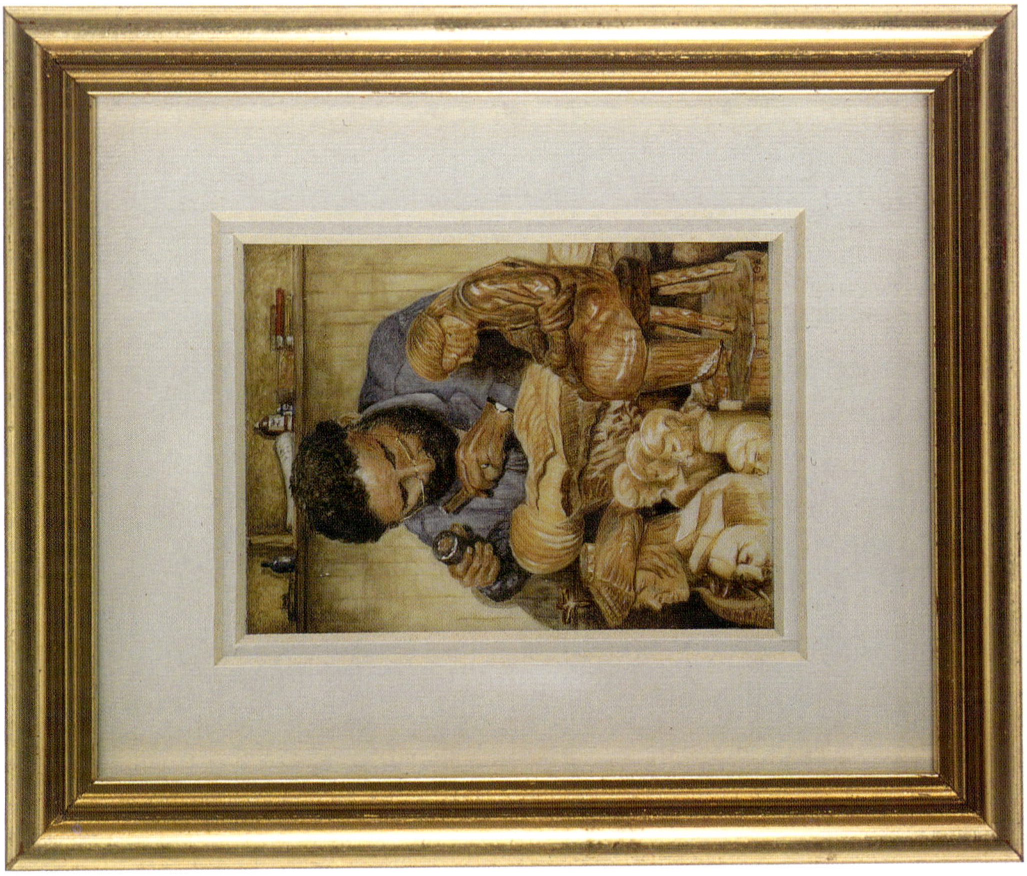

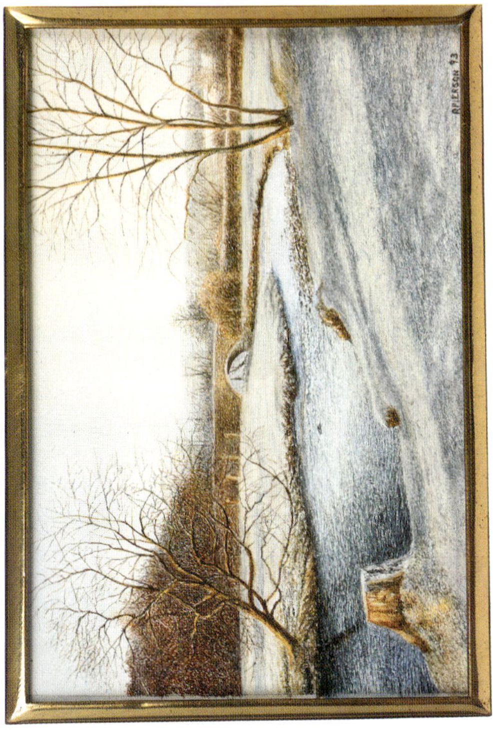

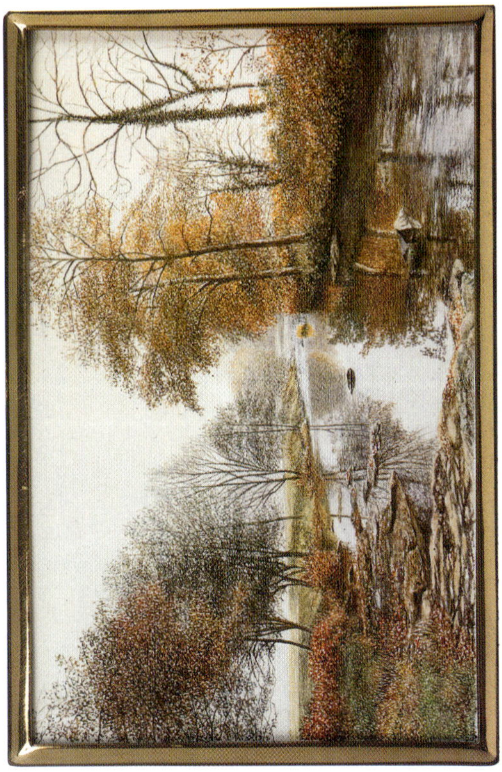

Alexander Prowse *ARMS*

Mountain Village, Tuscany
(water-colour on board)

Born in London in 1949, Alex trained at Harrow School of Art where he obtained a Fine Art Diploma. He continued part-time studies while teaching at Lockers Park Preparatory School in Hertfordshire where Lord Mountbatten was once a pupil. He developed a great interest in boats and inland waterways which became the theme of many of his paintings. Using a boat as a studio was a natural progression, culminating in the restoration of a 1930's Regent's Canal Barge moored at picturesque Little Venice in the heart of London. It has been featured in national and international publications and television videos.

One-man shows include Liberty's of Regent Street, London, V.A.U.W. Gallery, Caracas, Venezuela and General Motors Corporation, Mexico City.

His paintings have been hung by the Royal Society of Marine Artists, Royal Institute of Painters in Water Colours, the Pastel and Royal Portrait Societies. He painted a picture for presentation to Jacques Chirac which hangs in the Hôtel de Ville, Paris. Alex has always been interested in good draughtsmanship which attracted him to miniature painting. A painting journey through Tuscany, Italy, experiencing the very different light and architecture, was the inspiration for a series of miniatures.

Josephine Mary Cooper *RMS SWA*

Incoming Night Tide
(water-colour on fine paper)

The Autumn Pool, Bidulph Grange
(water-colour on fine paper)

In 1973 Josephine began painting miniatures of flowers in oil for an exhibition in Welwyn Garden City. 1974 found her in Paris at the Salon showing three miniatures, gaining the Médaille d'Argent, and in July being elected a Member of the Society of Miniaturists.

In 1977 she won the Prix Rowland at the Paris Salon and was elected an Associate Member of the Royal Society of Miniature Painters, Sculptors and Gravers.

From 1980 to 1985 she showed in the Small South Room at the Royal Academy Summer Exhibition and during this time changed her medium to water-colour on fine paper. In 1983 she was elected a Member of the Royal Miniature Society, and in 1984 was awarded the Gordon Drummond runner-up prize. In 1986 she exhibited at the Barbican, in November 1987 was elected a Member of the Society of Women Artists and in 1989 she won a Gold Memorial Bowl Honourable Mention. She shows her work in London and locally, winning the Welwyn Trophy in 1993. In 1994 she was elected to the Council of the Society of Women Artists and made Chairman of Welwyn Garden City Art Club in its seventieth year.

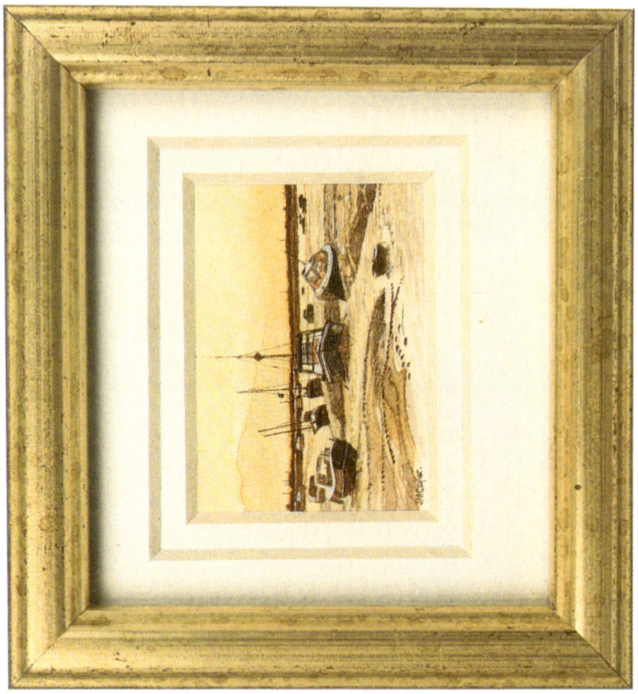

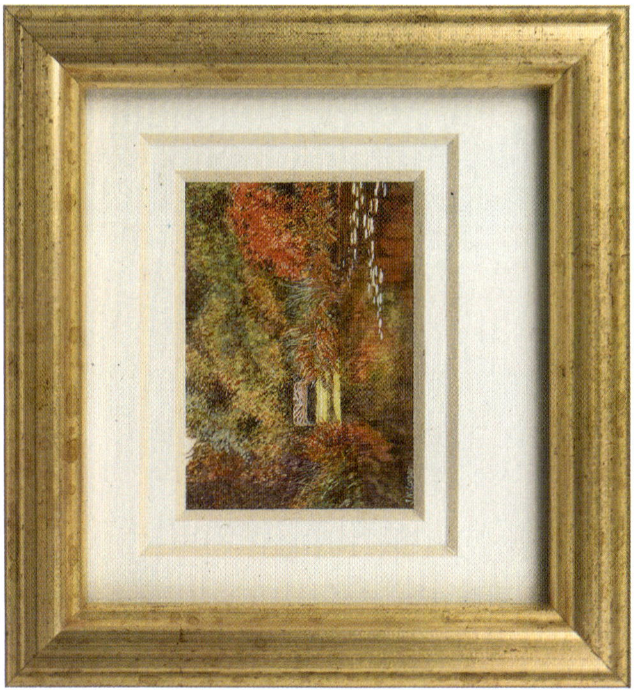

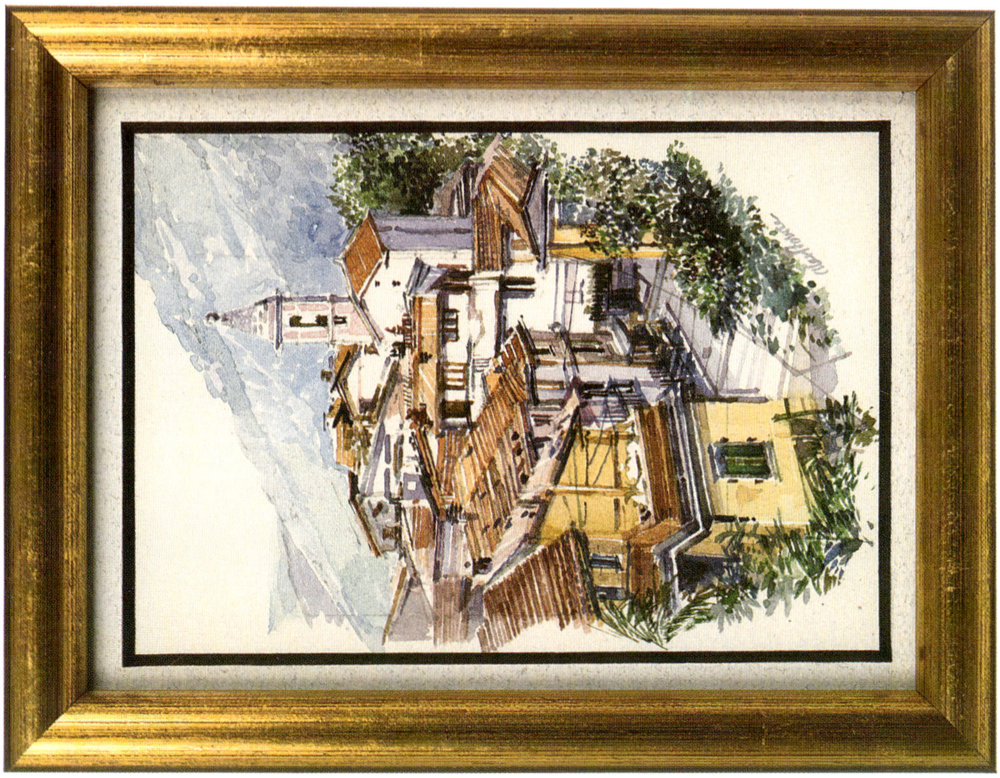

Ina Maria Harris *ARMS HS*

Yogini Rawal
(water-colour on Ivorine)
kindly lent by Yogini Rawal

She was born in Merthyr Tydfil in 1956. Her mother, from Prussia, and her grandmother were caught by Russians driving towards Berlin and they endured hardship and danger before reaching the West. From her mother she inherited her talent and her love of horses which, as an accomplished horsewoman, she trains. Ina's Welsh father was a cabinet-maker, who once made a table for the Queen, and from whom she derives her appreciation of nature. From childhood she rescued hurt animals and had a tawny owl living in her room! It drove her family to distraction because it was inconvenient to cover the furniture with tarpaulins. This owl used to groom Ina's eyelashes with a delicacy of touch worthy of a miniaturist.

She had no training but began painting small bunches of flowers, roots, cobwebs, lichen and any insects happening to live there. She wanted to paint miniatures but knew that it could not be forced. Two terrifying attacks by terrorists, in Uganda and Lesotho, and the resultant nervous breakdown made her embark on this venture. She lives in Lesotho, with domestic help giving her time for her horses, her considerable orchid collection and, above all, painting.

Judith Young
NDD ATC ARMS HS SLm

Mughal Emperor and Family
in the style of C17 Indian Miniature Painting
(water-colour on Ivorine)

Judith Young studied art at the Wimbledon Art School soon after the war and was awarded the National Diploma in Design, followed by the Art Teachers' Certificate. This early training proved invaluable in the management of the many aspects presented by a long primary school career in teaching.

Elizabeth Davys-Wood introduced her to miniature painting in 1988 and a new life began! Her work was accepted by the Royal Miniature Society in 1991 and she was privileged to be awarded a Gold Memorial Bowl Honourable Mention at that year's exhibition. Recently elected to Associate Membership, she also belongs to the Hilliard Society and the Society of Limners.

Her subject matter for miniatures is varied, but it must contain one vital element – a decorative quality. She is at present studying for a degree in Art History at Kingston University and is intending to present a thesis on the contemporary miniature for her finals.

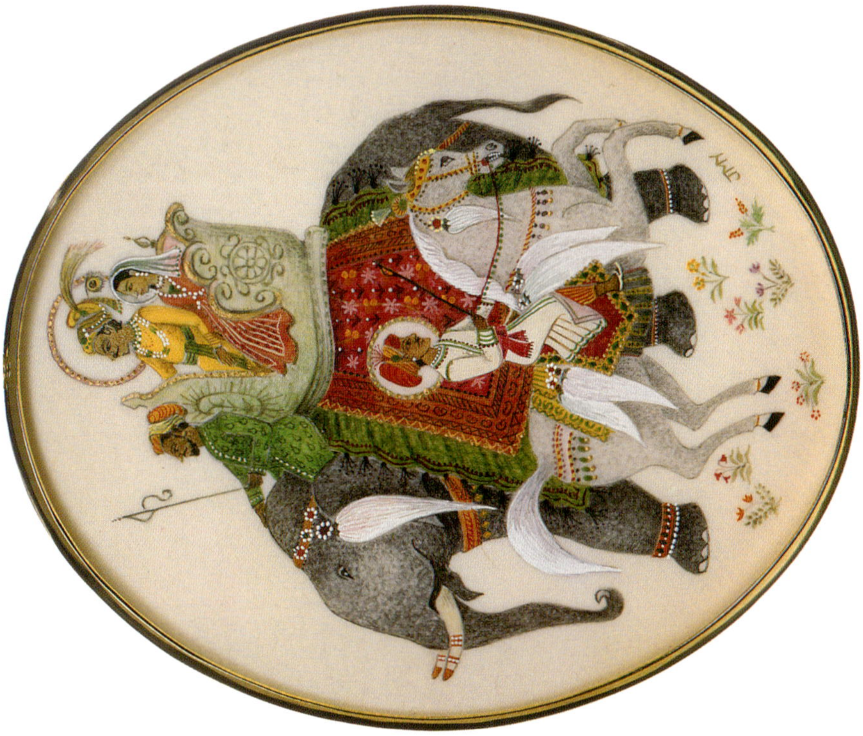

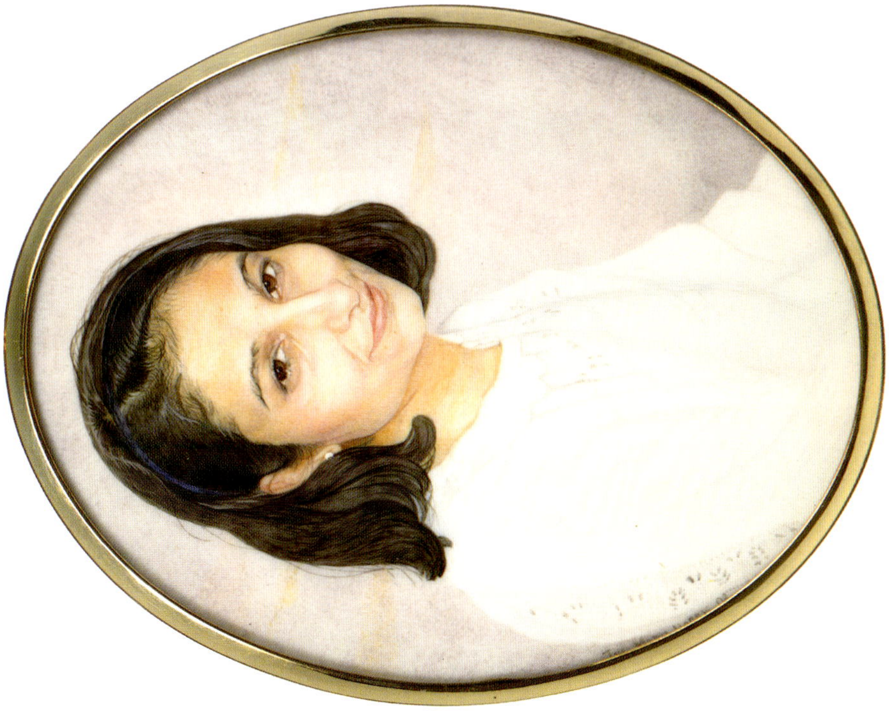

Harold Coates *RMS*

Three Stones, Pearl and Pin
(water-colour on Bristol card)

Two Stones, Two Shells
(water-colour on Bristol card)

Harold Coates was born in London. He now lives and works on the borders of Herefordshire and Wales as well as in France, Département des Yvelines.

He trained at Willesdon School of Art and Hornsey College of Arts and Crafts.

Working in water-colour, gouache and mixed media, his main sources of inspiration include stones and shells. Looking at these evokes ideas of a tiny, ageless and imaginative world: the extra drama of subject contrast can be achieved by introducing everyday objects.

He exploits fully the dramatic effects of the opposition of light and shadow and a strong impression is helped frequently by using artificial light. These artistic methods colour his work which has always been on a small scale.

He has exhibited at the Royal Academy since student days, as well as other London and provincial galleries, which led to his being a finalist in the 1985 Hunting Group Competition. He was also presented with The Three Friends Award for a miniature at The Royal Academy in 1987.

His work is in private and public collections in the United Kingdom and abroad.

C. Elisabeth M. Lake *RMS HSF*

Bluebells Lying on a Chair
(water-colour on Ivorex card)

She began painting in water-colour, but it was her interest in printing and the suggestion she should try miniature painting, with its particular techniques, which led her to pointillism using the four basic colours of printing inks. First she lays the warm colours, then works with cooler shades. By this method she achieves the lovely soft finishes, as on the cottage flag-stone floors, unattainable with a single wash of colours. Concentrating on interiors with an impressionistic approach, particularly to light and tone, she is fascinated not only by the beauty of a house but also by its atmosphere.

She lives in an old cottage, much like her paintings, where she creates her small masterpieces.

Elisabeth exhibits with the Royal Miniature Society, of which she is a Member, and the Hilliard Society where she is a Founder Member, and in 1988 won the Suzanne Lucas Best in Exhibition Award. In 1986 she exhibited in the Royal Academy Summer Exhibition and won a prize in their Christmas Card Competition. In 1988 she received the Ulster Miniature Society's Overseas Trophy and First Prize for Water-colour at the Canadian International Miniature Exhibition. In 1995 The Llewellyn Alexander Gallery awarded her a Commendation of Excellence.

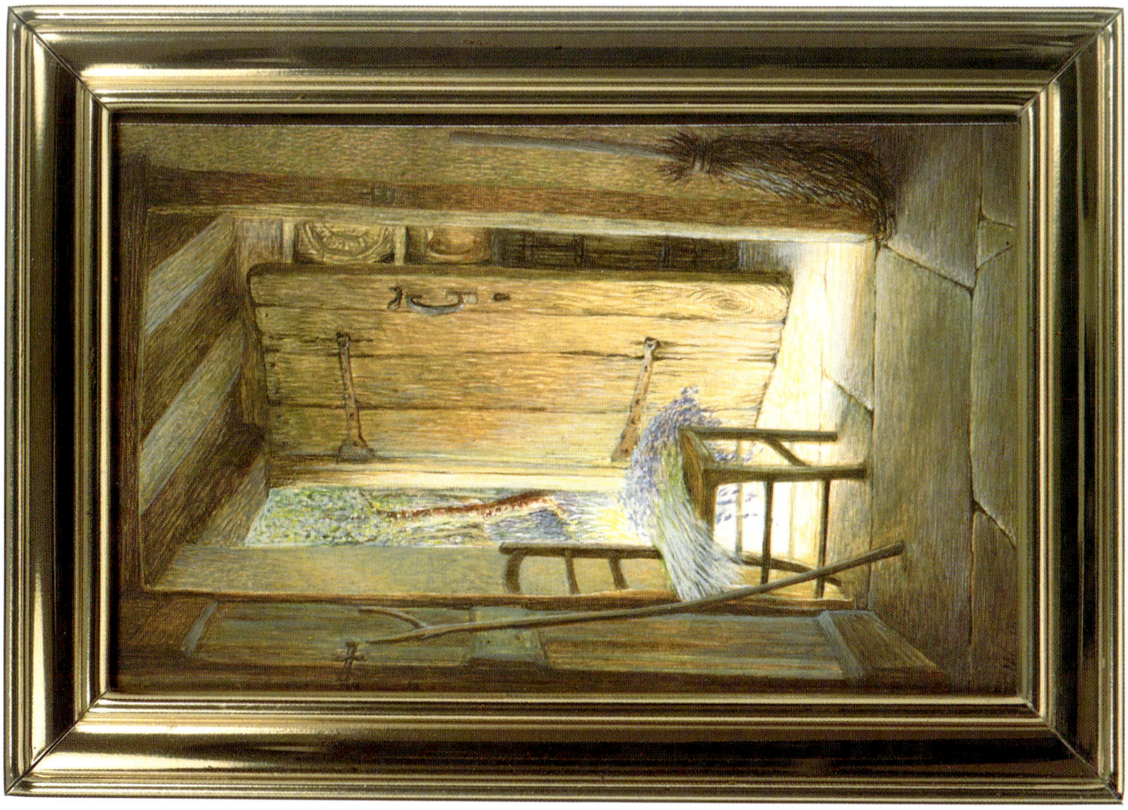

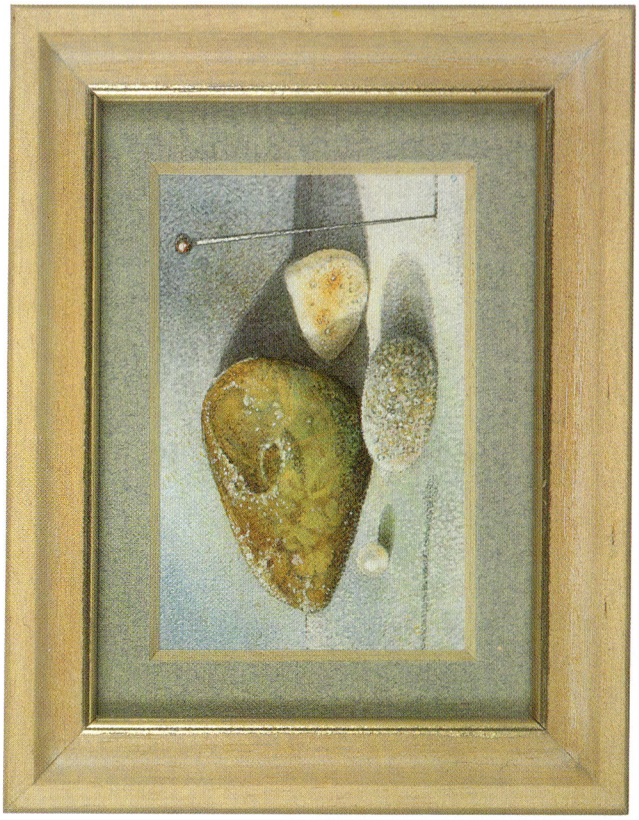

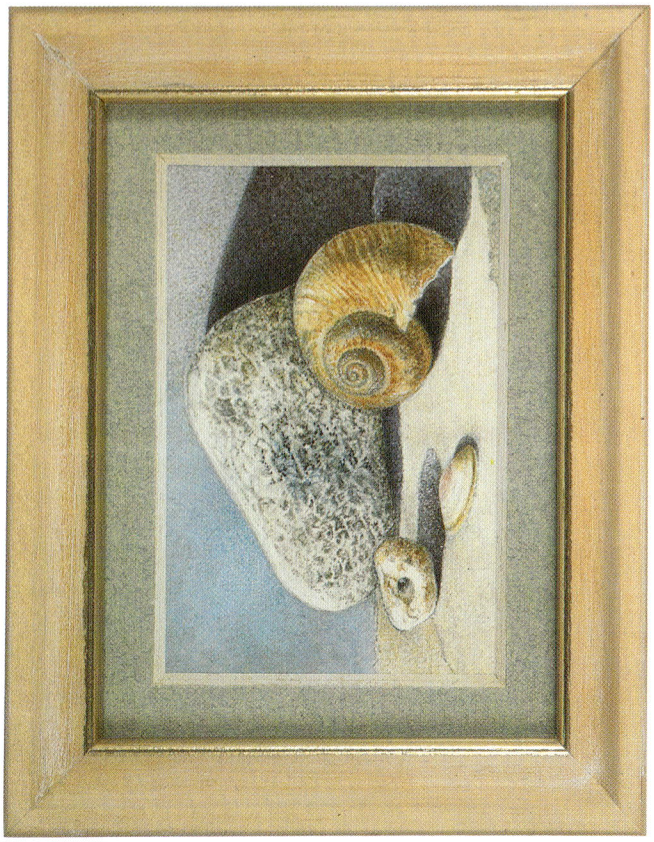

Index

Glossary

A	Associate
FP	Founder President
F	Founder Member
Hon.	Honorary
P	President
PP	Past President
PVP	Past Vice President
VP	Vice President
AE	Artist Enamellers
ARCA	Associate of the Royal College of Art
ASAF	Associé de la Société des Artistes Français
ASMA	Australian Society of Miniature Art (New South Wales, Queensland, Tasmania, Victoria)
ATC	Art Teachers Certificate
ATD	Art Teachers Diploma
BA	Bachelor of Arts
BAG	British Artists in Glass
BSOE	British Society of Enamellers
BWS	British Watercolour Society
CPA	Cider Painters of America
DA	Diploma of Art
Dip AE	Diploma of Art Education
DFA	Diploma of Fine Art
DSR	Diploma of the Society of Radiographers
FGE	Fellow of the Guild of Glass Engravers
FIGMA	Fellow of the International Guild of Artisans
FLS	Fellow of the Linnean Society of London
FNCM	Fellow of the National College of Music
FRSA	Fellow of the Royal Society of Arts
FSDC	Fellow of the Society of Designer Craftsmen
FSSI	Fellow of the Society of Scribes and Illuminators
GMAS	Georgia Miniature Art Society
HS	Hilliard Society of Miniaturists
IAL	Imperial Art League
LL.B (Lond)	Bachelor of Laws (London)
MA	Master of Arts
MAA	Miniature Artists of America
MASF	Miniature Art Society of Florida
MASNJ	Miniature Art Society of New Jersey
MASSA	Miniature Art Society of South Africa
MMAS	Montana Miniature Art Society
Mod. BA	Honours in Science at Trinity College, Dublin
MPSG	Society of Miniature Painters, Sculptors and Gravers (Washington)
NDD	National Diploma in Design
RBSA	Royal Birmingham Society of Artists
RI	Royal Institute of Painters in Water Colours
RMS	Royal Society of Miniature Painters, Sculptors and Gravers
RN	Royal Navy
RWS	Royal Society of Painters in Water Colour
SBA	Society of Botanical Artists
SEq.A	Society of Equestrian Artists
SLM	Society of Limners
SM (London)	Society of Miniaturists
SWA	Society of Women Artists
UA	United Society of Artists
UPA	Union of Polish Artists
USWA	Ulster Society of Women Artists
USM	Ulster Society of Miniaturists